A Path and Many Shadows & Twelve Stories

Rajelakshmy (1930–1965) was an eminent novelist, short story writer and poet and the first woman novelist to win the Kerala Sahitya Akademi Award for *Oru Vazhiyum Kure Nizhalukalum* (*A Path and Many Shadows*) in 1960. This novel was later serialised in the TV and broadcast as a play by All India Radio. Her other notable works of fiction are *Njanenna Bhavam* (*Self-conceit*) and *Uccha Veyilum Ilam Nilavum* (*The Noon Sun and Soft Moonlight*). Her short fiction was published in the weekly *Mathrubhumi* and the monthly *Mangalodayam*, two of the most prestigious literary journals of the period. Rajelakshmy committed suicide in 1965, leaving behind fragments of an unpublished novel.

R. K. Jayasree retired as associate professor of English literature after a long career of 27 years teaching in various government colleges in Kerala. She has published numerous translations of Malayalam short stories in English, and two English-language books in Malayalam – Paulo Coelho's *The Winner Stands Alone* and Jack London's *Short Stories*.

A TRANSLATION INITIATIVE OF THE THUNCHATH EZHUTHACHAN MALAYALAM UNIVERSITY

This is part of the translation project of Thunchath Ezhuthachan Malayalam University, aimed at unlocking the creative power of Malayalam, enhancing its reach and enriching world literature through translation.

A Path and Many Shadows & Twelve Stories

RAJELAKSHMY

Translated from the original Malayalam by

R. K. JAYASREE

തുഞ്ചത്തെഴുത്തച്ഛൻ
മലയാളസർവകലാശാല

Thunchath Ezhuthachan Malayalam University

Orient BlackSwan

A PATH AND MANY SHADOWS & TWELVE STORIES

ORIENT BLACKSWAN PRIVATE LIMITED

Registered Office
3-6-752 Himayatnagar, Hyderabad 500 029 (Telangana), India
e-mail: centraloffice@orientblackswan.com

Other Offices
Bengaluru, Bhopal, Chennai, Guwahati,
Hyderabad, Jaipur, Kolkata, Lucknow,
Mumbai, New Delhi, Noida, Patna, Vijayawada

ISBN 978 81 250 6351 3

Typeset by
Le Studio Graphique, Gurgaon 122 001
in ITC Veljovic Std 10/12

023560
14072016

Printed at
Glorious Printers, Delhi 110 095

Published by
Orient Blackswan Private Limited
1/24 Asaf Ali Road
New Delhi 110 002
e-mail: delhi@orientblackswan.com

Contents

Publisher's Acknowledgement

The stories listed here

1. A Suicide/*Aatmahatya*
2. The Apology/*Maappu*
3. The Defeated One/*Paraajita*
4. A Teacher is Born/*Oradhyapika Janikkunnu*
5. The Daughter/*Makal*
6. A Pretty Girl and Her Pals/*Sundariyum Koottukaarum*
7. The Curse/*Saapam*
8. A Winding Sheet for Mathai/*Mooduvaan Naadan*
9. In the Abode of God/*Devaalayathil*
10. History Did Not Repeat Itself/*Charitram Aavartichilla*
11. Mistakes/*Tettukal*
12. Handkerchief/*Handkerchief*

were first published in *Samyukta: A Journal of Women's Studies*, Vol. VIII, No. 2 (July 2008). The permission to reproduce the stories in this collection of works of Rajelakshmy published by Orient BlackSwan was granted gratis.

Rajelakshmy, my Cheriamma

Cheriamma (mother's younger sister) was everyone's favourite, be they elders or children. Her golden complexion gave her the pet name 'Thankamma' among family members. I was only ten years old when she passed away. My knowledge of her literary activities was very limited, except that my brothers and I used to surround our mother while reading her novels published in *Mathrubhumi* as a serial. Another incident which comes to my mind is how she stood her ground when Shri N. V. Krishna Warrier wanted to change the title of one of her novels.

Being the only girl among three boys, I was her pet. Cheriamma's ambition seemed to make me put on some weight. To this end, she saw to it that I had Ferradol, a tasty syrupy jam-like tonic, every night, much to the envy of my brothers.

Rajelakshmy lived in a small but nice house in Palapuram, surrounded by paddy fields and coconut trees, while working at NSS College, Ottapalam. That itself might have given some background for her novels. During the holidays we used to visit her and we children had great fun. In the country-brick (laterite stone) quarry in the backyard we used to stage Shakespearean dramas interspersed with a lot of nonsense and Cheriamma would thoroughly enjoy herself along with us.

Cheriamma was a free spirit. One day, my brothers collected worms, tackle and fishing rod to catch fish from the pond in the family compound. The plan was to have fried fish for the meal. I sneaked this 'fishy plan' to Cheriamma who marched out and confiscated the fishing equipment. Her logic was, 'you are enticing the fish with bait only to kill it. This is treachery' (*chathi* is the word she used). Once one of my cousins found a baby squirrel. Cheriamma let him keep it on the condition that it would be let free when it grew older.

She and her sisters used to speak in a secret language developed and mastered by them. That is, they would talk each word backward and so fast no one could understand them.

Cheriamma has gone, but her warmth remains, fanning all the embers into a rosy glow.

June 2016

BHARATHY MOHANRAM

INTRODUCTION

Rajelakshmy, the Tale and the Teller

P. P. Raveendran[1]

'Never trust the teller, trust the tale,' D. H. Lawrence is famed to have advised fellow artists and writers in the course of a discussion on the evolution of American writing.[2] Whether Lawrence intended it or not, the above maxim has often been proffered by later critics as a hermeneutic comment on an artwork's creative potential to communicate layers of truth, all of which may not be perceptible to the artist in a conscious manner. The artwork has a biography of its own, as Lawrence apparently implies, which nevertheless cannot be reduced to the life story of the artist.

Trusting the teller however has become a way of life with the institution of literature in the present-day world. There are myriad ways in which the literary institution today fosters the metaphysics of the teller, what with advertisements and previews of literary works before they are launched, their reviews and commentaries, and interviews with the authors after their launch. Writers often transform themselves into public icons and social celebrities through such gestures in the contemporary scenario of readymade fame that precedes those among them who are willing to indulge the illusions of the market. Art cannot be delinked from the 'artworld,'[3] its institutional environment. The teller, sometimes to the exclusion of the tale, is what gets privileged in this environment.

The biography of Rajelakshmy's fiction is truly significant in any consideration of her writings, because Rajelakshmy is one of the few authors of her generation who has left behind

---

[1] Professor Emeritus, Mahatma Gandhi University, Kottayam.

[2] Though this is the form in which Lawrence's dictum is often phrased in critical debates, what he actually stated in the opening pages of *Studies in Classic American Literature* was: 'Never trust the artist, trust the tale' (Lawrence 1969/1923: 2).

[3] 'The artworld' is philosopher and art critic Arthur Danto's formulation. See his essay of that title (Danto 1964).

no serious account of her own self worth retelling. The only personal statement that she had made about herself in the thirty-five years of her life was a crisp suicide note which merely stated that were she to live, she would live only as a writer and that she was leaving because she did not want to appear to be continually hurting others through her fiction (Menon 2002: 23). For long after her death her biography contained scant information about her person, and even after two or three decades following her death very few book-length studies on her life and works had come out.[4] From the accounts printed on her book-cover blurbs, we know that she was born in 1930 to middle class parents in a village in Palakkad, that she had her university education at Banaras Hindu University, Varanasi, from where she obtained a postgraduate degree in Physics, that she worked for brief spells of time as a lecturer at the Nair Service Society (NSS) colleges at Peruntanni, Pandalam and Ottappalam, that she received great acclaim for the little that she had published in her short life, that she was the first woman writer to win a Kerala Sahitya Akademi award – which she received for her novel *Oru Vazhiyum Kure Nizhalukalum* (*A Path and Many Shadows*, 1958) – and that a new novel was being serialised in a Malayalam weekly magazine when she committed suicide in 1965. Her laconic biography provides little beyond these sparse details about her personal life. One may therefore have to fall back entirely on the biography of Rajelakshmy's fiction in order to reconstruct the contours of her creative personality. One might perforce have to scrutinise the 'tale' a little more closely than is usually done before one can think of making any conclusive statement on the 'teller'!

Let us bring the focus closer on the 'tale', then. Rajelakshmy's creative output – some of them published in her lifetime, some others published posthumously – includes two novels, a fragment of a novel, about a dozen short stories and a couple of poems. These constitute the total oeuvre of a writer whose creative life lasted for about ten years spread over the 1950s–60s. The fact that her published works appeared in some of the most prestigious literary journals of the period such as the weekly *Mathrubhumi*

---

[4] Things have changed after the turn of the century, especially after the new-found scholarly interest in women's writing in Malayalam. A comprehensive study of the writer and her work in the Sahitya Akademi series on 'Makers of Indian Literature' was published in 2002 (Menon 2002), and this was followed by a few other accounts, including a new biography (Gramaprakash 2013).

and the monthly *Mangalodayam*, points both to the quality of the works and the great esteem that the reading public must have placed on them. Rajelakshmy came into the limelight with the publication of the short story 'Makal' ('Daughter'), which first appeared in 1956 in *Mathrubhumi*. N. V. Krishna Warrior, the scholar-poet and the editor of the weekly at that time, writes in a posthumous tribute to Rajelakshmy that reading the short story 'Makal' in the manuscript form was an exciting experience for him. The story represented the emergence of a new voice in Malayalam fiction, and he was struck by the confidence and authority with which it spoke. 'I have read somewhere about the thrill that an astronomer scanning the vast skies experiences at the sight of a new star moving towards him in the telescope. It was a similar thrill that I, a journalist leading an otherwise dreary existence, experienced on reading Rajelakshmy's outstanding work,' says Warrior (quoted in Menon 2002: 45).[5] Some of her other short stories and the two novels, *Oru Vazhiyum Kure Nizhalukalum* and *Njanenna Bhavam* (*Self-conceit*, 1965), were also published in *Mathrubhumi*. So was her novel *Uccha Veyilum Ilam Nilavum* (*The Noon Sun and the Soft Moonlight*), parts of which were serialised in *Mathrubhumi* in 1960 and the publication of which was discontinued midway through at the author's request. The novel survives in this fragmented form serialised in the weekly, as the manuscript of the complete novel was subsequently recalled from the newspaper office and burnt by Rajelakshmy herself.[6]

There are two distinct approaches that contemporary critical establishment has adopted in appraising Rajelakshmy's works and in assimilating her into the tradition of present-day Malayalam literature. One of these is to view Rajelakshmy as a highly talented writer of the generation of M. T. Vasudevan Nair, T. Padmanabhan, Kovilan and others, and to consider her as one who could not attain the creative heights of these other writers because of a deep flaw in her personality that ultimately drove her to suicide. Her great promise remained unrealised owing to her

[5] Translations from Malayalam appearing in this introduction, unless stated otherwise, are by the present writer.

[6] See *Mathrubhumi*, volume 37, nos 45–50 (26 January–28 February 1960) for the published fragment of the novel. N. V. Krishna Warrior, who has read the entire manuscript, is of the opinion that had the novel been published in full, it would have been regarded as the best fictional work of Rajelakshmy (quoted in Gramaprakash 2013: 81).

untimely death. Critic D. Benjamin articulates a characteristic version of this position when he states that though Rajelakshmy's stories cannot, in terms of craftsmanship, 'claim the structural compactness of the short stories of M. T. Vasudevan Nair or T. Padmanabhan, they are remarkable for the spontaneity of their self-expression' (George 1998: 274). Extended perhaps from MT's own early appreciative comment made in a commemorative essay originally written in 1965, which stated that 'Rajelakshmy was a gifted and ingenious short story writer of my generation' (Rajelakshmy 1993: *xi*), the position has been elaborated in diverse ways by a number of critics including K. P. Appan, the 'official' spokesperson of literary modernism in Malayalam. The argument here – though often couched in a facetiously approving vocabulary – is that though Rajelakshmy's works are expressive of subjective emotions and experiences unique to her personality, they lack refinement because of the author's temperamental insufficiency and inability to connect with the external world. The image of a lonely writer traversing a secluded path cut off from the common road of social intercourse recurs again and again in discussions of Rajelakshmy's works. 'The Lonely Traveller' ('Ekanta Pathika') is the title of MT's commemorative piece on her (Rajelakshmy 1993: *xi–xvi*). MT recognises that Rajelakshmy's stories are affirmations of life, but for several of her critics they exemplify life-denying fiction that alienates the reading subject from the world of real-life experience. If aesthetic works are generally considered life-enhancing, what one comes across in Rajelakshmy's fiction arguably are morbid and unpleasant emotions emanating from a sick mind. In her fiction Rajelakshmy practices a kind of 'linguistic asceticism,' according to Appan. Appan uses the attractive phrase 'death's poignant premonitions' ('*maranattinte hridyamaya munnariyippukal*') as an effective metaphor to describe the bleak and sombre atmosphere pervading Rajelakshmy's writings (Appan 1994: 167).

A second approach, favoured by critics like M. Leelavati (2008), is to consider Rajelakshmy as a sober representative of the tradition of women's writing that was slowly emerging in Malayalam literature in her time. The word 'sober' is important here, because Rajelakshmy comes immediately after K. Saraswathi Amma, the militant feminist, the author of a number of short stories that aggressively championed the idea of gender equality in a male-dominated society, and the writer who had just stopped writing in the decade Rajelakshmy entered the literary scene. It was as though the older author was passing the baton on to the younger writer to carry the race forward. The race, an international event of wider dimensions, in the case of Malayalam had begun much earlier and had – as indicated by the early writings on gender by women from Kerala put together by J. Devika (2005) – received great impetus from the social reformist initiatives of the late nineteenth century. These writings throw light on a context of public debate in which the idea of reform was linked with issues such as gender equality, women's education, widow remarriage, voting rights for women and women's space in the public domain. That literature is also integral to this debate has been proved by the huge reception accorded by successive generations of readers to *Indulekha* (1889), Chandu Menon's novel that brought some of these issues to the centre stage. The short stories of Saraswathi Amma and of Lalitambika Antarjanam, who had entered the world of literary writing a little before Saraswati Amma, obviously arise from this context of larger debate. The legacy of late nineteenth-century women writers such as Kuttikunji Thankachi and Thottaikat Ikkavamma, who had to fight for recognition as writers in a space occupied largely by the male literati, seems to have merged with this context and taken a strident form in the works of Saraswathi Amma. The readers of the 1940s, used as they were to the humanist and quasi-sentimental literary appeals of the patriarchal variety found in the social realist fiction of Thakazhi, Kesava Dev and others, must have been shocked by the brazen and harsh-sounding – though somewhat cerebral – tone of Saraswathi Amma's feminism.

There is no documentary evidence to prove that Rajelakshmy was personally interested in this debate, though there are ample pointers and subtle suggestions in her fictional works to her sensitivity to the question of gender justice. MT, in the commemorative essay mentioned above, likens Rajelakshmy to Virginia Woolf (Rajelakshmy 1993: *xii*). According to MT, both Virginia Woolf and Rajelakshmy suffered a feeling of 'spiritual isolation' arising from their conflicted relationship with the social world (ibid.: *xii*). The heart functioned as a lonely hunter for both, and the pangs of creativity shattered them as individuals at the psychological level. Rajelakshmy herself seems to have been conscious of the commonality of identity that she as a woman writer shared with Viriginia Woolf. A rare set of draft notes titled 'Changalakal Pottikkan Iniyum' ('More Chains Left to Break'), which Rajelakshmy apparently prepared for a lecture, and which was recovered after her death from among her papers, begins with a reference to Woolf's radical essay, *A Room of One's Own* (1929) that raises serious questions about the unjust way in which patriarchal societies have always treated women writers. Though *A Room of One's Own* is today regarded as a classic in feminist scholarship, it must have been a strange text for a Malayali writer to consult in the early 1960s, a period in which the literary-minded people in Kerala were talking excitedly about such fashionable things as existentialism, phenomenology and Jean-Paul Sartre. It was when feminism was not yet a distant star on the horizon of the Malayali literary imagination that Rajelakshmy chose to talk about Woolf's tract on feminism in preference to her more celebrated short stories and novels. 'This book is more interesting than some of Woolf's novels and short stories. Even if her short stories are set aside, she can take pride in having written this single piece,' observes Rajelakshmy (1993: 164). It is perhaps not so much an elevated sense of spiritual isolation as a more down-to-earth feeling of material isolation that binds her with Virginia Woolf. Rajelakshmy's reading of Woolf's diagnosis of the malaise affecting the patriarchal social order of her day is precise and pointed. She agrees with Woolf on the basic requirements of a woman writer – a room of her own and a steady income. Alluding to the inevitability of having better material conditions for the birth of good literature in her own culture, Rajelakshmy says, 'The social condition today is such that one cannot hope to earn a decent living by creative writing alone. One has to have a second job, a bread-winning job, which naturally will have a better claim over the writer's physical and mental resources. This lands the writer in the paradox of having to employ her creative energies in a somewhat stealthy fashion and to consider her real occupation, the act of writing which is part and parcel of one's innermost being, as a kind of clandestine activity' (ibid.: 165).

It is in the general context outlined above that the present volume of Rajelakshmy's writings become significant. As already implied, fiction constituted life for her – it was part and parcel of her innermost being – and this is generously illustrated by the contents of this volume. The twelve short stories and the novel included here are important both for their value as literary artefacts that weave a vision of life into textures of words and for the way they lay bare the working of a woman's mind at a time when radical transformations were taking place in the social fabric of Kerala. Writing as a texture of words – though difficult to realise fully in a translation – is particularly important in the novel *A Path and Many Shadows*, which draws heavily on language's immediate resources for communicating shades of meaning that are linked to the emotional life of the characters. Language here functions not as an instrument to communicate experience, but as experience itself, to narrate which one has to shed one's personal self and allow oneself to fuse unconsciously with the object of narration. This is the reason why capturing in a meaningful image the many shadows from the past haunting the path of human life becomes primarily a narrative question for Rajelakshmy. What is imperative here is to reconstruct reality from the plethora of inchoate feelings that lie dispersed in the large assemblage of shadowy, ill-defined impressions crowding the mind of the novel's protagonist Remani. As in some of the novels of Thomas Hardy, C. V. Raman Pillai, D. H. Lawrence, Gopinath Mohanty, Willa Cather and others, in *A Path and Many Shadows* nature acquires a new cultural significance and functions like a human character. It is through vivid and graphic descriptions of the natural environment surrounding the subjective, emotional world of the protagonist that the author succeeds in communicating the uncertain and shadowy aspects of experience. Look, for example, at the following description of the natural world in the first chapter of the novel:

> Every year for a couple of months the barren hill would wear green. Once the rains were over, some crop or the other was always grown on the slopes. Every year different people would lease the land.
>
> The gingelly had been harvested before the *vela* in the *kaavu*. Only their stalks stood about, drying in the sun.
>
> The girl flitted among the dry gingelly stalks. A little further, wild chrysanthemum was in bloom. Clutching her books and the box in one hand, she plucked a couple of the yellow button-like flowers with the other and pushed them into her hair. (Chapter One, *A Path and Many Shadows*, translated by R. K. Jayasree)

There is an emotional continuity established between the girl flitting among the dry sesame stalks and the barren hill that wears green for a short period every year, and this continuity has been sustained through the narrative with the help of words that are materially significant. Hence the reference to the texture of the words deployed in the novel – the way one can feel their materiality. Rajelakshmy's short stories included in this collection can also be seen to partake of this linguistic felicity.

Equally significant is the status of these works as representations of women's subjectivity. *A Path and Many Shadows* narrates the story of the growing up of Remani, a sensitive young girl, who stumbles through a life that in her perception has consistently been unkind to her. Both as a child at home and later as an adolescent in college, she is thrown into environments that are inherently hostile to her. They seek to curtail her freedom and slash her innate spirit of individuality. At this juncture, a comparison with the novels of her contemporary MT is in order. There is a remarkable similarity between the domestic environments appearing in the works of the two writers. The disintegrating feudal household described in *A Path and Many Shadows* is comparable in several ways with the environs of the Nair *tharavad* sketched in some of MT's fiction. Both Rajelakshmy's and MT's protagonists are lonely and frustrated individuals fighting large alienating structures of families and societies that refuse to understand them. They are also hunted by their own lonely hearts. There is, however, an important difference. The difference is that MT's male protagonist, in spite of all the reverses he may have suffered in the initial days, wins the 'battle' in the end, whereas Rajelakshmy's female protagonist chooses the path of defeat, knowing fully well that she has other, better options before her. The heart turns out to be both the hunter and the hunted in her case. That is why at the end of *A Path and Many Shadows*, Remani turns down the marriage proposals of some of her better-placed acquaintances, lovers perhaps, and resolves to choose a lover afflicted with tuberculosis as her life-partner.

Remani in *A Path and Many Shadows* finds her womanhood to be a curse in the patriarchal social order that she cannot escape from. The characters appearing in Rajelakshmy's short stories are no different. Look at 'Daughter', for example. The story here is that of Sharada, a young woman lawyer, who finds her domestic environment utterly alienating and suffocating. The only earning member in a family of eight children, she considers it her responsibility to take care of her aged parents and her siblings. She is perpetually torn between self-interest and her sense of filial duty. Her self-centred father, once a Gandhian political activist, lives in a strange world of futile idealism that is related more to the distant past than to the immediate present. Nothing matters to him except the memories of his activist days and the newspaper with limited circulation that he has started in order to spread his obsolete ideals. There arises some possibility for Sharada to escape from this stifling atmosphere through her friendship with Bhaskara Menon, a colleague who offers to marry her and take her away to Delhi. Though she has tender feelings towards Bhaskara Menon, she spurns his love for the simple reason that he happens to be the son of her father's arch-rival Damodara Panicker. Her father dies under the shock she inflicted on him by refusing to marry a cousin he had chosen for her. Amidst such jolts and tensions, towards the end of the story, Sharada takes the crucial decision to leave home for Goa in order to take part in the campaign to liberate the territory.

'Daughter' presents the protagonist's conflict between lust for life and the social compulsion to renounce it. This perhaps is the running theme of Rajelakshmy's fiction in general. The tension between individual desire and the institution's – especially patriarchy's – attempt to control it recurs in several of her short stories, such as 'Oru Adhyapika Janikkunnu' ('A Teacher is Born'), 'Sundariyum Koottukaarum' ('A Pretty Girl and Her Pals') and 'Paraajita' ('The Defeated One'). All these stories certainly have some connection with the life of a woman, perhaps that of an eccentric woman, that Rajelakshmy had purportedly lived, a point acknowledged when we agree to consider her fiction as contributing in some ways to her biography. Some of her critics ascribe suicidal tendencies to her. While this was the thrust of Appan's critical evaluation of her, in another sense, as feminist critics Sandra Gilbert and Susan Gubar would argue, the eccentric persona appearing in women's fiction could be regarded 'the author's double, an image of her own anxiety and rage' (1979: 78). Feminists, however, would not interpret this as the symptom of an individual's shortcoming, but would choose to consider it as a culturally acquired characteristic that comes from society's gendered division of labour. Rajelakshmy's 'Aatmahatya' ('Suicide') could be read as providing an illustration of this. 'Suicide' narrates the story of Neeraja Chakravarthy who, along with her husband, a top-ranking officer in the navy, had lived as a neighbour in the rented house next to the narrator's. She lived there only for a short while, as she had to vacate the place and leave for home for her confinement soon after. But during the short period they were neighbours, Neeraja had become friends with the narrator and had started treating her almost like an older sister. Neeraja had never discussed her marriage, but the narrator sensed that hers was not a happy marriage. 'She never said anything. She never used to talk about her family. But you can always make out if anything's amiss. I read a tale of sadness in every movement of hers and even in her intimacy with me' ('Suicide,' translated by R. K. Jayasree). Now, after Neeraja's departure for her home in North India, the narrator says that she feels unnecessarily apprehensive about Neeraja whenever she hears people talk about suicides. 'Every time I come across a news item about someone committing suicide, I cannot rest till I have read the person's name' (ibid.).

'Suicide' is a story that a feminist scholar might use to illustrate a theory regarding the contiguity between fictional and autobiographical discourses and between real and imagined subjects. These instances reveal fiction's subliminal layers that of necessity sustain the idea of an archaeology for the tale. One might also use it to substantiate arguments concerning the 'subject in process' as extended to literature (Eagleton 1986: 351). Did Rajelakshmy know that there was no material basis for treating her personal self as an entity more real than the several selves that she acquired in fiction? Did she know where the biography of the teller deviated from the archaeology of the tale? Perhaps her critics who recognised that the tale was more reliable than the teller knew. That was why some of them decided that a short story like 'Suicide' should be read as offering an early premonition of the author's eventual suicide.

WORKS CITED

Appan, K. P. 1994. *Kalapam, Vivadam, Vilayiruthal*. Kottayam: D.C. Books.

Danto, Arthur. 1964. 'The Artworld'. *The Journal of Philosophy* 61 (19): 571–84.

Devika, J., ed. 2005. *Herself: Gender and Early Writings of Malayalee Women*. Kolkata: Stree.

Eagleton, Mary, ed. 1986. *Feminist Literary Theory: A Reader*. Oxford: Blackwell.

George, K. M., ed. 1998. *Adhunika Malayala Sahitya Charitram Prasthanangaliloode*. Kottayam: DC Books.

Gilbert, Sandra and Susan Gubar. 1979. *The Madwoman in the Attic*. New Haven: Yale University Press.

Gramaprakash, N. R. 2013. *Ekanta Pathika: Rajelakshmy Jeevitavum Kritikalum*. Kottayam: SPCS.

Lawrence, D. H. 1969 [1923]. *Studies in Classic American Literature*. New York: Viking.
Leelavati, M. 2008. *Stree Swatwavishkaram Adhunika Malayala Sahityattil*. Thrissur: Kerala Sahitya Akademi.
Menon, Rathi. 2002. *Rajelakshmy*. Bharatiya Sahitya Shilpikal. New Delhi: Sahitya Akademi.
Rajelakshmy. 1993. *Rajelakshmyyude Kathakal*. Thrissur: Current Books.
____. 1994 [1965]. *Njanenna Bhavam*. Thrissur: Current Books.
____. 2002 [1958]. *Oru Vazhiyum Kure Nizhalukalum*. Thrissur: Current Books.

SHORT STORIES

ONE

Suicide

'Taking one's life – surely that's a sign of cowardice. – of inadequacy and cowardice.'

'I won't grant you that it's cowardice. Is it cowardice to throw yourself before a moving train?'

'Oh, no, brave of you, then? Just go and take your own life when things don't work out your way. If you ran away from reverses because you lack the guts to face them, I would say you are a coward.'

I generally believe that when heated discussions on topics such as this were taking place in a predominantly male gathering, it wouldn't be wise to intervene.

If you want men to say approvingly, 'Oh, she's nice,' about you, you'd better listen to both sides of an argument politely with a smile (if you happen to have a pretty smile, good) but you'd better not commit yourself.

I hadn't kept quiet remembering this little bit of practical wisdom. I cannot bring myself to listen to statements on suicide without feeling apprehensive. Every time I come across a news item about someone committing suicide I cannot rest till I've read the person's name. And I feel disturbed when my younger brother reads aloud his favourite death and disaster stories in the newspaper.

One fateful day will it feature Neeraja Chakravarti's name too? Neeraja Chakravarti – Neeraja – who was very fair, with black hair shot with brown and eyes faintly suggestive of grey.

Neeraja. The ill-fated heroine of Tagore's 'Malancha' also had the same name. I haven't come across an English or Malayalam translation of 'Malancha'. An older male cousin who knows Bengali once narrated the story to me. Though he never wrote stories himself, Kuttettan could tell them so well they touched your heart. Every time I see a sliver of the moon through silver clouds, I am reminded of the pretty feet of Tagore's Neeraja glimpsed through the folds of her white shawl.

It has been three years since I made Neeraja Chakravarti's acquaintance.

I was walking around in our yard, revelling in the fact that I didn't have to go to work on a Sunday.

'Oppole, the woman who stays in the house on the south wants you,' said my younger brother, running up.

It was only a few days since somebody had moved newly into the big house on the south. We had learned that he was some big shot in the navy and was a North Indian. When I went to the fence on the south, I found the maid waiting for me.

'She would like to know whether Amma spoke either Hindi or English.'

'I don't speak Hindi but I do speak English.'

The maid went back into the house. My patience was running out when Neeraja finally came out.

I noticed the beauty of her slim, shapely figure even that day.

When she asked me something, I put on airs and uttered a few sentences in English.

'I studied in a Hindi-medium school,' she said timidly.

I was immediately sorry that I'd tried to impress the poor thing. Her request was simple – the maid turns up at eight in the morning, which wouldn't do at all; she is to come earlier.

I conveyed her request to the elderly Muslim woman who worked as her maid, and she agreed. Neeraja and I stood around, talking for some more time. Her husband leaves at eight in the morning; the maid leaves at nine or nine-thirty. After that, she is all alone in the house. Sometimes she got scared, she said. I told her to come right over if she got scared or if she needed something. I showed her where a stile had been built into the fence.

The former tenants had been on good terms with us. The stile had been put when they were there.

Next evening I had come home from the office and was having my tea when she came in hesitantly. She had a small packet of caraway seeds in her hand. She wanted the Malayalam word for it. She took it down in Hindi and, after staying around chatting for a short while, left.

I cannot say for sure just when our acquaintance deepened into friendship. She used to come over as soon as I got home from work and stay till her husband turned up at six. And almost every Sunday her husband was assigned some special duty or other. As soon as he left, she would come over.

My younger brothers named her 'Oppol's White Mouse'.

She, who had never known the hardship of having to work for a living, found my busy schedule and always being rushed for time a novel experience. Bringing pending work home and poring over files till midnight – she didn't seem to have seen a woman work so hard. Soon she picked up enough Malayalam to call me 'Chechi'.

I hate doing chores round the house. But there was no getting around them. I have to cram everything into a Sunday. Once she happened to find me ironing my sarees, sweating over the work. From then on she used to come over, iron and fold my sarees. Or, at times, especially when my younger brothers were at home, she'd take the sarees over to her house quietly and return them neatly ironed.

Amma used to pick on me.

'She's the wife of a big officer. Do you think it right to let her do all this for you?'

If I tried to stop her, she'd only be upset.

Her life with her rich, powerful and middle-aged husband wasn't a happy one. Everyone drinks in the navy, don't they? She never said anything. She never used to talk about her family. But you can always make out if anything's amiss. I read a tale of sadness in every movement of hers and even in her intimacy with me. She never told me whether she had a Romeo back home in her village that nestles in the valley of the Bareilly foothills with snow-capped mountains for a backdrop. Maybe she did. Maybe she didn't.

To get away from the busy routine and to rest awhile, I availed of all leave due to me and went and stayed with an aunt in my village. When I returned, a little bit plumper and a shade darker, I learnt that Neeraja was going to be a mother. Her problems would soon be over, I thought.

Even when she was extremely tired, big belly and all, she came over to do my hair and iron my sarees.

Her husband did not accompany her when she went home for her delivery. It was some peon or orderly that went along with her. The day after she left for home, her maid came and told me she'd found a bottle of pills in the laundry basket. She showed it to me. They were iron and vitamin pills taken as dietary supplement. Neeraja's doctor must have prescribed them. She had taken only one pill or maybe two. What made her hide the bottle in the laundry basket? Certainly not because of the bitter taste. You only had to swallow the pills. Then why?

'Amma has always been like that. There was some medicine which she was supposed to drink. How many times have I seen her pouring it out the window!'

'Now look here, don't talk nonsense. She might have misplaced the bottle.'

'If you say so, Amma.'

For a few days I kept thinking about the pills that were hidden in the laundry basket and the medicine that had been poured out the window.

It was my brother who told me the news. He'd met and spoken to Mr Chakravarti on the way. Neeraja had given birth to a child but it was no more. And she was down with a very bad fever.

She came back only after three months. When she arrived I wasn't there to meet her. I was in my office. She came over in the evening to my place. She had been reduced to a ghost of her former self and had aged by at least ten years. And for the first time, I saw her in tears.

'I never thought only one of us would go. I was so sure that both of us would.'

I didn't know how to console her.

She didn't remain my neighbour for long after that. Her husband was transferred to some other place.

I offered to help her pack but she wouldn't let me.

'Someone has been sent from the naval base. He'll do the packing. You just sit here, Chechi.'

I took leave the day they left. I was afraid that her husband wouldn't like it if I turned up at the railway station, so I stood at the gate to see them off. She took leave of my mother with folded hands and cuddled my elder brother's child.

She was not crying. Her face was unusually pale. She said '*Goodbye*, Chechi' without looking at me.

'You mean *au revoir*,' I said. 'No, it is *goodbye*.' I wasn't sure whether she realised the meaning of the term. A small voice from inside me spoke: She is right. You will never meet her again. This really is the final goodbye.

I used to receive letters in her beautiful hand every other month or so. She never seemed to have anything to say about herself. They were letters written just to elicit a response from me. They say those who commit suicide are cowards and fools.

My Neeraja, who was capable of so much love – Neeraja, who didn't know what fear meant—'

('A Suicide' first appeared in *Samyukta* Vol III. No. 2. pp. 29–33)

TWO

The Apology

'So the most disgusting of pronouns is—,' she paused.

'She!'

It came from a bench in the back.

The class fell silent.

The young teacher turned pale.

The most hated pronoun in the language.

'She!'

The class consisted of only twenty students. There was only one girl. And she happened to be absent that day.

The only female of the species present in that small room with nineteen boys was the young teacher herself. The most disgusting word – 'She'.

The voice was only too familiar.

And she also knew only too well that she ought to haul him up and take him to task.

She stood before the students for a moment, her face pale as paper. Then she walked out of the class, not even bothering to pick up her book lying on the table.

When she returned to the staff room right in the middle of a period, all the other teachers were there.

'Ah! Let off classes whenever you feel like it! Well, well, not bad. Lucky the principal didn't see you.'

Kartha Master said, half in earnest, half in jest.

She couldn't hold out any longer. She rested her head on the table and started to sob – sobs which simply couldn't be held in check.

'Oh! What's wrong?'

Everyone rose to their feet.

'What did you say to her, Kartha Mash?' everyone was getting to be chivalrous.

This is a great shame, she told herself, it's so degrading, breaking into tears like this before all these men. They are all nice people but they're strangers.

She told herself all this, but could not hold her tears back.

Somebody went over to another department and fetched a woman lecturer.

The men trooped out.

The lady – a nice woman, mother of three kids – didn't ask her any questions, but drew up a chair and sat beside her, patting her head gently.

Gradually the sobs subsided. The lady brought her a glass of water. 'Wash your face.'

Going over to the window, she washed her face. She made a pretence of wiping her face dry with her colleague's dainty handkerchief.

'May I go? I don't feel like engaging any more classes.'

'Yes of course, Rema. I'll tell them. Go and sleep it off. You need come only tomorrow. I'll get someone to engage your classes.' She accompanied her to the gate.

People who were on the verandah or out in the yard at the time noticed her as she left, hiding her face behind her umbrella.

What really happened?

There was furore on the campus. Kartha Master himself called one of the students and spoke to him to learn about the affair.

The news spread like wild fire. It was something like an event in the history of the college.

A teacher to leave a class and burst into tears! And poor Rema Teacher at that!

As a teacher, she had never given cause for complaint.

The incident grew more dramatic in the telling.

The teacher had been crying when she left the class.

A boy stood up in the class and said something obscene.

And she walked out, crying.

Poor Rema Teacher who wouldn't hurt a fly. And the person who made the comment was Paul Verghese, President of the College Union.

Complaints against Paul Verghese which no one had heard before began to come out.

He is something of a rogue. Now that he has become the president of the students' union, he's getting too big for his boots.

Someone came up with the discovery that he was hanging around the girls' waiting room all the time.

There were others who had seen him enter a liquor shop through the back door.

It took only twenty-four hours to make a villain out of Paul Verghese. What really transpired in the class? Only this? Were the other students lying to shield him? If this was all that had happened, why should the teacher have taken it to heart – well, nobody rushes to the staff room and breaks down just like that, do they?

What really did happen for her to have taken it so much to heart – that was what Rema too had been wondering about.

Why did she have to break down like that? Just because the boy said that? Was she really so ineffectual? If she couldn't even handle just one student – or was it Kartha Master's teasing that did it? Oh, no! She wasn't that touchy.

Okay, she was fond of Paul Verghese. A smart boy, very bright and lively. When she heard that in his voice ... still, did she have to—

Could it be that she was reminded of something she had lost – lost irrevocably—

Or could it be that she glimpsed the emptiness of what she called Life as it stood unveiled in the unkind glare of the moment?

The anguish of yesterdays, the emptiness of today and the futility of tomorrows – did she glimpse them all, in that moment?

Was that why she broke down?

The next day she walked into the department without raising her head.

Everybody was considerate. The Professor came to tell her that she need no longer engage the Final main class.

No longer engage the class?

It ought to have made her happy. It was there that she was insulted. She ought to be happy that she did not have to go there or meet them any longer.

Paul Verghese—

He would never have imagined that this affair would be blown out of all proportion.

What will he be thinking of her now? Will he think, she brought on all this trouble by bursting into tears?

Why did the boy have to say that? Did he mean to insult her?

In Stratchey's essay, the phrase 'most disgusting pronoun' stands for the first person singular.

And she had been teaching the essay.

A predilection for the word 'I', the most disgusting pronoun—

Being saddled with a big 'I' – had not that always been her trouble?

Let me not, oh Lord, be troubled by the feeling of 'I'.*

She'd been to the class, thinking how akin the sahib's thought was to Vedanta.

And there, after the introductory remarks, she'd been warming up to the topic, when – Paul Verghese—

The tall, slender, handsome boy, what did he hope to gain by insulting her?

The issue was becoming serious.

She was told it had reached the Principal. And that he had taken the whole thing seriously.

Paul had been asked to bring his guardian.

Oh, that'll be the end of it, Rema consoled herself. The guardian will come, chat with the Principal and leave. The case will be closed.

What a relief it will be!

If only the whole thing would be over and done with—

It did not turn out the way she expected it to. Paul did not fetch his parent.

The Principal was getting more and more incensed. Paul was barred from attending classes.

Someone so good in his studies, she agonised, cannot attend classes just because of my—

Why can't he bring his father?

Nobody in her department discussed the affair in her presence.

Oh, damn! She said to herself, maybe they thought, the woman might start to bawl—

But this was the topic of conversation in all the other departments. And there were women in those departments and there really was nothing to stop them from discussing it in their presence. So Rema also got all the news fresh and hot.

It was not solely Paul's fault that he could not bring his father. His parents did not get on well. Apart from paying for his studies, his father never concerned himself with his son's well-being. He was not likely to turn up to settle the case. If he came to know about this hullabaloo, he would only ask him to quit right away.

---

* *Translator's note*: From Ezhuthachan's poem 'Harinaamakeertanam'

Except for his father, he had no close relatives either. So it came about that he did not fetch his guardian.

The Principal got more and more angry.

She had been told that the place was the kind where you could get any number of guardians for a couple of rupees. At any rate, that was said to be the standard practice among the students.

Why can't he do the same, she wondered, anyone might claim to have a couple of uncles.

He did nothing of the sort. The President of the College Union had been out of classes for over a week.

He had to appear for the final year examination that year.

Just because of me, she censured herself, the boy—

Does this mean, she asked herself, that I can only set the wheel rolling and not stop it?

He might have blurted it out without thinking about it, maybe with some practical joke in mind.

For which—

Just because of me—

Why not go and meet the principal, she wondered, tell him my breaking down had nothing to do with what he said. If he were to ask her why she broke down in the first place—

There was nothing to say.

She kept thinking it over in her mind and finally decided to meet the principal, come what may.

He welcomed her with a beaming smile.

She recalled that students referred to the man, well past middle age, as The Tiger.

The exchange of civilities over, she had to broach the topic—

'Sir, that boy Paul Verghese—'

'Why, did he create any more trouble for you?'

'No. He doesn't attend classes these days.'

'I told him not to.'

'He's very smart.'

'That isn't enough.'

'Sir, why don't you stop this and let him attend classes?'

He laughed. A couple of teachers present in the room joined in.

Does he take me for a damn fool, she asked herself, breaking down over something said by a student and then demanding that he be let off?

'You needn't have any compunction in this case, Rema. Lack of discipline – that's what's wrong with their generation. What's more, he's the president of the union. The elected representative of the students. He's supposed to be a role model for others. I intend to punish him severely. Let him be an example to all.'

'Oh, no, Sir! Just because of me, I don't want a student—'

'Since you took the trouble, Rema, I'll do this: I'll give him a choice. Let him apologise before the whole college. If he doesn't, let him get his Transfer Certificate and leave.'

'Apologise before everyone ...'

'It won't be embarrassing to you, Rema. We'll all be there. You only have to be present.'

'Still, in front of all the students, the boy—'

She had a feeling that the principal was looking at her oddly.

Oh God!

'I have a class next hour. I've to go.'

The whole college came to know about that too.

She was told Paul Verghese had agreed to apologise.

In front of two-thousand-odd students who had elected him their leader. It was to be on Monday. The notice requested everyone to be present in the main hall as soon as classes were over precisely at four.

She could not very well keep away, could she?

The principal arrived ten minutes past four. The seventy-odd teachers were on the platform; below, a sea of students. She wondered whether all the two thousand pairs of eyes were riveted on her.

The principal waited impatiently till quarter past four.

Paul Verghese did not come.

The very same day, a notice to the effect that Paul Verghese, no. 3572 of III DC, had been expelled from the college for indiscipline was put up on all notice boards.

Not heeding the words of her friends, she took leave for a week and went home.

She returned, her heart more or less calm.

As soon as she entered her room, Raman Nair, the watchman brought her a packet.

'The day after you left, a boy came here to meet you. When I told him you weren't here, he gave this to me. He told me to hand it over to you personally. It's a book. When I told him you weren't here, he wrapped it up and gave it to me.'

It was a collection of poems by Pushkin.

Inexpensive Moscow edition. On the title page, quoted in a beautiful hand was:

When I came to kneel before thee, thou closed the door on me.

– Paul

('The Apology' first appeared in *Samyukta*
Vol III. No. 2. pp. 34–40)

THREE

The Defeated One

Nirmala quickly pulled her hand away. The papers slipped out of his hands and fell on the table with a 'pish' sound. She quietly picked them up and rose to her feet.

'Well, get those changes made.'

'Yes.'

She stepped out of the room. The half-door closed behind her. Oh, damn, she thought, I shouldn't have pulled my hands away like that. He must have caught on.

What a shame ...!

Mother of a seven-year-old boy and still ... shame!

She sat down before the microscope.

She could hear Bhaskaran humming a tune in the next room. He must have stumbled upon something worthwhile. Or he wouldn't sing. A nice person, Bhaskaran. He and his white mice, insulin doses and Hindi songs. No hassles. He is destined to go up the ladder. He knows that himself. And he is also young.

Youth – when you are young, there's no problem you can't solve.

He must be twenty or twenty-two, and ready to take on anything.

Like him, I too—

Damn! There was no need for that little scene in the Director's room. Forget it.

She took out a bottle or two containing mites from the incubator.

If only I could immerse myself totally in my work like Bhaskaran does ... But how can I, with all these problems?

Even otherwise, how can I ever hope to be on par with him, I who turned to research because I will have nothing else to do for the next three years when my husband works abroad.

It was Ravi's acquaintance with a Mr Verghese, who was on the Board, that got me this scholarship.

I might have done something worthwhile if I had landed here, like this fellow Bhaskaran, fresh out of college. Well, what can you expect if you start out after having managed a house for eight years and forgotten everything you ever knew?

What would I have done, if I hadn't had even this? With Rajiv in boarding school and Ravi in England, if I didn't have even this to hold on to, I ...

'Are you busy, Mrs Panikker?' Thomas came in from the verandah.

'Oh, no! I'm not.'

'Bhaskaran is singing away.'

'He's been singing all the time. Great excitement.'

'He should've taken up something like biochemistry instead of coming to marine biology.'

'He'll be done with this soon. He's done enough work to submit his thesis. After which, he's sure to land a nice job.'

'That'll be the end of it,' said Thomas. 'Look at me! My teachers too had sent me off, saying I would come up.'

'I don't see what you've got to complain about, Mr Thomas.'

'I really am not doing anything now – no research, nothing. The stipend is much more than what I'd get in the college. That's why I'm here in the first place. And, why not put in three years here like this?'

'Ousep! Bring the coffee over here,' he called out into the verandah.

'I had ordered coffee. Let's have it here, shall we?'

'Okay.'

'Ousep, will you please ask Krishnankutty and Unni Menon also to come over here? Hey! Pakkara! If you want your coffee, come over.'

'Thommi Chetta, aren't you my very own Thommi Chettan? Will you please send it over here? I really can't come over there now,' Bhaskaran called from inside.

'In that case, you can go without it.'

'Please, Mrs Panikker, will you tell them to bring my coffee over here?'

She poured the coffee into a beaker and carried it over to where Bhaskaran sat huddled over the microscope.

'*Rompa* thanks.'

She closed the door and left. Why disturb the fellow by staying to chat with him. The other three had pulled up stools from somewhere and were seated round the table.

'Please serve the coffee, Mrs Panikker.'

She poured the coffee into four beakers.

'Mrs Panikker, did you show your paper to him?' Thomas asked, in between sips of coffee.

'Yes.'

'What did he say?'

'He wanted a few changes made. That German journal we subscribe to – he said a paper relating to this had appeared in it in '58. He told me to look it up.'

'Well, you must grant him one thing. The man knows his subject.'

'That's right,' Unni Menon agreed with Thomas.

'And if there's anything the fellow doesn't know, it's not worth knowing either.'

'The rascal!'

'Mephistopheles.' That was Krishnankutty's contribution.

'Who can that be?' Thomas wanted to know.

'Satan.'

'He took Krishnankutty to task yesterday, didn't he?' Unni Menon laughed, 'Didn't you know, Thomas? Krishnankutty's theory on the evolution of Protozoa – he killed it and buried it yesterday.'

'Oh, leave it,' Krishnankutty was provoked into saying. 'This has nothing to do with his views on my paper. He told me what was wrong with my paper and I was convinced. So this has nothing to do with that. He is rotten, doesn't have a conscience. Satan!'

'Dark ... Sinister ... Will you stop Krishnankutty! Your Protozoa theory was no good anyway.'

'Protozoa ...'

'Leave that out of this, Menon,' Thomas came to Krishnankutty's rescue.

'The fellow is bad. He thinks only of himself.'

'Everybody else is into *Sarvodaya*,' Unni Menon was just not prepared to give in.

'Others will at least have a wife and a couple of kids to worry about. He doesn't even have those. No family, nothing. Single. Cares only about his pleasure.'

'Isn't he about forty?' Krishnankutty wondered.

'Of course. He's been here for seven or eight years.'

'He doesn't look that old.'

'Mrs Panikker, have you seen his bungalow?' Thomas turned to her.

'No, I haven't.'

'First rate building – tennis court, swimming pool, Alsatian dogs. Great form!'

'You won't catch him sober after dark,' Krishnankutty said.

'I don't think Mrs Panikker relishes this kind of talk,' Unni Menon wanted to put an end to the discussion.

'It's alright. Don't mind me.'

'He's tough, Mrs Panikker, tough to the core.'

Satan – did he deliberately take the paper – what a shame anyway!

When she returned to the YWCA in the evening, a letter with Rajiv's school seal was waiting for her.

Dear Mrs Panikker ...

That was the superintendent's letter, the report that she sent twice every month. Rajiv's brief note was also there.

My dear Mummy

he wrote in English,

Got your letter. Thanks, I am all right. How are you? I had a letter from father. He sent me three stamps. Have you got stamps?
Yours affly,
Rajiv Panikker

The paper had straight lines made on it with a ruler to help him write neatly. She must have sat with him while he wrote it. Rajiv – before he was born she had wanted a girl and had even decided to call her 'Chitra'.

She must somehow manage to get him stamps. The Director had received a letter from Finland only the day before. He said he had received a letter from a Professor in Helsinki.

If she asked him, he might give her the stamps. He keeps getting letters from all over. Wasn't it only last year that he went on a tour of Europe?

Damn! The Director—

So it's back to him after drifting around.

Mephistopheles ... Dark ... Sinister ...

Two weeks went by.

She didn't ask him for the stamps. Unni Menon's brother works in Ceylon. He gave her a couple of worthless stamps. She sent them to her son.

Every time she went into his room, she would see the envelope with the Finnish stamps among a heap of papers in a corner of the room.

'You don't need it,' she wanted to say. 'Can I have it, so that I can send it to my son?' But somehow, she did not have the nerve to ask.

She did not even relish going into his room.

The smell of expensive, imported cigarettes that permeated the room. The way he sat beneath the whirring ceiling fan, his hair falling carelessly forward. The never-ending roar of the sea in the background—

Once inside, you always got the feeling that you were somewhere far away from other human beings. You felt uneasy till you got out. And you couldn't do without going into his room at least once or twice a day.

You've got to consult him, haven't you?

You've got to get things done.

Or was it just that ...?

Two weeks went by – what with Hindi songs from Bhaskaran and small talk from the others.

She was beginning to give herself up to the wonder of watching the mites grow and multiply.

She prepared five or six good slides.

When she showed him the diagrams, he wanted to see the slides. She walked to her cabin, with him following her.

Bhaskaran was not in. The other three shared a bigger cabin at the other end. Her cabin couldn't be seen from there. She mounted the slides one by one. After the fifth, she mounted the sixth and raised her head a moment too late, precisely when he lowered his.

A gentle collision.

Blood rushed to her face.

A few minutes later, when she looked up, he was rubbing the spot.

It didn't hurt her much, so it shouldn't have hurt him either.

'I am sorry,' he said.

Then he smiled.

There was no regret in that smile.

She bent her head again.

'Very good. Congratulations!' He was preparing to leave after having examined the sixth.

She did not speak.

She had the feeling that the point where his head touched hers was burning.

She heard Thomas' voice from the verandah. He was coming that way.

She couldn't meet anyone just then.

She hurried out into the verandah on the other side.

When she had gone down a couple of steps, she calmed down.

On the ground floor, Kittan rose to his feet to greet her. He was on friendly terms with her. He seemed to have a feeling that those who did research on the first floor were also required to drop in on the fish on the ground floor.

It was in the darkness inside that she felt normal once again. There was a crowd. She tagged on to the tail end of the queue.

She had watched those goldfish and sea snakes umpteen times.

Does the spot where my head bumped his, glow in the darkness, she wondered. Is there anything on my face that screams – 'Look at this woman, she's different from ordinary women. Despite having a husband and a son, in her heart another man—'

Where was she going?

The two turtles must have fought each other as usual. The glass case was full of blood. Turtles, she felt like saying, you don't have problems like us human beings, then why—

She tried to linger but reached the exit too soon.

Should she go out? Or take another round?

Kittan opened the door to let in another group of people. She went out. What shall I do, she mused, go back to that microscope?

No. She stepped out into the yard. It was only three in the afternoon. The sun was still blazing. There will be no shade on the beach. Never mind. A group which looked like college kids hung out in the shade of a grounded country boat, munching peanuts.

She sat in the shade of another boat.

She remembered another time when she had sat in the same place under an umbrella in the scorching sun. Ravi had been with her then.

Trouble was brewing at home. Ravi had sent a note saying he wanted to meet her. She was the one who fixed the time. And she had met him also. What nerve she had in those days!

The result of all that daring and pigheadedness – she stood firm till she was allowed to marry him. If she had not been so stubborn—

Stubbornness—

If her sister-in-law had not returned from her confinement and spoken disparagingly of Ravi, would she have stood firm?

'He is the son of a *nellu kuthukari*. I don't approve of this,' her Chettathiyamma had said. Even Ravi's grandmother, she claimed, had been their servant.

Chettathiyamma made it very clear that she would never ever let her marry him. And that was what made her obstinate. Who was Chettathiyamma to say yes or no? One's parents had the right. They were no more. And, as for her elder brothers and their wives, she knew only too well how much they cared. They absolutely had no right to talk. As a matter of fact, she had been actuated more by her resentment towards them than by anything else.

Ravi had been staying in a lodge next door. She had seen him, but had never even spoken to him. It was just like any other proposal of marriage. There was nothing special about it. If that particular Chettathiyamma hadn't seen fit to interfere, it might not even have worked out. She had not been particular about it till then. When she heard her Chettathiyamma's words, she made up her mind to marry him.

She had gone to her Valiyettan's room and spoken to him: 'You had better decide in favour of this. Or I might go away with him.' The words might not have been the same but that was the general idea.

It was on the previous day that she had come over here in answer to Ravi's request and sat talking to him.

After having spent close to two hours here on the deserted beach at noon, talking and planning, Ravi had not so much as touched a strand of her hair. And it was to him that she was being – Oh God! she thought, where am I going?

She had never had any special feelings towards Ravi, either at that time or now.

Stubbornness is one thing; respect and regard quite another. With Ravi, she had never felt the difficulty to meet his eye or anything.

Eight years of marriage. A seven-year-old son. And now—

Simply because a man had wavy hair – or because he had large eyes streaked with red at the corners, under thick eyebrows that threatened to meet in the middle – or because his moustache looked attractive on his dark face – or because he knew how to smile, revealing a row of small, even teeth – or because he had long, slender fingers – or because he appeared to be strong as steel—

It wasn't as though she had been an *akathamma*, living in seclusion without meeting men.

How very frequently had she played mixed doubles, attended parties in the company of men. Yet—

Frailties of middle age … aberrations of fading youth.

But I'm not middle-aged yet—

Fading youth – but the mirror doesn't say so.

God, what a trial!

If only I had a father, a mother and a home—

Couldn't I have set up home in these eight years? That wasn't what I did. I tried to be a society lady.

I wanted mine to be the best family quarters in the whole company – the prettiest cushions – kitchen with all the latest gadgets – took care to dress well – to be fashionably modern – to go to parties every evening – the club – tennis—

Since my son had to be brought up to be modern, I packed him off to a boarding school, spending a large sum every month.

Except for all this, I never set up a proper home. Now that Ravi is in England and Rajiv in Bangalore …

What a mess …

What was the point in sitting here? Ousep has to leave, after locking up the place.

She rose to her feet and walked back. She climbed the stairs noiselessly. After locking everything up, she got her umbrella and left the room. Only Bhaskaran saw her. He wasn't in the habit of asking questions.

The hostel was only a few minutes' walk from the bus stop. There was a stationery store in between. She saw it every day. She went into the shop.

'Do you have a picture frame that you can keep on the table?' It didn't take long to find a suitable one.

Back in her room, even before she changed her saree, she took the album out of the suitcase.

Which photograph?

The one taken when Ravi was about to leave would do: it had all three of them.

She removed the photograph from the album. Inserting it into the frame, she placed it on the table so that she could see it from her bed. Yes, she told herself, these are the faces that I should see first thing in the morning and last in the night before I go to bed.

They were the men in her life.

She did not go to work the next day. She sent in her application for leave.

How long shall I keep away like this, she thought, and what was the point in keeping away?

However much she tried, her thoughts kept returning to the same point.

She went back the next day. He sent someone to ask her over to his room. He was very matter of fact. And extremely courteous too.

Still more days went by.

Once she arrived in the morning her attention was focused on one thing.

Was that the sound of his car? Most of the days the place would be noisy with the cars of the visitors who came to see the fish.

But in any commotion she could always tell his car from the others' by its horn. She could even make out the sound of its door closing.

He used to drive himself. As soon as he drove in, Ousep would run up to meet him. There would be files and books on the rear seat. His room was at the other end, next to the staircase. She could not hear him going up. She could only make out from the sound of the car whether he had arrived or not. Sometimes he would turn up late, at eleven or half past eleven. And she would be distracted till then.

Then she simply had to go to his room on some pretext or other.

One day he was on leave. It was on that day that she realised how far gone she was.

Ten thirty ... eleven thirty ... no sign of the man. She could not hold on any longer.

Who do I ask to find out what the matter with him is, she wondered.

Had he come in early? Did I miss him? She went up to his room. No. The door was locked. On her way back, she met Ousep in the verandah.

He might know.

'Ousep, hasn't the Director come?'

'No, he hasn't. He's not keeping well.'

'Anything serious?'

'Oh, no! Just a cold. That's all.'

Even though she stayed till four, it was no good. Work gets done only if you can keep your mind on it.

She went back to the hostel and, taking the photograph of Ravi and Rajiv, placed it on her lap and kept staring at it a long while.

This was not the one that should have been kept on the table. It was taken just before he left – after he had put on weight – after he had lost half his hair to baldness. The wedding photo would have been better. In that Ravi and—

She removed the photograph from the album. It was only after she had replaced the photograph in the frame with her wedding photograph that she remembered – it didn't include Rajiv. She selected a good snap of his and inserted it into a corner of the frame.

She placed the frame on the table and spreading her letter pad before it, sat down to write to Ravi. She wrote in English,

Dear darling of my heart,

What do I write?

Do I write, 'I am so infatuated with a man that I cannot hold out against him. It's not that I haven't tried, Ravi. It's as though the very ground under my feet is being swept away?'

Or do I write, 'Darling, please do come. I long for a sight of you?'

Ravi will not come.

'Nimmi, it's easy for you to say. It'll cost me two thousand rupees to get there. How will I ever raise it? As it is, I can only just about meet Rajiv's expenses.

'How can you be so childish? What a whim! You were never very balanced. Keep yourself occupied, body and mind. Then you won't have time to think up these crazy ideas.'

That would be the tone of his reply. Ravi was the kind of person who wrote once a week, at an appointed time on Sunday evenings, to his wife.

No. There will be no help from that quarter.

Days went by.

There were times when she would think why she alone should be so upset. She knew that many of her acquaintances had had such affairs.

When your husband is two thousand miles away, on his own ...

Even if he were in the habit of chasing other women ... Poor Ravi!

Her seven-year-old son – eight years from now, he ... God!

It was a Saturday.

Bhaskaran had gone to Delhi as a delegate to the Science Congress.

Thomas had not returned in the afternoon. The other two were busy in their cabins.

She went to the Director's room to clear a doubt.

He was alone.

Drawing a picture, he explained it to her. Placing a hand on top of the table, she leaned over to get a better view.

Suddenly, she noticed that his voice had trailed off.

She didn't raise her head.

His left hand was resting idly on the table a little away from where she had placed her own for support.

Dark, slender fingers.

'A five-headed serpent.'

Suddenly, his hand closed over her fair, smooth one.

Without conscious volition, her hand turned palm up.

Her soft fingers were crushed in his powerful grip for a moment.

Then she jerked her hand away and ran out.

She met no one even when she ran down the stairs.

Without raising her head, she made her way through the crowd below to the road.

There was a bus waiting. As soon as she got in, it started to move.

Listening to the roaring sea breeze, she cradled her head in her hand and huddled into a corner of the seat.

She woke up well past her destination and had to walk back.

As she closed the door securely behind her, she heard the clock striking four. She paced the room for a long, long time.

She heard a song being played loudly in the cinema nearby. The matinee show was over. She went to the table and hugging the frame that held the photographs of her son and husband, knelt down. My son, she cried, only you can save me!

Taking her suitcase, she placed it on the bed. She stuffed a couple of sarees and blouses into it. The train was at six thirty. She would catch it only if she hurried.

She'd been paid her stipend only the day before. Thank God! She had money in her bag. She locked her room and went looking for the matron to leave the key with her.

The matron was in the front yard.

'I am going to Bangalore. I couldn't meet Miss George. Will you inform her? If I'm late, I'll miss the train.'

'What's the matter?'

'I got a letter from my son. He's not well.'

Those who were standing here and there gathered round her.

'What's wrong?' 'How is he?'

My son, may you be hale and hearty!

'No, he's not all that bad. But he wrote he'd like me to go over. He's all alone there, isn't he? See you. If I don't hurry, I'll miss the train.'

'You could have asked Mathai to carry your case.'

'Oh, I didn't think of it.'

'Mathai!'

Mathai came running from where he had been watering the garden. 'Hey, take this suitcase. And go to the station, please.'

The train was about to leave. Having bought the ticket she boarded a ladies' compartment. And the train pulled out.

She huddled into a corner. A woman in the opposite seat, happy to have found a prey, started talking to her. Her son was studying in a boarding school in Bangalore. She was going to meet him. It would be enough if she told the woman just that.

'Is he in college?'

'No.'

'School kid! Will he stay on his own, without seeing his mother? How old is he?'

'Seven.'

'Seven? My Kuttappan, when he was seven, wouldn't go to bed on his own.'

She wanted to tell her, 'This is not your Kuttappan, but my Rajiv,' but she did not. She just smiled.

'Is your husband with you?'

'No.'

'You are alone?'

'Yes.'

'I suppose it is okay, once you get used to it.' She kept quiet.

'What is your husband doing?'

'He isn't here. He's in England.'

'England?'

'Yes.'

'Working?'

'He's studying.'

'Oh, so you are staying alone, having seen off your husband and son to different places?'

That's exactly what I am doing. Oh God, this woman – 'Where are you staying here? With your mother may be?'

On the final day of judgment, when, like this, you'd be required to answer before that ruthless judge – when you'd be required to settle all accounts, balancing debit and credit—

The train stopped. Somebody else entered the compartment and occupied the next seat. The questionnaire came to be directed towards her. Fine, she's been let off.

Or, has she really been?

When the woman kept asking questions, her whole mind was busy thinking up answers to them. She had no time to worry about anything else.

The questions ceased. The tempest again started to rage in her mind.

She felt strangely calm for a short while, when at an unearthly hour she had to disembark at Trichy and board another train.

Unfamiliar place. It was night. She needed to remain alert. There simply was no room for idle thoughts. The train was so crowded that she had to stand till a few people got off two stations further on to get a seat.

She opened her eyes to the realisation that she was hungry. The morning was well-advanced. She had not eaten anything since the previous afternoon.

The thought that she was nearing the safety of her son's presence made her think of food. She rose to her feet. The crowd had thinned. She had not packed her tooth brush and paste. She had forgotten everything.

She washed her face and with great difficulty managed to order a cup of coffee and a couple of dosas.

There was no one who spoke Malayalam in the compartment. She wished she could talk to somebody. There was no one. The place was teeming with Tamil and Kannadiga women in gaudy sarees.

She was left alone with her thoughts.

It was nearly noon when the train reached Bangalore. Taking her handbag in one hand and lugging the suitcase with the other, she walked out of the station.

She took an auto to her son's school. She was driven to the school building first. The children were in the boarding for the break.

By the time she located the building and got the gatekeeper to find the matron, the bell rang.

Will he be gone? Won't she see him now? She had to wait for fifteen minutes in the parlour before the matron turned up.

She agreed to call the child only when she insisted it was urgent and she had to meet him straightaway.

She was getting tired of waiting when he finally turned up. Khaki trouser and shirt, green tie and school badge – her darling son. Before she could get up from her chair, he went over to her and extending his hand, spoke in English, 'Oh Mummy, how are you?' And there he stood, smiling and holding his hand out.

She wanted to hug him close to her.

'You are a brick to have come just now, mum. I would have caught it from old Ghosh, this period. Peter called me a lucky guy,' he told her in English.

Is this the child whom she'd borne in her womb and held to her breast—

'Which class do you have now?'

'Dictation. I go wrong always.'

'Why don't you speak Malayalam?'

'You are fined for talking in the vernacular here. Four annas from your pocket money if you are caught.'

'We are alone here.'

'You can't be sure.'

It was she who used to tell him in English: 'Talk in English, Rajiv. You must develop the habit. You have to learn it.'

'Who's Peter?'

'Peter Zakharia, my best friend. Head boy in our form.'

The superintendent came in. Maybe he thought the mother and son had talked enough.

'Can I take him with me? I shall bring him back tomorrow in time for class.'

'Oh, we have a feast here tonight. But, of course, if you are particular—'

'Oh, not tonight. I promised Peter ...'

He was speaking in Malayalam!

'I'll buy you whatever you'd have for your feast.'

'It's not that. Peter ...'

'Hmm. What's the matter with Peter?'

'He promised to teach me magic.'

'Tell him you will do that tomorrow.'

'You see, this is a moonlight feast. He needs moonlight for the tricks.'

'You'll have moonlight feasts again. In fact, you have them every month.'

'Oh no! Peter will be so cross. I nagged him till he agreed. Now, Amma, if I left with you ...'

When she left him here for the first time, he'd cried, 'Amma, please don't leave me here. I'd rather go to school there. I don't want to be on my own.'

It is for your own good, son.

Be a man, son!

Removing his little hands from around her neck and putting him away, she had walked away. Now that she came to him to beg—

'Don't go then,' he said in Malayalam. 'You stay here. Ask Mr Austin if you might.'

Mr Austin was an Anglo-Indian from Kerala. He had been following their conversation.

'I am afraid that's difficult, Mrs Panikker. There is no room to offer you. I am very sorry.'

Her son did not need her. There was a time when he needed her but then she hadn't stood by him. Now when she needed him ...

'I am sorry, mother. Peter will be so angry.'

Peter ... Peter Zakharia, you are everything to him now – whatever I should have been and whatever I never have been to him. Take care of him, please. This is the plea of a feckless mother. Watch over my child, will you? Lead him on the right path!

Will he also grow up to be a rootless drifter like me?

My son! My child—

'Can I get you a cup of tea?' Mr Austin was in a hurry to be rid of her.

'No. Thanks.' She rose to her feet. 'Rajiv, my son—' She clasped both his hands and pressed them to her breast.

There was only bewilderment on his face.

You, my child, who have my eyes and eyebrows, when you grow up and sit in judgment on your mother, you must recall this moment. This moment when she came to kneel in front of you, holding out her hands to you. My son, please remember this.

She heard a bell ring.

'That's the games recess for us.'

She let go of his hands and walked out with her head lowered. She collapsed into the auto that was waiting for her.

A mother whom her own child no longer wanted. She buried her face into the end of her sari and wept. She sat alone in the cave-like cab with its canvas-covered sides and sobbed ... sobbed louder and louder.

The driver stopped the vehicle. It had reached a junction. She removed the sari from her face. He had climbed down from the cab and was looking at her. He couldn't speak her language.

'Railway station,' she said. He stood there staring at her some more time.

Then he got back in. Railway station – the gateway to damnation.

('The Defeated One' first appeared in *Samyukta*
Vol III. No. 2. pp. 41–56)

FOUR

A Teacher is Born

Ravi died here in the isolation ward yesterday.

Her younger brother brought the letter to her as she came out of the kitchen wiping her hand on her saree.

Express delivery.

She opened the envelope after signing her name against a number pointed out by her brother on a piece of paper.

Express delivery was common enough, but she had forgotten the last time she got a letter.

In her hurry, she even failed to notice the handwriting.

Ravi died here in the isolation ward yesterday.

Ravi ... Ravi ...

Ravi is dead.

Ravi died here in the isolation ward. Where was it?

New Delhi. 10-6-

New Delhi—

Was he in New Delhi?

It was signed by Susannamma Varghese.

Susannamma—

Susannamma Varghese, Nurse, Safdarjung Hospital, New Delhi.

Ravi died ...

Ravi ...

It was septic fever. He'd caught his foot on a rusty old nail or something. The infection became septic. He was brought here too late.

Whatever modern medicine could do, was done for him. You can console yourself with that thought. When he was conscious he asked me to inform you, should anything happen to him.

God bless you!

—Susannamma Varghese

Ravi died, swallowing the pain of a wound which had turned septic.

Ravi who was nothing but laughter and sunshine. And he died, miles from home in a big hospital in an unfamiliar place, with no one by his side.

He was a mountain brook of vitality that surged forth, laughing.

Ravi – who had curly hair combed back forming a bird's nest in front and large, well-opened eyes—

Ravi is dead.

How can he be?

She would never see him again!

Those smiling eyes—

She raised her left hand and bit hard on her arm.

It hurt.

I am not dead, she told herself.

It was Ravi who was dead.

'You are born with a sick conscience,' he'd said to her once, in English.

Ravi ...

'Who is the letter from, dear? What's new?' She crumpled the sheet of blue paper into her palm.

It was all these people who killed Ravi.

'It's from a friend of mine, Amma. It's nothing.'

She went in and sat on her cot.

I'm sure you'd realise some day, Indira, that what you're doing now is wrong.

Ravi ...

'Aren't you going to school? It's well past nine.'

I must go away, she told herself, it'd be better for me to go away from here.

'What's wrong with you? You don't look well. If you are not feeling well, send an application for leave through the kids.'

She rose to her feet.

'I have to go, Amma.'

Seeing her change into a saree, Amma went to the kitchen.

She smoothed the crumpled letter and after folding it, slipped it into her blouse.

Indira, you're throwing your happiness away with both hands—

'Aren't you coming, Chechi? It's nearly nine thirty,' Rema called to her from outside.

'You go. I'll join you later.'

'Why go alone, dear? Let them wait a bit,' Amma came into her room once again.

'Rema, wait! Don't go.'

These people—

'Never mind, Amma. Let them go. They'll get into trouble if they're late. You get along, kids.'

If only Amma also would leave – Somehow she managed to set off.

'Where's your bindi?' Amma had been watching her.

'Not today, there's no time.'

'You could have done without all this rush if you had started everything a bit early, couldn't you?'

They've killed Ravi, now—

'Wait, Indira! You forgot your umbrella,' Amma was hurrying after her with it.

Oh Lord!

She hooked it, still furled, on her arm and walked on.

Oh, if only I too were to catch a fever—

Ravi ...

She had to pass in front of her college.

On the last day of examinations, it was here on the western verandah of the History Block that—

It was there that she got to know Ravi and came to lose him too. It was the final year of Honours. She got to know him only because she was on the editorial board of the college magazine. Or, she would have counted Ravi among those silk-shirted, perfumed fools hanging about the campus with nothing to do, hair combed back to form a kind of bird's nest in the front.

Ravi had come to find out whether his piece on the pre-Independence days would be published in the magazine. 'The Nineteen Forties' – that was the title of his essay. If he had not written it, he would not have come to meet her. Their acquaintance started from that day.

Ravi – whom she had in her mind named 'Butterfly'—

And she who disapproved of the chatting and flirting that went on in the corners of the verandahs and under the stairs—

Her plan of action had been chalked out in advance. There was no place in it for dalliance with butterflies.

She had to do well in her studies and get a job. She had brothers but they were all younger than her. She had to bear part of the burden with her mother.

There was no time to fool around. Yet, Ravi who was known as a mischievous devil—

Ravi who used to sketch caricatures of teachers during the class and smuggle them out to the girls' side through the back, making it difficult for them to hold in their laughter – Ravi who was the darling of the girls—

Many girls had wept the day Ravi's people flew him to Madras because he had broken his nose playing cricket.

What canards had been spread at the time!

One group had it that his nose was gone—

While another had it that he had been taken away for plastic surgery. What a hullabaloo there was!

And Ravi came back in a week, with the same handsome nose and mischievous smile.

Ravi could have had any flirtatious young thing dancing attendance on him with a flick of his fingers.

Yet, Ravi ... Ravi ...

On the day the college closed for the Christmas vacation—

The way he cut a foolscap sheet of paper into half-inch-wide ribbons so popular with students who wished to cheat in the examinations, filled them with 'Many happy returns of the day' written in very small hand, folded them into matchstick thin strips and handed them to her—

How on earth did he find out about her birthday? She had never had birthdays celebrated at home. She herself had never felt that the day on which you were born was in any way a memorable one.

The things that he got up to! Things which ordinary people would never do.

Then—

On the last day of examinations.

As soon as he set eyes on her, he blurted out, 'Let's go get married, Indira.' It was just like him. 'This is the day when everyone is supposed to go their own ways. But why should we? Come with me!'

'Come with me! How easy!'

'Why not? I've made up my mind to marry you, Indira. And you—'

She interrupted him to quote poetry at him.

King Cophetua swore a royal oath
This beggar maid shall be my queen.

'Shut up!'

'Aren't I right? Don't you think that this is somewhat like that?'

'Stop being silly, Indira. Answer me straight.'

'I'm not being silly. I'm very serious. We live in two different worlds. Everyone has a background, don't they?'

'Background, my foot!'

'Do you know the Hindi word for background?'

She had tried to while away time by being facetious.

'I don't know Hindi.'

'What's wrong with Hindi? Our national language—'

'Stop talking nonsense, Indira. Are you willing? Tell me.'

'My father is no more.'

'I know that.'

'There are seven of us.'

'Yes.'

'My first duty is towards them.'

'If I'm ready to do something which my people wouldn't approve of—'

'There's a difference. You are rich.'

'There you go again. Being rich doesn't make you love your parents less.'

And so it had gone on and on. And in the end—

'So your answer is no. I'd expected this all along. Indira, you are a fool to throw your happiness away with both hands. Born with a sick conscience. Leave it. What's the point in wasting time, talking to you? I am going. You'll realise someday, Indira, that what you've done just now is wrong.'

I realised it, Ravi, she cried, I realised it only too well and long before you expected me to.

It hadn't taken her the past six years to realise it.

She, who had prided herself on her intelligence, got only a third class and ended up as a school teacher.

She had been dead set against becoming a school teacher. 'Those who cannot, teach.' Everything the white sahib said was gospel truth in those days. She didn't want to be a school teacher. She became precisely that.

What else can you expect with a third class honours in History?

She realised her mistake only too well.

It didn't take the arrival of people with a proposal from the innocuous Kumaran Master to make her realise that.

Really, it didn't take her long to realise that she tended to measure everyone against him.

There never was any question of time, Ravi, she cried, I'd known it when I sent you away with a no.

I did whatever I thought was right. Forgive me, Ravi, forgive me.

I would have broken down if I hadn't played the fool then.

You, with your big heart, would have caught on to that, wouldn't you, Ravi?

Right and wrong—

Duties and responsibilities – Ravi ...

This cursed school, and the teachers condemned to share a single room, and the unruly students—

Ravi ...

You went away and died—

You'll never see him again, she told herself, you'll never see Ravi who walked away, hiding the wound that you inflicted, saying with a smile that you'd realise your mistake some day.

Ravi ...

Here's the damn school, she muttered to herself. The children didn't mill around the gate. Thank God for that!

The staff room was right near the entrance. It was a single large room, almost like a hall. The men sat beyond a screen.

There weren't enough benches for everyone. There was a single desk, which was crammed with lunch boxes and packets. In the middle of the room, three or four people huddled round a table with a broken leg. They had to exchange tittle-tattle accumulated since four o'clock last evening till this hour, hadn't they? What a lot of carping had to be got over with!

A snatch of film music floated in from the other side of the screen.

The odour of cigarette smoke. And laughter too.

Ravi ...

Suppressed giggles from the corner nearest the window. They did this every day. Savitri was right in the middle.

Savitri and Kunhikuttan Master.

They commute by the same bus. He'd get up to something every day for her to carry over here and laugh about.

On the other side, they will be carrying on from where these people left off.

Ravi ...

'Indira, what are you doing here?' said Meenakshi Amma. Where is she coming from now, with a bundle of papers?

'Well, the Headmaster is kicking up a row over there, saying that there's no leave application and no sign of the person either. You have a class during the first period, haven't you? What happened to you?'

A class during the first period.

She walked out just as she had come in. What day is it? What day is it today?

Oh God!

The Headmaster was waiting by the door. That ought to be her class, since teachers would have reached every other room.

Giving her a look, he moved away.

She stood bewildered before the boys, the umbrella still hooked on her arm.

What do I do now, she wondered ...

'Please, Teacher, may we sit?'

It was followed by laughter. She waved them to their seats.

She still carried the umbrella. She placed it on the table. The boys were laughing still. She should not have kept it there. What was she to do? What was she supposed to teach them? Oh God, she prayed silently, what am I to do with them?

The racket was growing louder.

Are these Ravis before me, she wondered, with their hair combed back?

Ravi ...

Was darkness closing in around her?

She stood leaning against the table, holding firmly on to it with her hands.

The class had fallen silent.

'Teacher, imposition.'

A boy stood before her, holding out a piece of paper.

Oh Lord!

Taking it from him, she looked at it.

Under the spreading chestnut tree.
The village smithy ...

Oh Lord! The six lines of that poem – that was what she'd been teaching them.

'Hey you! Hand in your papers, quick!' She heard a voice from the back.

Five or six others came up with the papers. Yes, the same poem.

'Someone please give me a book,' her voice sounded as if it was coming up a deep well.

A boy in the front bench sprang up, holding out a textbook.

As she took it from him, she felt tears moistening her eyes.

Children, I love you all. In the name of the sons I do not have – that I will never have – I love you.

('A Teacher is Born' first appeared in *Samyukta* Vol III. No. 2. pp. 57–64)

FIVE

Daughter

1

Sarada hugged the bag a little closer. Two currency notes must be laughing away to themselves among assorted papers and odds and ends in the bag. Brand-new blue ones!

This was the first time she ever made such a tidy sum at one go.

'The First Fee' – it was a nice title for a story. But this really was not her first fee. Fifteen ... twenty ... fifty ... once she had even made a hundred. But two hundred at one go – that was certainly something new.

Poring over those blasted accounts during sleepless nights, she had cursed the judges, lawyers, courts, everything at the same time.

Two hundred rupees – three months of hard grind!

His lordship the judge had said, holding on to the door of his car, 'You are Krishnan Kutty's daughter, aren't you? I wish I could really help you. But what can I do? The times are bad. Nothing ever seems to go one's way. This job isn't really difficult. You don't have to argue your point or cross-examine someone or anything. Two, may be three weeks. You only have to check the accounts. That's all. You'll be paid a tidy sum as fees.'

Paid a tidy sum as 'pees'. Two hundred rupees!

A good turn to Krishnan Kutty's daughter, indeed! Since no one else could be bothered with those moth-eaten ledgers, he dumped them on her. The conundrum that nobody wanted went to Krishnan Kutty's daughter. He gave it to her, knowing very well that she'd be glad to have any kind of work and would not refuse. And now he acts as though he has done her a great favour! Anyway, it was over. She was rid of it. Now for a few days of peace and quiet.

While hurrying on, she ran her eyes around. She had reached the bazaar. Lord! What a relief! She can walk leisurely.

This was not such a bad day, she thought. If only my bicycle would break down every day of the year! She would be able to walk home just like other women do.

Achan ought to hear this. When you are sure you are not doing anything wrong, he would start off, it is foolish to be bothered by what others have to say about it. In a way he was right. But all this philosophy comes in handy when somebody else is at the receiving end of all those snide remarks from passersby. It is a little hard when it concerns you.

If one walked, home was a long way off. Still it was better than careering through the main thoroughfare on the bicycle. It had been a long time since she started commuting this way but the kids still found her a novelty. They delighted in booing at her. Instead of riding straight as an arrow, if she happened to look this way or that, well, she would have it!

She did not mind the jeering kids. It was the stares from the adults that really got on her nerves. She always wondered why the sight of a woman cycling to her office should elicit stares and snide remarks from these people.

All that was required of her was to think: let them jeer if they must and stare too. Women had to be smart, hadn't they?

Well, if you pick someone who loved to curl up with a book in some corner, rig her out in a neck-tie and a black gown and set her off to the courts on a bicycle, how do you expect her to cope? She wished she had done her MA. There would have been no need to dress like this. She would have been paid a regular salary – however small – had she taken up a teaching job in a college. And if it were a women's college, she would not have had to deal with catcalls either. Instead of poring over those blasted accounts, she might have lounged about reading poetry.

Oh, why think of all that now? How adamant Achan had been! If you must study, do your BL. If not, nothing. Why was he so stubborn? Cost-wise, it would not have made a difference either way. Did he expect that if she studied law, she would turn to politics of her own free will?

She made way for a motor car and a rickshaw, running abreast.

What a rush!

A small signboard caught her eye: Readers' Book Stall.

She was reminded of the money in her bag. Why not be extravagant for a change? After all, it was only once in a blue moon. During her stay in the hostel, how many times had she watched others blowing away money! Why not spend something on herself just this one day? After all, she had been paid for three months' slogging.

It has been a long time since she laid her hands on a good book.

She stepped into the book stall.

Books everywhere.

Pocket books with smooth red and green covers. Penguin books with orange and white covers. Thick classics.

Her eyes shone.

Books wherever one could reach. What a long time it had been since she was in a place like this. Not since leaving college. In those days, what fun it used to be in the library! It did not matter if you read nothing. Just tiptoeing among the book-filled cupboards was a pleasure.

How Radha and Vimala used to tease her, saying she was going to be a writer someday!

Writer!

Now she had dry-as-dust legal tomes for company. She moved towards the less-colourful fat volumes. *Complete Works of Shakespeare*.

Small print in two columns covering over a thousand pages on thin paper. A very handy volume. Everything that Shakespeare ever wrote. She had been longing for a copy. She glanced at the foot of the back cover.

Twelve rupees!

It cost twelve rupees ...

She replaced it on the shelf. She took the other books out one by one: Galsworthy, Tolstoy, Dostoevsky ... She wanted to buy the whole lot.

Money?

Money?

Only this morning she had listened to the milkman leaving in a huff over the money to be paid to him. And the rent on the house had not been paid for two months. I should never have thought of buying a book, she told herself, I have no right to. Books are a luxury, meant only for the rich.

Lord, how do I get out of this place, she panicked, what will the stall owner think? After hanging around for so long, if I went out without making a purchase—

There was no way she could slip out. There was no other soul in the whole place. How could one leave without a word?

What was there to say anyway? Were he to learn the cause of her discomfiture!

She had a brilliant idea. 'Do you have *Brothers Karamozov*?' she asked, turning towards him.

She was sure she had not seen it on the shelves.

What if he were to say, 'Yes, I'll get you a copy from inside'?

God! Don't let him have one!

'Sorry, we don't have it. The last copy was sold out yesterday.' The courteous young man was crestfallen. Why did the young woman have to demand a book that happened to be out of stock? He was very proud of his bookshop. Normally he stocked every book that people were likely to demand.

'I'll get it for you. It won't take more than a week,' he continued, as if he wanted to make amends for some great mistake on his part.

She regained her composure when she saw him perturbed.

'No, it's really not essential. I just thought I might buy one if it was available. There is no need to send for it.'

'No, it's really no trouble,' the poor man continued, none the wiser.

'No, I'll come some other time.'

'If you had come this time yesterday you would have got it.' Being well-versed in the basics of his business, he could not shake off his feeling of guilt.

'Never mind. I can always get it some other time. See you.' She went out.

'Miss Sarada!'

She turned when someone hailed her from behind.

Bhaskara Menon.

'It was I who bought the book yesterday. It was to complete my collection. I've read it. I don't mind letting you have it.' He paused.

She didn't know what to say.

Someone who had never shown her a sign of recognition coming to talk to her right in the middle of the road! And Bhaskara Menon, at that!

He paused and then continued, 'I'll bring it tomorrow.'

'I ... I don't need it particularly. Thought I'd just read it. That's all.' Damn! She ought to have refused it straightaway!

'I'll lend it to you. You can take your own time returning it,' he said, as though he sensed her reservations. She wanted to refuse that too. By the time she had framed a refusal in her mind, he was walking alongside, wheeling his bicycle.

What was wrong with borrowing a book? She had meant to read it when she saw it in somebody's hands three years back. She could not till now. Now someone was offering it to her. Borrow the book, read it and return it to him. That's all. What's the big deal?

Nothing? He is Damodara Panicker's son. It was with him that she was beginning this business of lending and borrowing of books. Even walking along the road in his company like this did not bode well for her.

'You have read a lot, haven't you, Miss Sarada?' He spoke after they had turned into the lane off the main road.

'Oh, no! I haven't read a lot. At any rate, I don't read anything these days. I don't have time.'

She should not have told him that. It slipped out unbidden. What was the need to have told him that she wanted to read and hardly ever got time? He made no reply to that. He walked on, eyes fixed on the ground. She was grateful for his silence. They walked on in silence for some more time.

Then somehow they started talking. The conversation began with Dostoyevsky and meandered in many directions. About writing and writers. Without realising it, they reached the place where the road forked into a lane which she had to take. They stopped at the junction.

'*Namaskaram*,' he said, glancing at her face.

'Namaskaram.'

After walking on for a while, she turned back and saw him riding away on his bicycle.

They had been meeting each other off and on for two years but their acquaintance had never developed into anything beyond a few smiles.

But this day—

As he came along the road, he must have heard her ask for the book and the shopkeeper say that it was sold out.

So what? You don't buy books to lend them to all and sundry, do you?

Wasn't it only the other day she heard the loud mouth Sankaran Nair say in the Bar Room that Bhaskara Menon would never ever let a soul into his library nor let anyone so much as open the cupboards?

They why did he offer to lend the book to her?

When she heard Sankaran Nair's talk, she only took it to mean that Bhaskara Menon had a lot of money, with which among other things he also bought quite a number of books and kept them, clean and dusted. He might never lend his books out, but he certainly must be handling them well himself. Otherwise, he would not be able to talk like this.

Who would have thought, looking at him lounging about smoking cigarettes all the time, that he was amazingly well-informed and well-read? People said he came to the Bar Council just to drink tea and chat. No one ever heard him argue a case. He came once in a while when the mood took him and scarcely ever came or left on time. They said he spent his days on the road and the grounds and his evenings in the cinema.

He had a lot of money. He could please himself, couldn't he? Yes, he did have money. His father had made lots of it.

Damodara Panicker's son! She ought to have said a firm 'No'. If Achan were to find out about this! It will only bring trouble.

As if he would remember! He would not even have meant it.

Anyway, it would be better if he forgot. Still ...

2

'Look, Valiyechi is home ...' when Sarada reached the gate, a cry went up from the yard. She got in and locked the gate. The children ran up to mill around her.

Her world.

Someone has compared children to flowers.

'The saree's freshly ironed. Take your hands off, boy!'

Did it make that bud droop a bit? Look at his chest sticking out! Has his Liver Cure got over?

'Gopalankutty, did you take your medicine today?'

'No.' So it was over and she had not bought it. He was not the only one who needed medicines, was he? Who would guess Ammini was all of nine? As if the other one was anything to write home about!

'Charu, why do you keep standing in the yard? It's five, isn't it? Come and have your coffee, dear.'

Amma came out holding the baby. So the noise made by the children must have reached the kitchen. She went straight to her room and closed the door. She was about to remove the end of her saree from her shoulder but she placed it back. Contrary to her usual practice, she moved towards the mirror on the wall. Just as Malati had told her that day, her eyes almost filled her face.

She took the mirror in her hand. Rubbing a finger against her cheek, she stood looking at it for a long while. As if she were studying someone else's reflection.

Small face, not bad. Small nose also. Nothing wrong with it either. But the shape of the mouth was all wrong, especially the lips. Not luscious enough. Should they not resemble red berries?

Altogether she needed a little more flesh. The cheeks should fill out a bit. Since they were not so, her eyes looked enormous. Hm ... Should put on a little more weight.

Put on weight!

She laughed softly to herself. She hung the mirror on the wall and changed quickly out of her saree. She was getting into another one she had taken off the clothesline when Amma brought her a cup of coffee and a banana leaf packet.

'I would've come over, Amma!'

'Have this before you change, Charu, it's late.'

'Do you know what I have got for you, Amma?'

'Is it money by any chance? The milkman came twice today. He had plenty to say.'

She got the two brand new notes from her bag and held them out to her.

'How much Ammu? Are they hundreds?'

'Oh, yes! You don't know your daughter yet, do you? Two hundred rupees. Just for a simple matter of checking some accounts – you know?'

'Two hundred rupees! I'll send for the milkman. We'll pay the rent also. Thank God!'

Thank God, she thought, I had not changed the hundred rupee note to buy the book.

'Your coffee has gone cold.'

She gulped it down and placed the cup on the table.

'There was just one banana left from that lot. It isn't ripe yet. I skinned it and grilled it with salt. Hope it's done nicely.'

Opening the leaf packet, the mother pushed it towards her daughter.

Sarada sat with one leg perched on the table, the other still planted on the ground. She had only stretched out her hand to take the packet when she felt somebody's presence at the door and looked back.

Three pairs of hungry eyes! How long have they been silently waiting there!

'Gopalankutty!' she called, breaking off a piece.

'Hmm. They're all here?' Her mother became aware of their presence only then. 'I brought it here so they won't know. But what's the use? All they do is have their fill of coffee well before the four o'clock siren and romp about the yard. Won't even let her have her cup of coffee in peace once she's home. And she has to make a pretence of eating a mouthful of rice in the morning and leave.'

'None of us got bananas.' It was Gopalankutty who said it.

She carefully broke pieces of the banana on which three hungry pairs of eyes were still fixed and gave them each a piece. She threw the last little bit into her mouth without looking at her mother's face.

Amma left with the cup. Sarada went to the porch.

For the past two or three months, she had been keeping her nose to the grindstone. Now that she had nothing to occupy her, she felt disoriented. She used to rush to the ledgers once she had had her coffee.

There was no longer any need for that.

She strolled about in the yard.

Padmini was stringing jasmine, sitting in the corner of the verandah on the eastern side of the house. Where did she manage to get the flowers? Must be a treat from some friend or other. So I can expect a piece of it today, she thought. You should keep Valiyechi in good spirits, shouldn't you? Don't you have to cajole an anna or two out of her once in a while for bangles and ribbons?

Sarada stood watching her for a while.

Once she finished the garland, she divided it into two equal portions and removed them on to a leaf. She shook her skirt out and stood up.

Then she started to take out the tangles in her hair.

She's a cute little thing, she thought.

Sarada went up to her. 'Would you like me to plait your hair? Oh, if I do it, it won't be nice and modern enough for you, will it?'

'Oh, no! It's dark after all.' She stepped in front of her sister.

Sarada laughed.

'So my handiwork is only good enough after dark?' Padmini too laughed.

'Make it tight, sister. Here's the ribbon. Work it into the plaits.' When it was over, she worked the flowers into her plaits herself and offered the other half to her sister.

'Shall I put them in your hair?'

'No, keep them.'

Sarada went to the kitchen verandah.

What's Parootty upto?

Just as she'd expected, Parootty was washing dishes near the water tap.

'Parootty!'

'Yes.'

'Come here, please!'

She took the dishes into the kitchen and came out.

'Finished your chores?'

'Rice is cooking. It won't be done for some more time. Everything else is over.'

'So you are not in a hurry, are you? Why can't you keep your hair in plaits, Parootty?'

Something like surprise or joy lit up the dark face.

'Where's the time? And anyway it's difficult to work near the hearth with your hair in plaits.'

'Okay, come here. Let me plait your hair. Let's see how it looks.'

She slowly worked her fingers into the darkness that tumbled out of a top knot.

What tresses! She had the best-looking hair of the lot. So thick you could not hold it with one hand.

Did nature bless her with long, thick tresses because she had not been blessed with anything else? Buck teeth, dull eyes, dark complexion, only the hair was beautiful.

Everyone else was fair. What went wrong with her? If not beauty, she could at least have been blessed with intelligence. She had failed in every class till she had been relegated to the kitchen to become a drudge!

A beast of burden hitched to a loaded wagon.

Why was she alone not given a pretty name? She was born when Achan was serving time in jail. Was that why her name began as Parukutty and ended up as Parootty? Perhaps they had foreseen even at the time she was destined for drudgery.

Why did she have to be born into such a wretched life? Is it right for human beings to be born with nothing to their credit, like this? It was injustice. Sheer injustice on the part of nature. Push someone to the battleground unarmed, with no armour or gauntlet.

'Kochechi ... Where's she got to?'

Calling to her sister, Padmini reached the kitchen yard.

'Hmm? What's it?' It was Sarada who asked.

'Rice is done.'

'So? Can't you see what she's doing here?'

'Amma told her to hurry and strain the rice. She said it would be overdone.'

'Why don't you do it yourself?'

'I'm supposed to light the lamp.'

'Oh! I haven't swept the porch,' Parootty got into a tizzy.

Sarada paid no heed to her.

'Listen, Padmini Amma. For one thing, you can go and see to the rice.'

'I don't know how to.'

'You take the pot off the fire, keep it on the ledge with the lid on, and tilt it ever so carefully. That's how it's done.'

'I still don't know.'

'You've got to learn anyhow. Try it once. And then, get the broom and sweep the front porch. Kochechi will be over there by that time.' Padmini pulled a face.

'She'd scald her hand and feet, Chechi! ... Let me go.'

'Don't worry, she won't. She's not a kid. It's time she learnt these things.'

Sarada plaited her hair slowly. She let the tip free so as to highlight the thick hair which spread out like a fan. She worked the string of flowers into her hair and let her go.

Who does Padmini think she is, ordering her sister to strain the cooked rice?

On top of everything else, she has to put up with her younger sister's haughtiness too. Poor Parootty. She has been born to suffer.

Is there no way she can get out of this?

Getting out!

There is no way. Not only for her. What about me, she wondered.

Gossamer thin strings bind my feet. There is no way I can break free.

No way at all.

For some inexplicable reason, she was suddenly reminded of the young man she had met on the road. Damodara Panicker's son. Achan and Panicker!

Did Panicker really do something dreadful? Achan believed it was he who had ruined his life. How far was that true? Did something really happen for him go on about it? He was a businessman. He did not want to miss an opportunity. That was all. There really had never been a question of integrity. He wanted his selfish way. That was all he wanted. He got it in the end too.

Why did Achan have to expect more than that? Why did he have to make friends with a rich man? The relationship went sour in their youth. So why harp on it now?

Even otherwise, did his action really change Achan's life to any great extent? Was it really due to him that Achan ended up like this? Was it not due to his own shortcomings? How can you say that someone else would not have taken Panicker's place?

God! What am I thinking! It is dangerous to doubt. One must believe blindly.

Prabhan Chettan had told her before he left: 'Sarada, there's hope for you till you lose faith. The moment you come to realise that your idol is mere clay, everything is finished. Before the idol crumbles, you must get out of the temple. You should never have to offer sympathy where you offered worship.'

Prabhan Chettan. It was when he left that she felt the saddest. That was the only time she wept.

How she longed to have a brother of her own like him!

Of all those who came to meet her father, she had a feeling of respect only towards him. How intelligent he was! Once he had left, the newspaper never looked up.

Everyone worth his salt had left. Only Ramankutty stayed back. He stayed because he was not good enough for anything else. He was her father's nephew, so he had the right to stay. He was older than her but she had never felt like calling him 'Chetta'. Imbecile!

Did all those young men leave because Achan really had nothing to offer them?

Does it mean that there is nothing behind the halo?

God, was her temple also beginning to grow desolate?

Deepam ... Padmini was bringing the lamp out. She had not washed herself.

She hurried in. The children sat round the lamp chanting the evening prayer. Taking a bar of soap and a towel, she went to the bathroom and closed the door.

By the time she finished washing herself, the children were sitting down to their rice gruel. It was a free-for-all in the kitchen. It was through the racket that she picked her way to the front porch. There was no one there. She made her way back to the kitchen.

'Amma, where's Aniyan? It's nearly eight.'

'Aniyan Chettan has gone for a movie.' It was Padmini who replied.

'Why did you give him money, Amma? He'd been to one only the day before yesterday.'

'I didn't give him money,' Amma replied, while ladling out rice gruel. 'He didn't ask me either.'

Hearing the sound of the gate being opened, Sarada went to the front porch.

It was Achan, with Ramankutty in tow.

Now they will go on and on about the newspaper, she thought.

3

Krishnankutty Menon threw himself down into the canvas chair on the porch. Looking at the haggard, bony face and sunken eyes, no one would guess the fire that he had carried within himself at one time. Everything had burnt down. A few embers lay smouldering in the ashes, giving out smoke that choked you.

He was the person who, twenty-five years ago, in a fit of patriotic zeal had thrown caution to the winds and set out ...

Twenty-five years ago ...

The whole country had been in turmoil. A time when people thought of prison terms as pilgrimages.

The north wind blew in the seed of revolution. It fell on fertile soil and sprouted quickly.

And a lawyer who was not thirty yet threw off his coat and gown and arrayed himself for battle in coarse khadi clothes.

It was not a well-thought deed at all. The atmosphere was sultry. The battle cry rang out, strong and strident. When a tidal wave came rushing in, quite a few were swept away. The young lawyer was sucked into the whirlpool. When he came up after a space of time, he found he had been swept a long way off from land.

His was a heart that could easily be swayed by strong emotions.

It was not on the higher planes of intellect that the revolt had been planned but on the quicksand of volatile emotions. He had been something of an intellectual among the young men of the time. But in the struggle it was emotion that took precedence over intellect.

Even in those days, there had been a family solely dependent on him. A wife and a child who could survive only by the sweat of his brow.

Who would think of that when one's blood was on fire?

Speeches were made and laws broken.

One fine morning, the red caps came to take him away. He went to prison as if it were a consummation he had been longing for.

When he set out on his crusade, there had been one who worked shoulder to shoulder with him – Damodara Panicker.

Was it patriotism, pure and simple, that made the heir to millions tread the thorny path? He had unlimited wealth. He did not have to work for a living. After a life of unstinted pleasure, did he set out in search of variety? Cloyed with a regular fare of sweetmeats, did he, even at the time, merely want to slum it with something hot and spicy for a change?

At any rate, he too had not been lacking in zeal. Panicker was there right behind Krishnankutty Menon in everything. They took part in meetings and rallies together. Faced the very first blows of the lathi also in each other's company.

But it was Menon who led the way. Panicker was always ready to do Menon's bidding. He was willing to follow blindfolded wherever Menon led. A kind of hero-worship. The warrant had come for them both at the same time. Panicker's father had been alive at the time.

The policeman came to the house of the mill owner, who could afford to buy up the whole village if he set his mind to it, with a warrant for his son's arrest.

Dawn was just breaking.

The inspector was met by the father. He took the officer to one of the inner rooms and closed the door. They were closeted together for about half an hour. Then the door opened and the inspector went back just as he had come in. Panicker's father accompanied him to the gate.

The son who lay fast asleep in his room knew nothing about it. The father left by the afternoon train, taking his son along. He put in an appearance only after six months when the storm had died down. They were accompanied by a third person. A cute little thing that definitely warranted a second look. It was only then that most people came to know of Damodara Panicker's marriage in exile.

After spending two years in jail, when Krishnankutty Menon came out, his friend had undergone a sea change.

Panicker was no longer his former self. His father had died suddenly, of no particular illness. The onus of running the mill had fallen on him. He had a wife and a child. He had responsibilities at home too. He took the householder's duties very seriously and was trying very hard to forget whatever he had got up to two years ago.

Menon took quite some time to grasp the situation. Once out of jail, he waited for a couple of days for his admirer to turn up and pay his respects. On the third day, he set out in search of him.

He had never set foot inside the house while Panicker's father was alive. Still, it was with great self-confidence that he walked up to the spacious porch.

A servant came and asked him what he wanted. When informed that he wished to meet Panicker, the man wanted to know who he should say was calling.

This was not what he had expected. Still, he managed to keep his cool and replied with a measure of self-possession.

It was to the next room that the servant disappeared. He could hear them on the porch.

There was no response for sometime after the servant had conveyed his message.

Three or four minutes must have passed.

'Tell him I'm not home.' Damu's voice.

The servant came out. 'The master is not here.'

Menon went back without a word. He never set foot in the house again.

He waited for some more days. There must be a mistake somewhere. Can Damu ever really say that?

At long last, he realised that it was futile to wait for him. Damu who had been his shadow was no more. Damu was dead, only Damodara Panicker survived.

He had a feeling that he had irrevocably lost something which had always been a part of him.

The very first blow to his ego. The wound healed in course of time. But the rancour remained.

They went their separate ways. Panicker continued to be a four-anna member of the Congress. Only, he no longer took part in agitations. He was evolving slowly into a first-rate businessman and was mastering the art of nosing out a bargain.

Menon went on, sometimes in and sometimes out of jail. He had time for nothing except politics. In his house, nothing ever grew except the size of the family. The eldest child died. Its mother cried a lot. Yet more children were born. Somehow or the other the house ran itself. Menon's wife had inherited a little something from her side of the family and with that the family pulled on.

Menon had launched the newspaper partly to meet the financial crunch. With a band of followers behind him, it did not seem difficult at all. He had a band of daring young men at his beck and call.

The newspaper did not exactly mint money but it did quite well for a while. One by one the followers began to desert him. In the beginning, new faces took the place of old ones but slowly that stopped. When someone left there was no other to take his place. Followers began to evolve into leaders in their own right. The newcomers began to leave in search of greener pastures.

Prabhakaran was the one who remained almost till the end. When he also left, only Ramankutty remained.

India won freedom. The country finally became ours. The wheel took a full turn. Khadi came into fashion. Politics became a rich man's sport.

Menon wanted to contest the very first election. He waited for them to ask him. No one did. The party fielded someone else and that person won.

For the next election, Menon offered himself as a candidate. No one responded.

Everyone filed their nominations. Menon learnt the name of the Congress candidate from the papers.

The same evening, Sri Krishnankutty Menon resigned from the Congress Party and joined the PSP.

Another election was declared. This time Menon was a candidate. Rumours were rife about whom the Congress would field.

The last day for filling nominations came. Everyone got to know the Congress candidate: Damodara Panicker!

The campaign was hectic. As far as Menon was concerned, the campaign had taken on the shades of a revenge drama. He still nursed the old grouse.

The former friends spoke at the same maidan. The same set of people listened to what both of them had to say.

Their followers indulged in a lot of mudslinging.

Panicker spent money like water.

The polling was over.

On the counting day, Menon's people waited, garland and all, ready to take out a rally.

The last box was opened. Counting was over. Congress was in majority. Was it party power? Or the glory of money? Or the charisma of the candidate? Whatever it was, Panicker won the election.

When the victory rally passed his gate, Menon went in and slammed the door. After that, he never again tried to enter the Legislature.

His new friends had hopes of exploiting his name. Their attitude changed when Menon refused to play along.

Now Menon did not belong to any party. In a way it was convenient. He could pick on every party. His newspaper criticised the government in power, so also the opposition which did not get a chance to govern the state. He spared none. A kind of unbalanced diatribe came to fill the paper.

He would be making the rounds till very late in the night. His nephew was always with him, hanging on to every word of his. He had to cover all the public meetings and speeches and finish the editorial work on the newspaper before the deadline. When he got home exhausted, he would flop down somewhere.

Krishnankutty Menon turned over in his chair.

This particular day, the man had returned, bored to tears, from a public meeting. As soon as he got home, he lay down and closed his eyes, not uttering a word to anyone.

Ramankutty positioned himself on a broken-down chair in the corner.

Sarada stood near, turning over the pages of the daily he had brought.

Menon stirred at the sound of pages being turned over. 'Is that you, Charu? Bring me a glass of cumin tea.'

Sarada brought him a glass of cumin tea from the kitchen.

'Here you are, Acha.'

He opened his eyes. He drank a little and kept the glass on the arm of the chair.

'There's a meeting tomorrow at the ground. Achutha Kurup is going to speak. You must go there at five. Ramankutty will come with you. It's no use sending him alone. I'm busy otherwise. Just go with him. Your piece should appear in the daily day after tomorrow. Make mincemeat of them.'

Sarada made no reply.

'Why don't you speak? What are you doing there?'

'Nothing. I'll go.'

'Don't forget to be home early from the court.'

'I won't forget.'

4

Thinking of Bhaskara Menon Sarada woke up the next morning. The man who had promised to lend her the book!

Will he remember to bring it?

As if he would! He'd have a whole lot of other things to worry about. He won't be dwelling on this all the time like me.

When it was time to go to the court, she plaited her hair in two and pinned the plaits up as usual. Somehow it took longer than usual.

After pinning up her hair securely, she stood before the mirror for some more time. Her face looked slightly oily. Why not put some powder on? Will there be some left in Padmini's tin, she wondered.

She took the old tin from the drawer and shook it. A pinch of talcum powder fell on her palm.

Has the girl hoarded it somewhere else?

'There's nothing in it, Chechi. It's been over for two weeks now.' Why did Padmini have to come in just now to witness this?

'You don't have classes today, do you?'

'No. Will you buy me a tin on your way back, Chechi? It's been ages since you bought me this one. I made it last this long because I refused to share it with the kids. Will you buy me a new one?

'Let me see.'

Sarada came out of the courtroom extremely tired. Even though she was used to the job by now, she went through hell every time she had to speak. All that she ever had to speak were a few words. Even that was hard.

To add to her difficulties, the bicycle had been repaired and she could not very well refuse to ride it.

Bhaskara Menon was not around. She heard someone say that a cricket match was being played on the premises of the court.

It was after turning into the lane past the main road that Sarada casually looked back.

There was Bhaskara Menon just behind her.

He got off his bicycle and extended a brown packet towards her. 'Here's the book.' She too got off. Somehow she could not bring herself to take it.

Since he had not even bothered to put in an appearance at the court, she really had not expected him to remember.

'Take your time.'

She took the book. She began to walk, with the book in one hand and pushing the bicycle along with the other. 'You can keep the book on the carrier.' She said nothing.

Without waiting for her response, he took the book from her and inserted it under the rubber band on the carrier.

They walked on, wheeling their bicycles along. Since they were talking all the while, the distance seemed shorter. Just as on the previous day, when they reached the place where she had to turn, he said 'namaskaram' and took leave of her.

It was nearly five-thirty when Sarada made it home. Ramankutty was waiting for her in the front yard.

'You are a nice one! You promised to be back early and here you are at half past five. I've been waiting here for over an hour. Ammavan told you that the meeting began at five, didn't he?'

Suddenly she remembered. The damn meeting!

'I'll come right now, just a moment, please.'

She handed her bag to Padmini, made a pretence of having her coffee and started out.

The meeting must have got under way at least half an hour ago, she thought. Why couldn't the fellow have gone earlier? Waiting for me indeed! Now, should Achan come to know that they were not on time!

Fifteen minutes of furious walking got them to the grounds. It was full of people. They took their seats in a corner.

When it was all over and they were about to leave, she looked at the watch.

It was past seven.

Was it so late? She was hardly aware of the passage of time. She began to panic. She had not been listening to a word. She was busy, thinking of this and that. She did not even know what the whole thing was about. Lord, if Achan were to ask—

'Why do you look tired, Sarada? You wouldn't have had a proper tea. Let's go to Maruti and have a cup of coffee,' Ramankutty said, when they started to move after the crowd had thinned a bit.

'No, thanks. I'm not tired.'

She certainly was not going to have coffee with him in a hotel at seven in the night. Not on her life!

'Would you like something cold then? There's a place round the corner.'

'No. I don't need anything.' As if all she needed now was a cool drink!

She quickened her pace.

When they got home they found Aniyan seated on the porch, his legs spread out before him.

The children stood round him.

So he has not gone to a movie, Sarada thought.

It was only when she drew near that she found that some kind of first aid was being applied to his leg.

A roll of cotton and a bottle of iodine stood near.

'What's wrong with your leg, Aniya?'

'I'm putting on iodine.'

'I can see that. I'm asking you what went wrong'

'Chettan hurt his leg while playing football.'

It was little Kuttan who replied. His voice rang with awe. 'It isn't serious, is it, Aniya?' Sarada continued.

'It is.'

'Is it very bad?'

'When you get hurt, it's always bad for you.'

'I'm not going to take you on.'

'Did someone ask you to?' She went in.

By the time she had washed herself, Achan was home.

'Charu, how did it go?' he asked, as soon as he came in.

'It was okay.'

'Eh, what do you mean, okay?'

Sarada found herself in a fix. She had blurted it out, without thinking. It was Achutha Kurup who spoke. What ill fate had made her say that his speech was okay? Oh, God!

'No, no ...'

'What exactly did he say? Tell me!'

'He – that is ...'

'Did you not go to the meeting?'

'Yes, I did.'

'Then?'

'Then ...'

'What were you doing there?'

'I ...' she gave up. What if she blurted out something and it turned out that it had nothing to do with what he had said?

'Ramankutty too was there.'

As soon as it was out, she wished it unsaid.

'I know very well that Ramankutty was with you. I'd told him to. Would he have kept away? Did I send you to come back and tell me that he'd been with you? Is this what you're supposed to do when you're sent on a job?'

She did not speak. She deserved all this for having day-dreamed through the meeting. This was not enough, she really deserved much more. 'Charu!'

She did not respond. Lord, why should I be harassed? Somebody must have made a report. He only had to look at it. Won't it be enough if he looked at that?

'If you carry on like this, Charu, where will we be?' he lowered his voice. 'If you don't care, who will? As for Aniyan, he has no sense of responsibility. That leaves only Ramankutty. His being here or not doesn't make a difference. If you didn't ...'

Sarada wanted to scream: 'I cannot do anything. I cannot possibly do anything.' Fortunately, the cry died down in her throat.

'Don't you feel well, Charu?

Here's a way out, she thought.

'I've a headache.'

'In that case why did you go? Would anyone in their right senses set out to listen to a speech with a headache? Would you be able to pay attention? Go and lie down, Charu. How can you be so foolish?'

5

Six months went by. Sarada and Bhaskara Menon met every day. In the evening, they made their way back together. Once they turned off the main road, they would get off their bicycles and start to walk, wheeling the machines along. They had a million things to talk about. There never was a dearth of topics. He brought her more books. She read and returned them. Days seemed to fly.

All the while her family was sinking deeper and deeper into trouble. Debts kept piling up. The circulation of the daily kept dwindling into nothing.

Once he was home, Krishnankutty Menon made it a habit of losing his temper with everyone. He was slowly cracking up under the stress. They were days that crowned a life that was a saga of failure.

It had been a long time since the burden of running the household shifted to Sarada's shoulders. Both father and daughter pretended not to notice the fact. As far as the father was concerned, it was an act that he put on, albeit unconsciously. He maintained the pretence even to himself. The man's ego needed it. He was supposed to be the breadwinner. It was, after all, his duty.

Time was running out for the newspaper. His final enterprise too was crashing down by the minute before his very eyes. Another chapter of failure was drawing to a close. How many more left? Was the epilogue at hand? Or was there anything more left?

Even at this juncture he was not willing to concede defeat. How could he bring himself to do so before his own wife and children?

He made it a habit of losing his temper with everyone. Ramankutty had to bear the worst of it. He put up with his uncle's rage and ridicule with the impassivity of a cart horse. Nothing seemed to penetrate his thick skin.

Complaints piled up about Sarada. With rancour arising out of a feeling of guilt, her father seemed to find fault with her all the time. Her lack of interest was the cause of every misfortune. Had she taken pains, the newspaper would not have been in this state. He could not really be expected to keep an eye on everything in his old age, could he?

He had educated his daughter, expecting her to take care of everything. But did she bother with any of this? She had a hundred other things!

Listening to this day in and day out, Sarada got fed up. At times, she pretended not to hear. She tried to make amends but it was of little avail.

The truth was that none of this ever really touched her. She had risen unconsciously above all this to a world all her own, a world of whose existence her people did not even know. In that world the rainbow had brighter hues and dusk acquired a brighter shade of red. Moonlight was dazzlingly white and the star-spangled autumn sky was bluer than ever.

It was an indefinable emotional experience.

She saw the familiar world around her decked out in a halo of colours. It was through an aureole of light that she looked at the universe.

There was beauty everywhere. Suddenly, she realised that the tree that she saw everyday on her way was in bloom. She read poetry into the rustling sound of the bamboo grove that stood arching its head over the road. There was music even in the insistent call of a kakkathampuratty bird from among the fronds of a coconut tree.

She was discovering something new by the minute. Invisible fingers made music in the dormant recesses of the heart of the girl who should have become a poet.

Every evening on her way home, as soon as the tall and slender young man, with an unruly shock of straight hair falling on to his brow and a straight nose that turned ever so slightly down at the tip, appeared at the corner where the road branched off into a lane, she felt herself being lifted cloud high.

Once past the corner, it would not take long to reach her own world of naked truths that could drag her down to earth or even below.

Padmini complained that she had no skirt to wear to school. Aniyan was getting to be more irresponsible and headstrong by the day. No question of studying anything. He went to movies every day; reached home only late in the night. As soon as he got home, father and son invariably fought over his late hours. Whatever anybody else had to say never seemed to touch him. The youngest boy, perhaps taking a leaf out of his brother's book, threw tantrums all the time. The younger children fell ill by turns. Neither making demands nor staking her claim to anything, but causing the most pain to her sister by her mute presence, was Parootty.

From time to time a voice seemed to whisper in her ears that her intimacy with Bhaskara Menon boded ill for her. But it died out soon. The melodious music that rose up newly in her heart instantly drowned it.

When her soul, which had begun to parch, longed for water, it was he who rained a droplet or two into it. The woman in her, who craved for compassion, recognised in him a mate with a mind and the will to share her emotions and feelings. At that particular juncture, she badly needed someone like him.

6

Looking back on that day afterwards, Sarada wondered many times whether a word or a look from her had prompted Bhaskara Menon into saying that. Perhaps not. Maybe he had come prepared. But to her, it certainly was unexpected. She had left the court later than usual.

They had been talking as usual.

He was telling her about the job that he had been offered in Delhi.

They paused when they reached the corner. He said, without preamble, 'Sarada, will you marry me?'

A thrill of pleasure coursed through her body.

A squirrel, its tail raised, was busy munching something on a low-hanging branch of the old jack tree. The wind made a rustling noise in the bamboo grove beyond the wall in the east.

When she did not respond, he continued, 'Did you not expect me to propose? You never even had an inkling? Did this feeling that fills my whole being never find an echo in you, Sarie?

'I had been waiting to land some kind of a job before I asked you this, Sarie. I am a lazy fellow. But if I set my mind to it, I really can change. I've never felt the need so far. And I've never bothered to change either. That's the truth.' He paused for a while.

'I really can make a living on my own.' That sounded puerile to her at the time. Had she ever thought him incapable of making a living? That he could not make money? A job! Even if he did not have one, to go with him where he asked her—

The squirrel trilled from the old jack tree.

It roused her.

'But, Achan—' she was, in fact, speaking her thoughts out aloud.

He understood her train of thought. 'Will he not give in, once he realises where his daughter's heart lies?'

'Achan will never understand. He doesn't think our way.'

'Destroy his daughter's happiness for an old grouse?' She said nothing.

'Do you think that the sins of one generation should visit the next?'

She had nothing to say to that too. She stood still, staring fixedly at the ground. He too stopped talking.

Five or six minutes passed.

'Can't you give me time to think it over?' she said in a low voice, without raising her head.

'Of course. How long?'

'Today is Monday. I'll give you an answer next Monday.'

'Okay. So we part. Please remember one thing. It takes a much stronger will to brush off the cobwebs that stick to your leg than to break iron chains. Namaskaram!'

Taking leave of him silently with her eyes, she turned away.

When she had taken a couple of steps, all the realities of life stepped away from her. In her field of consciousness only one thing remained. There was someone to love her. And for her to love. Every beat of her heart proclaimed it. Her whole body throbbed with the knowledge.

He loves me ... loves me ...

When she reached home, in spite of herself, her lips were curved in a smile.

7

On the following day too they returned home in each other's company. They did not speak much. The same thought filled their minds. But they had made up their minds not to talk about it. So they could not express what was in their hearts. And they were left with nothing to talk about. They had no quarrel with this silence. After walking on for three-fourths of an hour in companionable silence, they bestowed a smile on each other and happily went their separate ways.

They were in a world where words did not matter. All her waking hours Sarada had just one thought.

After mulling over it for a long time, Sarada would make up her mind to follow where her heart led. Once she was home, she was confused all over again.

How would Achan take it, she worried. Would he ever be able to bear it if she were to tell him she was going as a bride to the house of a man whom he took to be his greatest enemy, and that too while that man was still alive?

Wouldn't there be opposition on the other side? Would Panicker be ready to receive Krishnankutty Menon's daughter? Did the son suggest they should leave the place because he knew only too well that his father would never agree?

What a mess!

Just shake the dust off my feet and take off to Delhi, that's what I must do, she thought. Together we can turn over a new leaf.

God! Who'll the kids have? Will it be possible to look after her brothers and sisters from Delhi? Can she, by right, demand that she be allowed to provide for her people, after setting the son and the father at odds? Even if he were to agree, will Achan ever deign to accept money from the wife of Damodara Panicker's son? Then the children ...

Once outside the confines of her home, she felt drawn to the other side. Her mind would begin to waver when that world of music and poetry beckoned.

All her misgivings were dispelled the moment she set eyes on her beloved. The man whom she loved was waiting for her, his eloquent eyes declaring his love for her ...

The seven days were thus drawing to a close.

It was about seven on Sunday evening. Sarada was taking a stroll in the eastern courtyard. Padmini came out in great hurry.

'Valiyechi, there's some kind of trouble in there. Amma is crying And Chettan's got the cupboard open and is pulling out everything. Come and see, please!'

Sarada went in. Just as Padmini had told her, having pulled out bundles of old dhotis and the children's old dresses, Aniyan was searching for something. Her mother squatted on the floor, crying. 'What is this, Aniyan? What does all this mean?'

It was not Aniyan who replied, but his mother.

'He says he needs money. As if I have any! There isn't a single paisa in there. I told him that and he's not convinced. He snatched the key from me and is messing about.'

Sarada did not speak. She just stood there.

'Oh, no! Don't make off with that!' her mother suddenly cried. 'It's Ammini's broken chain. I promised to get it repaired and I kept putting it off. Don't take it, please. She'll be shattered. Oh God! What shall I do?'

He was opening a packet that he had found among the pile of dhotis.

'Aniya, put it back!' Sarada said, without raising her voice.

He paid no heed to her. He took a tiny gold chain out of the packet, looked at it and replacing it in the packet, slipped it into his pocket.

'Aniya! I am telling you, give it to me!'

He was stuffing the clothes scattered on the floor back into the cupboard.

'This is the limit.'

Having stuffed everything back into the cupboard and locking it, he threw the key at his mother.

She took a couple of steps near him. 'There is a limit to your impudence.'

'Really? Give me cash. And I'll let you have this.'

He stepped on to the porch, gently pushing his sister, who was blocking the door, to one side.

Sarada followed him. Full of sorrow and rage, she had no idea what to say to him.

'Give him money! Where does he think it'll come from? Do we have a money tree or something in the backyard to pay him every time he asks for money?

'Shameless boy! You don't spare a thought as to how we pull on here! All that you ever do is drink tea and go to movies! And on top of everything take a chain which belongs to a kid who's no bigger than your thumb! I'll not let you do that!'

'It doesn't hurt you if I drink tea or go to movies,' he turned back to throw at her. 'And I don't drink tea at your or anybody else's expense. So forget it. I'll never again disturb you – will that do? I badly need some money today. You can say whatever you like, but I'm going to take this.'

'How very manly!'

'Oh, perhaps not. Okay. I'm not manly enough, I grant you. At any rate I'll not trouble you again. I'll take care of myself. I'm going. You no longer have to feed me. I'll take this chain, instead. Take it as my share of the property, if you please.'

'Property! There's a whole lot waiting to be picked up! Where are you going, if I may ask?'

'That is none of your business. I'm leaving.'

'None of my business, is it? He says he'll go. Your parents, who brought you up—'

'I will go. I'll get out of this hellhole somehow. I can't go to a movie. If I take a cup of tea somewhere, all hell breaks loose. If I turn this way, you pick on me. If I turn that way, again you pick on me. Every time I come home, there's a showdown. I am not supposed to ask for money even if it's absolutely necessary. I'm fed up, listening to your nagging. A nice job of bringing up children my parents have made!'

'Did they ever deny you anything deliberately? Was it not because they could not afford to?'

'Exactly! They will never be able to afford anything. If you can't give your children a proper childhood, you shouldn't have them in the first place.'

'Aniya!'

'Yes, you should realise that you have the responsibility to bring up your children properly before you have them in the first place. It isn't enough if you just have them. Moth-eaten politics and a newspaper not worth the paper it's printed on. A nice upbringing indeed!'

'Aniya!'

'Don't provoke me. I'm leaving. I want to see if I can survive.'

All the children stood in a group near the inner door. No one spoke. No sound. Amma stood leaning on the wall. She'd stopped crying. He walked out through the gate.

Her mother did not move. She stood still, looking at the road her son had taken. Silence hung heavy in the room.

The minutes crawled by. Sarada looked at the gate. It was still open.

He has left without closing the gate, she thought.

He is gone.

The gate is open.

He will not come back. That gate must be closed.

All feeling froze. She was obsessed with the open gate. She could be at peace only when she closed it.

She went out.

It was on her way back that she looked that way.

Somebody was sitting on the verandah in the dark. Achan!

From where he sat, he must have heard everything.

8

No one ate anything in the house that night. The children holed up in different corners and eventually went to sleep.

Krishnankutty Menon continued to sit on the porch for quite some time. Finally, when Sarada called him he went in and lay down.

The house did not shake off its funeral air even the next morning. The children were unusually quiet. No one seemed to have anything to say to the other.

It was around noon that Sarada came to think about the case which had been posted for the day. There would be trouble if she did not get a postponement. She changed her saree and hailed a rickshaw. She could not even think of riding to work that day.

She had to wait for quite some time before her case was called. It was three o'clock when she finally got a postponement for two weeks.

There was no rickshaw at the gate. If she were to send a peon to hail a rickshaw, she would have to go back into the building. She felt it would be better if she walked.

She joined the crowd on the road. Shops lined either side of the road. There were different kinds of signboards. She saw them but nothing registered in her head. Her mind was somewhere else.

She turned into the lane and after passing two turns, reached the old jack tree. She turned back when she heard a sound behind her.

Someone was getting off a bicycle.

Bhaskara Menon!

'Why did you leave early? I thought your hearing will not be over before four o'clock and I'd just slipped out for a while. When I got back you'd left. I came rushing after you on my bicycle. It was only by speeding madly that I managed to catch up with you. What was the hurry?'

'I didn't feel well, so I got a postponement.'

'You are not ill, are you? You were late too.'

'No, I'm not ill.'

After which, there was silence for a while.

'Sarada!' he said at last.

'Hm?'

'This is Monday.'

Her surprise was not feigned.

'You don't remember? One week is over. You promised to answer me today.'

She said nothing.

'You forgot? Did you never even think about it?' She really had forgotten. She had kept turning it over in her mind for a week. For the past six days and six nights, all her waking and sleeping hours, this one thought had filled her mind.

But today – when she had to give him an answer – she did not remember! She had to be reminded by him!

One picture kept pushing every other picture off the screen of her mind since last night. The son who walked out through the door and the father who sat in the dark, witnessing it.

'Sarie!' There was pain and remonstrance in his voice.

Still, she kept quiet. It was a nerve-racking weariness that she felt. She wanted to curl up somewhere and close her eyes. She had had enough.

She wanted no more.

'Yes or no? You have nothing to say?'

She exerted her will to retain her grip on her consciousness, which was slipping toward darkness. She must give him an answer. She had to. What was the point in putting it off? She had to answer him some day. Why not now? If she put it off, would it become less bitter? Without lifting her eyes off the ground, she said, 'We shouldn't.' She could speak only those words.

As soon as they were out, she felt she had known for sure every moment of the past one week, her answer finally would have only been this. All the while she had been turning it over in her mind, she had known only too well that her answer could be no different; that she would be forced to turn back at the threshold to a world of dreams.

'Shouldn't? Why shouldn't we?' He was piqued. 'I didn't ask you whether we should or not. I asked you whether you'd marry me or not.' She said nothing.

'Sarie!' he said after a while. His voice was caressingly soft.

'Look into my face and tell me. Don't you love me, Sarie?'

Her eyes brimmed with tears, as, in that deserted lane, in a corner away from the bustle of the city, his beloved voice articulated the question for the first time ever. The man whom she loved was asking her tenderly: 'Don't you love me?'

In spite of herself, she raised her head. He stared into the moist depths of her eyes. He read whatever he wanted to learn in them.

The moments seemed to freeze.

'Sarie!' His voice was replete with all the tenderness in the world. 'My Sarie!'

She closed her eyes. She felt that the sweetness of the moment was more than she could bear.

'Sarie, we're meant for each other,' his voice went on. 'There really is nothing to think over.'

There is nothing to think over. No need to do so either. She really can unburden everything and relax. Give everything into his strong hands and relax.

Peace – Happiness—

Do I really have a right to them, she wondered.

The picture of her father sitting absolutely still, his head bent, on the verandah in the dark suddenly appeared before her eyes. Achan!

The eldest son had left. How can the eldest daughter too leave after him? Shatter completely that feeble life?

Oh, if only everything would just blow up, this very day!

He was waiting for her to say something.

Should I tear my flesh into bits myself, she asked herself.

What was the use of hesitating? 'We should never become one.' It was in a very firm voice that she got it out at last.

'Why not?' He got ready to battle it out once again. 'I love you, Sarie. And you love me. Then, why not?'

'I don't deserve it.'

'Isn't that for me to say?'

'No. We live in two different worlds. There's another world much different from the one you are familiar with. One which belongs to my father, mother and my people. That—'

'Suppose I'm willing to share it with you—'

'You'll never be able to come to terms with it.'

A labourer came up the path with a bundle of firewood on his head. Struggling with the load, he hardly noticed them.

When he had walked past them, he spoke again. 'Why can't I? Where there is a will—'

'Your father ...'

'There is no need to drag my father into this. As far as this is concerned, he doesn't exist for me.'

'So, he too doesn't approve.'

'The question of his approval or disapproval does not arise. This is my life. I'll do whatever I please with it.'

'Don't you have to live with him hereafter?'

'Why? Isn't that why I waited till I got a job? I can very well do without his money. I'll stand on my own feet.'

'Setting father and son at odds ...'

'There has to be some kind of relationship for that. Had my mother been alive, I would have thought twice before marrying someone she did not approve of. Where my father is concerned, I've no such qualms. For him, his son is another one of his assets – a live one. There's no place for finer feelings there.'

'My case is different,' she spoke after a while.

'I cannot abandon them just as easily. Those who depend on me ...'

'I'm not asking you to abandon them. Just because you throw your lot in with me, you needn't stop helping them out.'

'From Delhi, I ...'

'People do send money orders from Delhi, don't they?'

'Not to people who are unwilling to accept them.'

'Do you mean to say they'll not accept my money?' She made no reply to that.

'Sarie, you can find some work there, can't you? Surely he'll not refuse his daughter's money?'

'Wife of Damodara Panicker's son!'

'That old tale!'

'To my father it's still fresh. He hasn't forgotten it. If I were to do this, it would be more than he could bear.'

'That's meaningless.'

'Perhaps.'

'Even if a person has such a feeling, is it right to destroy other people's lives for it?'

'Perhaps not.'

'Leave your father out of this. I want to know your view. Are you prepared to sacrifice your love for the sake of somebody else's mistaken notions?'

'There are seven children younger to me. No, six. There are only six now. He's gone. He won't come back. He told me to count him out.

'Yes, there are six. For those six ...'

'Who's gone?'

'My brother. He walked out last night. He said before he left that he won't come back.'

'Why did he go?'

'Said he couldn't go on with this life that was choking him.'

'Yes, you shouldn't let it choke your soul.' After remaining silent for a while, he spoke again, 'Yes, the boy set out to live life as it should be lived. The path he's taken is still open. Come away. Don't strangle your love. I tell you, come away!'

'Six children!'

'You can take care of them even afterwards.'

'Achan won't let me.'

'That's sheer stubborness.'

'Perhaps. That doesn't make me love them less. They've no one but me. He walked out on them.'

'Does my love mean nothing to you then, Sarie? You don't set any store by it?'

'Don't set store by it!' her voice cracked.

He bit his lips. 'I know, Sarie. You do love me. Don't you think, that love is worth something? How can you trample over it like this? You live only once. How can you let others make a mess of your life?'

He paused for a while. 'Look here. You adore children. Don't you want a child of your own? To bring up, taking pains and dreaming of the future? ...' his voice dropped till it was hardly a whisper.

Her own child – her son.

She stood looking down, relishing the sweet thought.

Her mind was in turmoil. One more word, and she'd have given in.

He paused, expecting at least some kind of gesture from her. But since she made none, he continued, 'They say that a woman's life is complete only when she becomes a mother.'

Had he seen her face, he would have said something different.

She got her voice back.

'To hurt other people to fulfil my life—'

'Whom do you hurt? Sisters and brothers! Those who have children are also supposed to look after them. Not a sister. That pack of brats ...'

'They are people whom I love, and you—' Suddenly she was angry. A pack of brats, indeed!

'Namaskaram! I'll leave you now.' She turned away. A pack of brats, indeed! If he truly loved me, she kept thinking to herself, would he have spoken of them in that tone?

A pack of brats! She was not walking home, she was almost running.

Pack, indeed! Are they not human enough? If only she could get home soon – a pack of brats, he had said. If I don't keep on chanting it to myself, she told herself, my anger will evaporate.

And that would make her burst into tears. It was anger that saved her from doing so. Imagine breaking down on the road!

Oh, why doesn't she reach home?

Oh! Home at last!

The gate was open. None of the kids was in the yard. Somehow she got in and threw herself on the bed.

9

Padmini brought her coffee even before she had rested for a couple of minutes.

Now there would not be any peace.

'I don't want coffee right now. I'll come and have it later.' Sarada somehow got it out without raising her head.

Her sister was not convinced. She went and fetched her mother.

'Why did you say you didn't want your coffee, Ammu?'

This is the girl's doing, Sarada thought, she has roped in Amma.

'I've a splitting headache, Amme,' she said, pressing down with her fingers on her temples. 'If I drink something I'll be sick.'

Her mother was taken in by her flushed face and swollen eyes.

'In that case, don't have your coffee now. You can have it later. Let the pain go down a bit.'

After caressing her face and head, she went away.

Sarada turned over to face the wall once again.

She had sought her bed because she was afraid that she would break down and cry. Now she did not feel like crying. It was a kind of heaviness that she felt in her heart.

Her mother came back in ten minutes with desiccated ginger made into a paste with God-alone-knew-what-else.

'Charu! Turn this way please! Let me spread this on your forehead.'

How could she refuse? Her mother applied the whole lot on her forehead.

'Now close your eyes and try to rest. You'll be alright soon. Then you may have something to eat.'

'Let me get some sleep, Amme! I have this headache because I didn't sleep well. If I don't get up for dinner, don't call me.'

'You'll be okay by dinner time.'

'In case I am asleep, don't wake me!'

'No. Go to sleep. I'll close the door.'

Her mother covered her legs with a sheet and went out, closing the door softly.

She heard the children saying their prayers in a low voice. A little while later, she heard them in the kitchen. They must have sat down to have their rice gruel.

One by one, they were making their way back.

Someone opened the door.

'Chechi is not well. Don't make noise. Come and lie down quietly.'

Parootty had come to make the beds for the children. Quietly, without making any noise, she was shaking the beds out one by one and making them. Only she can manage to make the tattered beds without pushing the cotton out.

'What is wrong with Valiyechi?' said a hushed voice. It was Gopalankutty.

'Headache. I told you to keep quiet, didn't I? Come and lie down, everybody. Go to sleep soon.' She went away just as quietly as she had come in.

The sound of even breathing filled the room.

She heard the sound of a pot falling in the kitchen, following which she heard mother's voice. She was telling someone off. Must be Padmini. She heard the front door close. Achan was going to bed after his dinner.

Somebody was standing near her bed.

Amma was calling to her in a low voice.

'Charu, don't you want dinner, dear? Everyone had theirs.' She spoke again, raising her voice slightly this time. She did not answer.

'Don't disturb her, Amme. She told you not to call if she was asleep. She must have been too tired to stay awake. If you get her up now, the headache will get worse.'

It was Parootty. Everyone else must have gone to bed.

'Go to bed on an empty stomach? Going without supper ...'

'How do you eat when you have a headache?'

'Supposing she wakes up hungry in the night?'

'Aren't I here? Don't pour water in the rice and don't set milk to curd. I'll do it in the morning. If she feels like it, I can make her a cup of coffee in the night.'

'Okay. And she did tell me not to call her. Anyway, keep a glass of cumin tea here. She just might go without a glass of water so as not to disturb you.'

She left.

Sarada heard the sound of dishes in the kitchen for some more time. Then she heard the kitchen door being closed.

Someone placed a glass on the window sill at the head of her cot.

It must be Parootty bringing her a glass of cumin tea. She heard sounds in the next room, for a brief while. Then they too stopped.

'Go to bed, Amma! I'm here, aren't I?'

'Hm ... I'm going.'

She looked out through the window.

Not a leaf moved.

The sky was just as empty as her heart was.

Not even a single star.

The room felt unbearably stuffy and hot.

She kept turning over in her bed.

Oh, will this never be over? Will the day not break?

The clock struck eleven in the house next door.

How many long hours more? Long hours. Long, interminable days.

Tomorrow would be just like this day. Day after tomorrow would be just the same too. No different, smouldering slowly. One who shattered her own happiness. One who perforce had to shatter it.

Why did this ray of light have to come into her life, to illumine for a fleeting moment, the realms of her dreams that lay steeped in darkness? Why did the curtain of black clouds lift for a moment to reveal a magic world enveloped in an aureole of light?

If I hadn't come to know what radiance meant, she thought, I wouldn't have resented darkness.

She had come away without even saying a nice word. Maybe she will never again get to meet him properly.

No. He will not come again.

Will he ever come to plead again for something which was denied him once?

No. He will not.

There is nothing to hope for.

No one will wait for me by the corner of the lane with his twinkling eyes and the shock of hair falling lazily on to his forehead, she thought despairingly. No one will bid me farewell beneath the old jack tree.

There is nothing to wait for. Nothing at all.

A vast desert lay before her. With no hint of green anywhere. Oh, God, she cried silently, how long will I have to go on like this? The minutes kept crawling by. Were they minutes or aeons?

Strains of soft music wafted in, dissolving the frozen stillness of the room.

'*Suhani raat dhal chuki/Na jaane tum kab aoge ...*'

A lonely sleepless lover seemed to have put on the gramophone.

The song floated in, wave after wave, in a deep male voice.

It was midnight. The whole world slept.

The heart-rending sound came rippling in, through the numbing stillness and the darkness unrelieved even by the faint glimmer of the stars.

'*Suhani raaat dhal chuki/Na jaane tum kab aoge ...*' The auspicious night is spent. I wonder when you will come ...

Familiar old song.

'*Na jaane tum kab aoge ...*'

Sarada could bear it no longer. She feared her ribcage would be crushed. She felt a great heaviness in her chest. She could not breathe.

If I don't get out of here, she thought, I'll go mad.

She got up and, groping around in the dark, opened the door.

Nothing moved outside. There was not a ray of light. She stepped out into the courtyard. The heart-rending song went on.

Tears, held back for hours, streamed out. She threw herself down on the barren ground, bare even of a blade of grass, and sobbed.

The earth, all-seeing, all-knowing, received her sobs into her bosom dispassionately. The trees slept, heedless of the human heart that lay breaking at their feet. The sky lay under her dark blanket, not bothering to open her starry eyes.

When she heard a whisper from inside, Sarada held her sobs back.

'Hush, baby! Hush ... Hm ... m ...' It was followed by a prolonged cough.

Her mother. The baby was awake.

She listened to the wails mingle with a lullaby.

'Hush ... sh ...'

She could hear footsteps. Her mother must be pacing the room, carrying the child.

The hollow, ringing cough.

The children, and poverty and hardship had gnawed away her health. She had been working the live-long day and now kept awake for her baby son. She never got rest. Will she ever get a moment's quiet before the end?

The lullaby stopped.

She heard the prolonged cough once again. And the sound of her clearing her throat. It came from a little way off.

She must have gone up to the porch to clear her throat so as not to disturb the child.

She bore the cross that others had fashioned out of their follies and foibles. A life that had never known a moment's comfort. Still she carried on. She was a mother. Since she had borne children she must bring them up. She had no time to be sorry.

Indulge in her weakness in the presence of that mute pain? It was a sin to weep over the lamp that went out near someone for whom the darkness had never lifted and would never lift.

Weep? I have no right to, she reminded herself. Tears are a boon. You have to earn them. You shouldn't weep. You are not free to.

Pressing her chest to the ground, Sarada held her breath. If she heard a sound, her mother might go looking for her to see how her headache was.

No. She heard her going to bed. She must have thought her asleep.

She got up.

The song was over by then.

She moved softly and stood leaning her head on the old pavizhamalli tree by the tulasi *thara*. She heard someone cough once or twice in the room. Then she pressed her forehead on the wilting branches of the pavizhamalli and, closing her eyes, stood there for a long time.

It was only when she heard a cock crow somewhere in the distance that she raised her head. Dawn was breaking in the east.

She walked back into the room. She closed the wooden lock quietly and went to bed.

10

Sarada got up before everyone else did and finished her bath. But when it was time to go to the court she did not, because she simply did not feel like dressing up and going out anywhere.

She had made up her mind to go the next day. After having her food, she had even started out. But when she looked at her diary, she found that no case had been posted for that day. She did not feel like going there. Changing her saree, she lay down on her bed. She spent the whole day in bed.

There was a letter for her in the evening post.

Her fingers shook as she opened the envelope. Just four or five lines. No clue as to the place and no salutation either.

If anything that I said hurt you, Sarie, forgive me. It was unintentional and was prompted by my pain.

I'm leaving this place today. I haven't made up my mind about where to go. I need reach Delhi only by the end of next month. I've got to do something with my time till then, haven't I?

Should you need me, all you have to do is drop me a word and I'll come.

I will wait for you.

And he had signed off.

So that's the end of it all. Never to meet again! Hmm. That's best anyway. There's nothing to wait for. Let the rainbow fade out just as it had appeared, slowly, on its own.

For a few days, she moved around keeping the very first – also the last – letter from her lover close to her bosom. She knew it by rote. Still she read it from time to time. That brought her a kind of relief.

Days and nights went crawling by. Days passed into weeks and weeks into months.

Sarada could no longer take an interest in anything. She seemed to be listless on the whole.

She felt that the first few days, when the wound was still raw and she still smarted under searing pain every moment, were preferable by far to these.

Immersing yourself in pain amounts to living, she told herself. To feel pain you must be alive.

During those days she had one more thing to see to. No one should come to know of the tempest that raged within her. No one should get an inkling of the fire that singed her heart. It took a lot of will to contain something which defied control within the confines of her mind. Even having to strive for something can bring you relief in itself.

Then the feeling in her unconscious mind that she was the one who let go of something well within reach might have increased her feeling of self-worth. Could there be anything sweeter to the ego than the bitter pain you bring on yourself for someone else's sake?

Thus there had been quite a few things helping her to hold her head high.

It was when the days crawled into months and only the excruciating pain, knocked about and worn out, lay across her heart like a dark shadow, leaving no space for bravado that she realised only too well that life had become meaningless for her.

Her mind had become numb. She lost interest in everyone and everything. She felt no love even towards her little brothers and sisters. She could no longer bring herself to cuddle them or take part in their games like she used to before. She no longer had the same regard for anyone at home. Instead of love, she could only feel compassion for them.

She had to pay with her love for the sacrifice she performed for their sakes.

She engaged herself rather mechanically in the chore of making a living for her family. She did everything from getting up in the morning to going to the courts but her heart was never in it.

Her father rarely, if ever, went out those days. It was Ramankutty who ran the newspaper single-handedly.

Her father got increasingly annoyed about his daughter who took no interest in the newspaper.

But she paid no heed to that. She had made up her mind not to have anything to do with the paper, notwithstanding what anyone had to say about it. It was a kind of revenge.

She began to feel irritated at the very mention of the newspaper. She regarded both the newspaper and Ramankutty, who prolonged its death-throes, as symbols of the forces that had blown out her life. Ramankutty had never willingly done anything to hurt her. Nevertheless, she reserved for him the bitterest hatred which she could never afford to expend on anyone else. He pretended not to be aware of her scornful behaviour. The more she tried to keep away from him, the more he tried to get closer to her.

11

Krishnankutty Menon was laid up. When someone is ill in the family, money will always be in short supply.

A large family had to live. The children had to be paid their fees. Medicines had to be bought.

And help in bringing out the newspaper, which no one ever subscribed to.

Money?

Even in the past, Sarada had never managed to land any worthwhile law suits.

Who would trust a girl who looked so patently ineffectual with a law suit? Only accounts which required laborious checking or commissions which no one else was willing to touch came her way. But still she had managed to eke out a living. But with her carelessness of the past eight months, she lost whatever little practice she had had in the beginning.

People usually approached a woman lawyer thinking that though she had no oratorical skill to speak of, she would be intelligent enough to come up with a logic, take pains to study a case, etc. If she lacked diligence, along with glibness and bombast, who would engage her services?

What with her father's illness and the shortage of money, Sarada was compelled to take an interest in her work. It was only when she sat up and took notice that she realised the practice she had so painstakingly built was slowly fizzling out. If she had to start all over again at a job which she had never liked to begin with—

Ramankutty was getting to be quite a pain in the neck. He asked her to write the editorials for him. It was always do this, do that, with him. He never left her alone once she was home. If she refused to oblige him, he would go straight to her father. He knew she would not dare to disobey him. For the past three or four days, he had not left her father's side. They seemed to be discussing something seriously.

It was evening. Sarada was sitting alone on the southern verandah. The children had gone to the temple. Her mother and Parootty were in the kitchen.

Lost in thought, she sat still for a while, the newspaper lying forgotten on her lap. When she saw Ramankutty walking up to her from the front yard, she picked up the newspaper and started to read. He came up to her.

'Are you reading the newspaper or just day-dreaming?'

She wanted to remind him that it was none of his business. She continued to read, not bothering to give him a reply. He sat down on the verandah beside her.

'Why are you so silent these days, Sarie?' Who was he to call her Sarie?

Someone had called her Sarie before.

Oh, ages ago!

What right did this fellow have to call her so? 'Are you angry with me by any chance?'

If she did not make a reply, he would not go away.

'Angry? Why?'

'Only you know the reason, Sarie.' She kept quiet.

'Ammavan and I were talking about you.'

'Oh?'

'Ammavan says we should get it over with as soon as possible.'

'Get over with what?'

'Do I have to spell it out for you? As if you didn't know! Poor thing!'

He gave a foolish grin.

Oh, Devi! That she had to endure his antics too! Trying to flirt with her, the creep!

'Ammavan is easily tired these days,' he started again. 'He's getting old, isn't he? Naturally, you can't expect him to live forever. I think he has a feeling that he won't get any better. Since he's not well, let him at least have this one relief. Where's the need to put this off any longer?'

'What relief? Put off what?'

'You will have me spell it out for you, won't you? You little liar!'

'If you have something to say, please get it out. We'll have the humour later on.'

'Pray, do not be angry.' He tried to laugh. 'It's this thing about our getting married. What else can it be?'

'What exactly does that "our" mean?'

'You and me. Who else?'

'You can leave me out of this. You need bother only about yourself.'

'How can that be? How can I get on with this on my own? This is not something you can do on your own.'

'Find someone else.'

'Why should I now? Sarie ...'

'Forget about it. That's impossible.'

'Why should it be?'

'It's impossible. That's why.'

'There ought to be a reason. Let's have it.'

'There's no reason. I'm not marrying anyone right now. That's all there's to it.'

'You mean to say you'll never marry?

'Yes.'

'A lot of women have said that. And do you think they are all spinsters now?'

'This woman is determined to remain so.'

'Suppose your father has something quite different in mind for you?'

'Impossible.'

'This is something Ammavan has always had in his mind.' He changed his tone to one you would use when you reason with children and began, 'Do you think your father will be pleased if you tell him that you won't agree to this?'

'This has never been decided before. And in any case, this is not something that you do to please your father.'

'Is it because you just do not like me in particular or do you mean to marry no one?' He spoke after a few minutes of silence.

'I told you in the beginning. I don't want to get married.'

'No? Even if it's Bhaskara Menon of Elanjiparambil?'

'Oh?' She was shocked. 'What did you say?'

'I said, will you agree to get married if it's Damodara Panicker's son Bhaskara Menon? If it were lawyer Bhaskara Menon in my place, would you say you don't want to marry at all?'

She rose to her feet. Sparks seemed to fly from her eyes.

He was still not prepared to stop. He too rose to his feet. 'Do you think that no one has come to know of all that chatting in the lane and flirting under the jack tree? It's common knowledge now. And the cat thought no one would know if it lapped up the milk with its eyes shut.'

'Stop it! Don't say a word more.'

She could say no more. She was trembling from head to foot.

She turned and, going into her room, slammed the door shut. She sat on the cot but could not keep still for long. So she got up and paced the room a couple of times.

So he had the nerve to say that!

He even sullied the memories that lay dormant in the recesses of her heart. The jerk!

He dared to tread where he had no right to!

Common knowledge, indeed!

Really?

Was it true that that merciless eyes had witnessed the rainbow appearing on her sky and fading behind the clouds?

No. He's lying. She would have come to know if it had been common knowledge. She had been treading the same road all these months, hadn't she?

He is lying. He must have found out by chance. Now he's pretending that it's common knowledge.

Now everyone might come to know because he was sure to talk. That was certain. And he was the type. He parted on bad terms too. He was sure to talk. He would fill the place with it. He might even take it to Achan. Lord! This too on top of his illness!

12

The day passed off with no further developments. Ramankutty did not venture to talk to her again. It was around eight o'clock in the evening the next day. The children were poring over their books on the porch after dinner.

Amma came and said to her, 'Charu, Achan wants you.' Giving it no thought, she went over to him and stood near the cot.

Her father lay with his eyes closed.

'Did you call me, Acha?' She spoke quietly after a brief silence.

He opened his eyes.

'Draw up that stool and sit by me.' She obeyed him.

He did not begin immediately. He cleared his throat a couple of times. Then he said very softly, 'Ramankutty tells me that you don't bother with the newspaper these days.' She kept quiet.

'I don't keep well these days, Ammu. Now it's for you to run everything.'

She made no reply to that too.

'I couldn't finish anything that I ever began. There's only you to run the paper now. You are intelligent enough. I gave you the education. That's why I made you do BL. You have to achieve whatever I could not. You can. I know that.'

After a brief pause, he continued, 'You possess a man's brain. But a brain is not enough. To run the show, you need a man behind you. It's all very well to talk about equality. It takes a man to do things which need brawn. You know what I'm driving at?'

She wanted to say 'No' but she just said 'Hm.'

'I know you are sharp enough to get my drift.' He lay quiet, as if lost in some thought.

'Ramankutty isn't smart enough. He cannot get anything done on his own. But he'll do as he is told. You only have to tell him what. He'll pull it off. If you put your mind to it, the newspaper wouldn't go to the dogs like this. I can no longer run these things. It's up to you now. You must get him to run it.'

Her anger kept mounting. She could have borne it had he told her, 'Take care of the younger children.' It was not that. He was not worried about bringing them up at all. He was still thinking about politics. Politics! What politics? It was all an ego trip. If whatever you started runs aground, it's a shame. It lowers your self-esteem.

What if your children starve? Your pride is intact!

Her eyes rested briefly on the gaunt face.

Shame, she told herself, you are losing your temper with someone who cannot not raise himself on his own. And he has hypertension. He must not be disturbed.

'I'll see to the newspaper,' she answered quickly.

'I knew you would. You've always listened to me.'

Her only thought was to get away soon. She wanted to slip out before he started on some other topic. But how could she, without being dismissed? Still ...

'I must send Ramankutty to fix up an auspicious day,' her father said, as if speaking his thoughts aloud. She panicked.

'Why an auspicious day?'

'Whatever people might say, you should never do anything without paying attention to these things. Let him consult Astrologer Embranthiri. He's good.'

'What's this auspicious day for?'

'You've got to conduct a wedding like everybody else does, haven't you? We must find an auspicious time. Don't you worry about all that. I'll see to everything. Ask Ramankutty to meet me. I'll get everything fixed without stirring myself.'

Lord! Everything is going to be a mess. If she kept quiet now to spare his pain, she will get herself into deeper trouble later on.

'Acha, who spoke of marriage here? I don't see why you should have an auspicious time fixed.'

'Eh? Who spoke of marriage, is that what you said? In that case, what did you speak of a little while ago?'

'I said I'd see to the newspaper.'

'Yes, that's it. Can you run the newspaper without Ramankutty's help?'

'Maybe not. Well, I don't know. In that case, between us, we'll run it. Just as it is being run now.'

'That's impossible. Once I'm gone, it wouldn't be a nice thing for you young people to move about closely like this. That's sure to lead to trouble.'

'No, it won't.'

'Even if it doesn't, this arrangement will not work out for long. He's sure to get married some day. Then will he help you run the newspaper if his wife tells him not to?'

'Even so, please don't ask me to do this, Acha. I can't.'

'Why not? What wrong has he done?'

'Nothing, but I cannot marry him. That's all.'

'There has to be a reason. Isn't he educated enough? At any rate, he's done his BA.'

'No, not that he's not educated enough.'

'Then tell me what's wrong with him.'

'Nothing perhaps.'

'Nothing perhaps, she says. A very satisfactory response!'

'Then what do you expect me to say?'

'Why do you refuse? There's nothing much wrong with him. You too admit that. And you need him if you are to get anything done. You certainly cannot do without him. That's another fact. And he says he's willing to marry you. Why don't you agree?' She made no reply.

As if the newspaper was a good enough reason for getting married!

'Charu, why don't you try to understand?'

'It's not that I don't, Acha. But I cannot marry him.'

Closing his eyes, he continued to lie for some more time. Sarada waited with bated breath.

He opened his eyes at last. 'Do you have someone else in mind, Charu?'

'No.' That was one question she could honestly answer in the negative.

'Are you in love with someone?' She made no reply to that.

'Are you in love with someone for you to refuse Ramankutty so categorically?'

'I only said I didn't want to marry.'

'You didn't say so to begin with. Even so, that's an absurd reason to offer. It's childish. It's foolish to offer such a lame excuse to your own father after you've come to realise the desirability of such an alliance.' She had nothing to say.

'Wouldn't do if you keep mum. This is no joke.' She still did not speak.

'You have nothing to say? I'll ask you the same thing once again: Are you in love with someone else?'

'Yes.' Her voice was firm. She had reached the end of her tether. If he were bent upon making her come out with it, let him have it. The blighter must have told him. The only question was, how much.

'Who's the person?'

'That's beside the point. I'm not going to marry him. Isn't that enough for you?'

'That's for me to say. Tell me who it is.'

'I won't.'

'Why not?'

'Don't make me take his name.'

'Eh ... You ... So, what that lad said was true? I very nearly slapped him. Charu ... you ...'

'Acha!'

'Is it true? Is that rascal's son your ...'

'Acha!'

'So that's how it is, is it? So you could do this to me. The son of the man who ruined my life ...'

'But I told you I won't marry him.'

'So you did.'

'Yes. I did. But that isn't enough for you. I ruined everything. I willingly sacrificed two lives. Still it's not enough. Oh, God! I buried my love for their sake. Why blame them? I did it for the sake of just one person's pride. Yours.'

'You ...you—'

'You made me say it.'

'For my pride ...'

'Acha!'

'Go! Get out of my sight!'

He turned over in his bed to face the wall. She waited for a while. Then she went quietly out.

Around eleven in the night, her mother came to where Sarada lay and called her. She was awake.

Achan was in a very bad condition. He had severe chest pain.

She ran to his room.

He lay with his eyes closed. There was only a whimper now and then.

Her mother had got Ramankutty up too. He was immediately sent to fetch the doctor.

By then Parootty too got up and joined them. One by one, the other children followed. Even Gopalankutty.

The children, dazed with sleep, looked on. No one spoke.

Her mother and Parootty began to massage his legs. For a while, Padmini stood still, looking on. Then she got hold of a fan, moved to the cot and began to fan him, without being told.

Sarada alone stood stock-still near the bed, never taking her eyes off the occupant's face. Even her lips were ashen.

Only once did the sick man open his eyes. For a moment, his gaze lingered on Sarada's face. He closed his eyes immediately. He never opened them again.

Everything was over even before the doctor arrived.

The weeping and wailing started. The eldest daughter had no tears. When he was dying, she didn't dare touch him. Now her eyes refused to weep.

13

Seven or eight months later, one Sunday after sundown, a tall, thin young man came along the lane, turning past the old jack tree. When he reached the old iron gate, he stood still.

An old man with his body smeared with holy ash was on his way to the temple. There was no one else around. The young man stood looking at the closed gate for some time and then crossed over to the other side. He took a few steps past the gate. Then he stood still, as if lost in some thought.

The old man stopped on his way and studied the young man for a short while.

'Lost your way?' he approached him at last.

'Oh, no!' the young man came out of his thoughts.

'I wondered, since you seemed to hesitate.'

'I haven't lost my way. In fact I came out for a walk. I stopped here because the place is familiar to me. That's all.'

'You have acquaintances in that house?'

The old man was not willing to leave him alone.

'Ah, yes, I know someone.'

'Whom do you mean? There is an elder and a younger brother.' He was happy to have someone to talk to.

'Neither the elder nor the younger. I know the lawyer.'

'Lawyer? There is no lawyer there.'

'How can that be? A woman—'

'There are no women at all in the house. Both of them are bachelors.'

'I'm talking about the house with the tin gate. Saradamma ...'

'Oh, that's it. You mean Saradakutty? Yes. She had indeed studied law. I thought you meant the present tenants of the house.'

'Present tenants? Doesn't she stay here any longer? Where did Saradamma go? Did they move house?'

'Move house? Don't you belong to this place?'

'I do. But I've been away for a while.'

'You are coming from a long way off?'

'Yes, I only landed today. As for Saradamma—'

'She was a nice girl. Not high and mighty like some of these educated girls.'

'Tell me where she is now?' His patience was wearing thin.

'I heard she was in jail in Goa or some place.'

'In jail?' The young man was shocked.

'Yes, she was a nice girl with a heart of gold, but when he died—'

'Who died?'

'That Krishnankutty Menon. The children's father.'

'He died?'

'Yes. It's really a year now. The girl got sort of queer after his death. If you ask me, I can't put my finger on it – something went wrong with her. It was then that some folks left boarding a train for a satyagraha in Goa or Portugal or wherever. She just left with them. Her mother and everyone else came to know of it only after she'd left. They wailed as if there'd been a death in the house. They had only this girl to tide them over. And she had no practice to speak of. Still, it was better than nothing. When she too left, they were in real trouble. There was a chap who was Menon's nephew. Once Saradakutty left, he never bothered about them. They stayed on for a while, selling this and that and somehow pulling on. They left when they could no longer fend off creditors. After that, there has been no news of them.' The old man stopped. It was when he received no response that he observed the other man's face.

'What's wrong with you, mister?'

'Nothing. See you later.'

'No. Wait. When I look at you – you seem to be – are they related to you?'

'What? Ah, yes. They are. See you!'

('The Daughter' first appeared in *Samyukta* Vol III. No. 2. pp. 65–114)

SIX

A Pretty Girl and Her Pals

A room in a busy office where about two hundred people of all sorts – married and unmarried, men and women – worked. The time was eleven o'clock in the morning.

A twenty-six-year-old IAS officer had assumed charge.

That was the event.

Seven people shared the space beneath the white concrete ceiling, suspended from which a fan whirred all the time.

Panicker, the father of six children and forever hard up. Muraleedharan, the good soul. Thomas, forever carping about everything and everybody. Raveendran, given to poetry and melancholy. Lalitha Devi, pretty and flirtatious. Nalini, asthmatic and stoical. And Malati, the pregnant one. These are the seven people. And now, a little more about them:

As mentioned earlier, Panicker has six children. The eldest is doing the pre-university course. The youngest hasn't left the mother's lap yet. Half of Panicker's hair has gone grey. He had entered service very young, and while in service he continued his studies and took his BA degree.

There never was a time when Panicker would not be chewing paan. If you asked him why, he would tell you it afforded him a perfect excuse to get out of the room.

Nothing much to be said about Muraleedharan, the nicest of the lot. The only thing special about him is that he is in love with, no, madly in love with, the pretty and coquettish Lalitha.

Thomas had been transferred there from somewhere up north for having ticked off his boss in rather discourteous terms. His school-mistress wife and two children stayed home. He blamed his former boss if he bit on a tiny stone in the rice served in the restaurant or if he got a letter from home saying his son had a cold or if his wife complained that, since her father was no more, there was no one to harvest the paddy or if he missed the morning bus after much waiting.

The melancholic Raveendran is in love with his cousin, his maternal uncle's daughter. What taught him melancholy was the awareness that it was his duty to marry off his sisters orphaned by his father's death. These days he is mostly engaged in only two things – writing poetry and waiting. And the only occupation of his beloved, the uncle's daughter, is the latter.

Lalitha is beautiful in every sense of the term. Fair complexion, curly hair, smooth cheeks and two darling dimples. She is everyone's favourite. An only child, she took up a job to get round her working mother, who insisted on her daughter doing her MSc. She would dally with the grey-haired Panicker, the pensive Raveendran and the carping Thomas.

Next, Nalini the stoic – right? Her stoicism was a direct consequence of her sense of duty towards her parents, who brought her into this world without having sought her permission, brought her up anyhow and educated her since she was good in her studies (also since there was, very conveniently, a college in the neighbourhood). Her salary was not sufficient to feed and clothe her three brothers and four sisters (all of them brought into this word without their consent), leave alone other matters.

She too had entertained hopes when she finished her studies, without ever having to seek anyone's help or cringe before anyone, and had landed a job soon after. Buy a few nice sarees, read books, see movies, have fun and fall in love – everything figured on her list.

The fan which whirred non-stop overhead blew her dreams away. It left a lot of space empty. She then gave herself up to the task of trying to save the rest of the space in her head from being overgrown. When she felt like seeing an English movie, she read, in three-anna weeklies, reviews by people who had seen the movie. She slaked her thirst for romance with the dog-eared novels – by the way, only novels get dog-eared since only novels have readers – that her brother borrowed from the college library.

Now she had advanced into *Katha Upanishad*. The asthma which troubled her every new moon day was efficacious in bringing her closer to Vedanta.

Malati, who comes to the office leaving her one-and-a-half-year-old first son at home in the care of a maid and carrying the second in her belly, is a fairly innocuous person. Since she felt tired and run-down most of the time, her work was handled mostly by the others.

Seven individuals of seven different temperaments – they carried on in the same room, sometimes on good terms and at other times on bad, from ten in the morning to four in the evening.

While Panicker talked of his son who flunked his examinations, Nalini waxed eloquent over her rascally brother's exploits. Thomas reported his daughter's cold in detail while Malati described her child's teething troubles. The pensive Raveendran never spoke much. But no one could say for sure whether he talked 'love' with Muraleedharan on the sly.

Everyone was thus getting on fine when the Government of India saw it fit to launch a twenty-six-year-old IAS officer into their midst like a tweed-suited Sputnik.

All hell broke loose.

Not here in the room alone, mind you.

It was as though a minor earthquake had shaken every single room and verandah of that sprawling building.

Officers come and go. But someone so young!

Eleven thirty.

Everything quiet in the room.

After the initial bout of small talk, everyone was engrossed in their work. Reading files and scribbling on them in full swing.

Time passed.

At last someone came to summon Panicker.

As the senior-most, it was Panicker who carried out transactions with the office on the first floor. He was about to become a superintendent.

Gathering up the files, Panicker moved toward the door, flashed a smile and left.

Just as they say in the stories, the minutes crawled by.

'Ah! He's coming now,' declared Lalitha, whose eyes had been riveted on her wrist watch. 'It's been half an hour since he left.' Panicker sat down and took out his paan box.

'Tell me what he's like, sir. Good-looking? What they said is true?' Lalitha had run out of patience.

Stepping out onto the verandah, Panicker spat out the betel juice. 'No family.' He winked. 'Stays in Palm Lands. I've gathered this much news. Isn't that enough for you?'

'Don't you have to pay eight or ten rupees per day in that place?' Muraleedharan the virtuous was concerned about that.

'Let him pay, sonny. He's young, let him pay,' said Thomas.

'How do I get to meet him, Panickar Chetta?' Lalitha had not been paying attention to any of these exchanges.

'He isn't shy. Wait for a day or two. He's sure to come this way.'

'Wait for two days? If I don't see him today, I won't be able to get a wink of sleep.'

'In that case, you can go without your beauty sleep tonight, child.'

'There's something you can do, if you will be happy with a peep through the curtain,' Thomas put in. 'Just stroll down the verandah. It just might work.'

'Is the window open, Panicker Chetta?' Lalitha grabbed at the suggestion.

'Yes.'

'Let me try. Are you coming, Nalini?'

'No.'

'What about you, Malati?'

'I don't want to loaf around on the verandah.'

'It won't be that. We'll go to the out-audit and see what Thankamma is doing.'

'No, you can count me out.'

'You are plain lazy, that's it.' Lalitha set out on her own.

'This is grave dereliction of duty, *saare*,' Thomas called after her.

When she came back in fifteen minutes, it was Malati who spoke to her first.

'You saw him?'

'Yes. When I was coming back, he had got up and was standing at the door. I saw him clearly.'

'How's he?'

'Tall, dark and handsome.' It was Nalini who replied in English.

'Did you see him, Nalini?' Lalitha took offence at that.

'No.'

'Then?'

'Okay, leave it. Am I right or not? Isn't he like I said?'

'Yes. He's a bit dark but very good looking. And so tall too!'

'So I am right!'

'Oh, great! Very smart of you!'

That day and five or six very like it went by. The craze about the new officer didn't abate. Even if Lord Krishna, beloved of Gopis and handsomer than Manmadha, the God of love, had come down, he could not have created a greater stir. The officer was the topic of conversation wherever people met.

One morning he went along the verandah on some business with the peon in attendance.

'Saare, here he goes. You haven't seen him, have you, saare?' Thomas called to Nalini.

Malati was on leave. And Lalitha was not in the room.

Nalini waited for her to turn up.

'I too have seen him,' she said when Lalitha turned up.

'Mohammed came to the mountain.'

'How's he?' Lalitha took it up eagerly.

'Unheard melodies are sweeter,' Nalini said in English. When Lalitha looked bewildered, unable to make anything of it, she felt like laughing. When Muraleedharan saw her laughing to herself, he said, 'What's the matter?'

'Nothing. I'm laughing at my own nonsense.'

By and by, Panicker unexpectedly went on leave one day. And Muraleedharan started out with a few files to the top floor.

He came back, looking none too pleased. 'Lalitha is wanted up there.'

'Me?' Usually no one sent for the clerk.

'Yes. He seems to have come across a few mistakes in the files that you put up.'

Lalitha left without a word.

When she came back, she didn't look as if she'd been taken to task.

'Now, Lali, did he tick you off?' Nalini wanted to know. She smiled and winked.

The whole day Muraleedharan was down in the dumps. When Nalini asked him why, he refused to elaborate.

It was Panicker who enlightened her the next day. It was when both Lalitha and Muraleedharan were out that he did so.

This is what transpired when Muraleedharan presented the files.

Being new to the job, the officer takes more than usual care about the files. He picked out a few minor mistakes.

Lalitha's file came last. Do beauties ever work?

Panicker used to go through Lalitha's papers carefully before he put them up. How was Muraleedharan to know that? The officer looked at this and that and said frowning:

'Send the person who put this up here.' Something, either a quixotic sense of chivalry or the ardour of love, made Muraleedharan say:

'It's a lady, sir.'

The brute's immediate response was: 'Is that so? In that case, ask her to present herself in a purdah.'

The next day when Panicker presented the files, he was told to keep them on the table and leave.

In about half an hour, the peon came to fetch Lalitha.

No one could make anything of it. Lalitha did not seem to be unduly upset.

She took about ten or fifteen minutes to return. Her face was glowing.

'Why did he send for you?' Nalini asked her quietly.

'After all, it was my file. There were a few mistakes.' She started to turn the pages busily.

Nalini did not say another word.

After a while Lalitha said in a low voice: 'Asked me whether he could get me a cup of coffee.'

'Oh-Oh! So he called you over to give you a treat? The conquest is over?'

'Come off it, Nalini.'

'Hey! Look at him twice like that, and he'll definitely fall for you, hook, line and sinker.'

'Look here, if you don't stop, I'll – well, it was his coffee break, that's why he asked.' Nalini laughed.

The next day at twelve the peon came to summon Lalitha. As soon as she was back, Nalini said:

'Had coffee?'

'As if I would share his coffee!'

'So he had another ready for you.'

She did not say anything. Only her dimples made a brief appearance.

Nalini said, 'From the look of it, this is going to get you.'

'What?'

'Well, carry on.'

'I' m fed up with you, Nalini. You're talking non—'

'I'm not talking nonsense, I'm talking sense.'

Lalitha came to be summoned to the first floor every day. When he saw the peon coming in the morning, Muraleedharan's face would darken. And he'd be touchy the whole day. If someone spoke to him, he would answer them in monosyllables.

These days the dimples never faded from Lalitha's face. The gloom on Muraleedharan's visage increased in direct proportion to the glow on Lalitha's.

One day Lalitha was sent for as usual. Muraleedharan sat looking down, his chin supported on his hand.

Thomas began to hum a song. Raveendran signalled him to stop.

Thomas paid no heed. The singing grew louder.

'Because of a girl of no worth ...'

'Shut up, you fool,' Muraleedharan shouted in English and sprang up. Thomas too rose to his feet. For half a minute they stood glowering at each other.

'Thomas!' Panicker rose to his feet and placed his hand on his shoulder.

Thomas didn't utter a word.

Muraleedharan turned and walked out.

'He's a harmless sort, Thomas,' Panicker said a short while later.

'My goodness! How was I to know that he was so badly bitten?'

'This has got to stop somehow,' Panicker said after musing on it a while.

'The girl can do as she pleases. What's the use of his pulling a long face over it?' Thomas belonged to the opposite camp.

'I think someone should speak to Lalitha Saar about this.' The usually reticent Raveendran spoke without raising his head.

'Bravo! Please take note of that, coming as it does from someone in the same boat.' Thomas was not prepared to leave well alone.

'Thomas, will you be quiet! Either Nalini or Malati might drop her a hint.' Panicker had taken it seriously.

'I can't,' Malati was unequivocal.

'Why not? It's with your tongue that you speak. It won't tire you out.'

'Lalitha will not listen to me.'

'In that case, let Nalini Saar speak to her.'

'Shh ...!' Nalini hissed in warning, since she saw Lalitha approaching.

When both the parties were absent, the others held an emergency meeting in the room. Nalini was entrusted with the task of getting Lalitha to understand the lie of the land.

During the noon interval, as soon as lunch was over, everyone 'vanished' this way and that.

As had been agreed upon earlier, Raveendran lured Muraleedharan away on the pretext of reading his poem to him.

Panicker set out in search of paan; Thomas to see whether he could cajole a cigarette off someone. Malati said she wanted to rest and remained in the waiting room. She didn't even return to the room after lunch. The stage was set.

Nalini tried to clear her throat. No sound. Lalitha sat as though she were unaware of these developments around her.

Nalini felt like hitting her.

'Lali,' she brought herself to begin. 'I want to tell you something important.'

'Oh!'

'To begin with, let me ask you something.'

'Yes?'

'Is our officer in love with you?'

'How do I know?'

'Do you love him?'

Lalitha laughed.

'Do you realise that these visits in the morning and the coffee breaks are not just the thing?'

'I didn't have coffee with him on a single day.'

'Still, these visits ...'

'Well, do you want me to refuse when he sends for me?'

'No, you can get him not to call you.'

'What am I supposed to do? Tell him not to send for me?'

'You can stop flaunting your dimples like this.' She smiled still more dazzlingly.

'Are you trying to drive that Muraleedharan crazy?'

'I'm not driving anyone crazy. Let someone go up and tell him not to send for me.'

'Lalitha Devi, this game is not good for you.' She smiled again.

'A crow in your hand is better than a koel in the forest.' Still she smiled.

'I am not joking.'

'No,' Lalitha agreed.

'Lali, have you made up your mind about marrying our boss?' Beating about the bush would get her precisely nowhere. Still the same smile.

'Do you mean to marry Muraleedharan?' Lalitha kept smiling.

'Whom do you propose to wed, madam?'

'A lecturer in my mother's college.'

'Praise the Lord! Really?'

'Yes.'

'Then it isn't our officer?'

'No.'

'And not Muraleedharan either?'

'No!'

'You wretch!'

The interval was nearly over. One by one the others drifted in. Everybody except Muraleedharan. These days he never arrived before time.

'Dear friends,' Nalini said, rising to her feet. 'I have something of the utmost importance to convey to you. Our very own Lalitha Devi is about to get married.'

'The lad's been caught, or what?'

'Mr Thomas, let me have my say. Lalitha is getting married. To a lecturer in her mother's college.' She took her seat.

'Hurray! Three cheers for Lalitha Devi!'

Thomas sprang to his feet. Muraleedharan appeared at the door, walking in with his eyes downcast.

('A Pretty Girl and Her Pals' first appeared
in *Samyukta* Vol III. No. 2. pp. 115–124)

SEVEN

The Curse

'Ramsaran, who is that girl?'

'She must be the priest's daughter. He lives nearby.'

'Bhargavacharya's?'

'Yes, my Lord.'

'Surprising! A rose on a blade of darbha grass.'

'I have heard that the maiden's mother was extremely beautiful.'

'Is she no more?'

'No. All that the priest has in the world is this daughter.'

'How ethereally beautiful!'

'She is said to resemble her mother greatly.'

The Maharaja could not take his eyes away from the direction in which she disappeared.

The sylvan nymph—

'Did you not feel, Ramsaran, when the fairy stepped out through the veil of mist, that spring was approaching?'

Ramsaran covered his mouth with his hand and tittered. 'Ramsaran, you are a spoilsport.'

The Maharaja turned his horse. He did not speak till he reached the palace.

Ramsaran knew his master too well to speak. They had meant to alleviate boredom by going for a ride.

The Maharaja lost himself in a daydream. It was because he was bored with the stifling monotony of his harem that he had set off, hoping to divert himself with physical exertion.

After the trials and tribulations of the battlefield, he had revelled in the luxurious life of his palace.

Oh, how soon it had palled on him!

There was no variety at all.

This day was so like the one that went before it. And the next day threatened to be just like this one. There would be no difference at all.

Yet, when he had mounted Dhavan in the morning and set out with Ramsaran, did he really expect an experience like this?

That a nymph would appear through the trees in the mango grove like a rainbow ...

The next day too, precisely on the hour, the king, in the company of Ramsaran, came to the mango grove.

Hours went by. He was tired of waiting. And he never got to see what he longed to see.

The fairy did not present herself, with a pitcher poised on her waist and the end of her sari drawn over her damp hair.

When the sun rose high, he went back. As on the previous day, pleasurable thoughts did not fill his mind.

The next day and the day after that too found the king walking through the grove to the edge of the pond. He could not ride through the low-hanging canopy of trees. He dismounted and started to walk. Many were taking a bath in the pond. The only person whom his eyes sought was not there.

He timed his arrival a bit early. All in vain.

Every day he returned without setting eyes on her, she became more alluring.

A child denied a bauble before he could lay his hands on it.

The more he was denied her sight, the dearer she became to behold. Ramsaran wearied of the waiting.

He made discreet inquiries. The priest's daughter did not make daily trips to the pond for water. She was the apple of his eye. Normally, she was never allowed that far alone. That day she had ventured thus far for some special reason.

There was a pond in their yard. She usually bathed in it.

It was futile to wait for her at the mango grove and the lakeside.

The early morning rides stopped. The king bore up valiantly for a week. It was becoming an obsession with him.

'Ramsaran!'

'Yes, my Lord.'

'I must have her!'

'The priest—'

'That was what I was about to say. Go talk to the priest!'

'A brahmin maid—'

'I am the lord of the Kingdom of Amber.'

'Lord, threatening the priest—'

'You might try the three methods.'

'He is not the kind of person who yields easily.'

'Is there anyone of that kind?'

'The brahmin – if you can, please rid your mind of this thought, my Lord.'

'Is there no way other than the use of force? The Queen Consort of Amber Raja—'

'Queen Consort, my Lord? What of Sunanda Devi—'

The priest's modest residence stood a little way from the bounds of the city, at the edge of the mango grove where the trees spread, brushing against one another, their intertwining branches forming a forest canopy.

It was with a certain amount of trepidation that Ramsaran went and stood in the front yard of the grass-thatched hut that evening.

When he cleared his throat rather noisily, the priest came out of the house.

The long beard reached his chest. The bones stood out on his gaunt face. In the hollows beneath his grey eyebrows, his eyes were piercing.

The exchange of civilities was over. Now Ramsaran had to broach the topic.

Where did one begin? If he did not introduce it before the brahmin's patience ran out ...

'When your wife passed away, Acharya, you did not—'

'No, I did not remarry.'

'So your daughter has no one for company ...'

'I am here.'

'No women ... the girl is of age, isn't she?'

The priest's eyebrows rose and met in a frown.

'I am here to seek the maiden's hand for another person.'

'Hmm.' That was the only response.

'The maiden's age—'

'Who is the man?'

There was no point in prevaricating.

'Master! Your daughter is Goddess Lakshmi herself.'

'Who is the one that seeks her hand?'

'The fame of her beauty has—'

'Tell me who he is.'

'Your maiden is a gem. The proper setting for all gems ...' The priest did not speak.

Ramsaran felt a curious unease which he normally did not feel. The sight of a whole army up against him had never discomfited him. In any gruesome battle he never left his master's side. Now, before this brahmin's gaze ...

'I have been sent by the king of kings. Your daughter, as the queen consort—'

'What!' The priest sprang to his feet. Ramsaran, too, rose to his feet.

'The king's consort – the queen of Amber—'

'What did you say?'

'Think of this: Your grandson on the throne ...'

'Stop it!'

It was a roar. Ramsaran was stupefied.

'How dare he? A brahmin maid ...'

'The Maharaja ...'

'The Maharaja ... a maid born into the Bhargava clan ...'

'He's a kshatriya.'

'Kshatriya ... low-born ...'

'There is nothing to prevent a kshatriya from marrying a brahmin maid. Our ancient scriptures do not forbid it.'

'Which is the ancient book that allows it?'

'Did not the daughter of Suka wed Yayati?'

'The daughter of Suka – No, do not say anything: One does not let dogs lick sacrificial offerings.'

'Dogs! Oh, priest! You speak without caution.'

'Out! Get out! Do not utter a word. I will not give my daughter in marriage to him.'

As he rode against the wind to the palace, Ramsaran's head cooled.

His anger subsided. The king was waiting impatiently for him.

'What did he say?'

'The priest will not give his daughter to you. He said he would not give a brahmin maid in marriage to a kshatriya.'

'Was that his final word? Did you not inform him that she will be made the queen consort?'

'Yes, I did. I told him everything, my Lord. He refused to heed my words.'

'I even offered to make her the queen consort in preference to Sunanda Devi—'

'To that brahmin ...'

'The brahmin! I will not rest till I avenge myself on him.'

'Bhargavacharya is the priest to many of the clans in this kingdom. If he were to be harassed or tortured in some way, the people ...'

'Who spoke of harassment?'

'My Lord! He is a fearsome sorcerer. It will amount to playing with fire. An old man's folly – pardon him, my Lord. As for the maiden, there are many who are more beautiful than her. The brahmin is sinister.'

'Do not be afraid. I will teach him a lesson. He will come falling at my feet.'

Ramsaran was entrusted with the task of studying the damsel's routine. He went about it half-heartedly. There was nothing he could do against the royal command.

The maid takes a bath every morning. In their own pool. And she would be alone.

Apart from the priest and his daughter there was only an old nurse-maid in the house; and there were no other houses in the vicinity.

One morning on her way to the pool, the maiden came across a weary soldier who had taken a nasty toss from his horse.

He wanted some water to drink. And she also helped him reach his horse, which stood a little way off. Back home after her bath, for some reason she did not tell her foster mother – in whom she confided everything – about this incident.

At dusk, when she sat down to her prayers, it was not the child Krishna, peacock feathers, anklets, girdles and all, that she saw before her.

A long-limbed warrior, who looked imploringly up at her from where he lay tired and worn out on the ground. Thus the old drama came to be played out again in that yard, away from the shade of the grass-thatched hut.

The sage's daughter and the warrior. There was neither Anasuya nor Priyamvada to gently tease her, nor the fawns to look on indulgently.

The wind that came in through the mango grove went whistling past.

The snowy-white grains of sand laughed in derision.

Only the white mantara plant, which the poor motherless girl tended lovingly, closed its eyes in sorrow. And she scarcely noticed its white flowers close their eyes. When the ecstasy of life assumed a human shape and beckoned to her, the stolen moments on the poolside alone meant life. All else was a reliving of those moments.

Months passed. Time which heeded neither the creepers blooming nor the leaves falling, rolled on unconcerned.

The poetry was over. Only stark reality was before her now.

At last, one day the priest too came to know.

'Who was it that deceived you? Tell me!' She was silent.

'Tell me! Tell me!' the old man roared. 'Tell me who it was.'

The priest dragged his daughter by the hair. She did not make so much as a whimper.

'Tell me! Speak!'

The old man was becoming deranged.

The sword employed for animal sacrifice lay before the idol of Kali. The priest scarcely knew how it came to be in his hand.

'Tell me! Speak!'

The old man's hand moved up and down.

That was the end of the poor maiden's travails ...

In the yard, fire blazed in the sacrificial pyre before the idol of Kali. The old man stood before his deity with the lifeless body of his daughter in his hands.

'Devi! If I have ever served you well, please punish the man who is responsible for this. Before one year is out, he too shall die a slow, agonising death as I do.'

He jumped into the pyre with the body of his daughter in his hands.

The lone witness to the deed was a goatherd who happened to be passing by. And he did not have the courage to stop the priest.

The ghastly story of the priest's human sacrifice spread through the kingdom. It reached the Maharaja's ears too. Ramsaran did try to keep it from him. In six months' time, the Maharaja was confined to bed. No one could diagnose the illness. Doctors and sorcerers tried hard, but it was of no use.

Come one blood-red evening exactly a year to the day, the Maharaja breathed his last.

(Hull in his *Annals of Amber* puts it thus: 'Legend has it that the sturdy and well-built Maharaja Ajit Singh died of a brahmin's curse.')

('The Curse' first appeared in *Samyukta*
Vol III. No. 2. pp. 125–131)

EIGHT

Winding Sheet

Ever since I could remember, he had been like this. Dark, tall, spare bodied. Long limbs and taut muscles. A statue chiselled out of rosewood (that was what he was like).

No one could say for sure how old he was. They say he had looked the same when Achan came to Ernakulam for the first time to do his schooling. Since he always kept his hair cropped short, I could never tell whether his hair had started going grey.

He occupies a very prominent place even in the earliest memories of my childhood. He had a never-ending stock of stories. I don't think I've ever enjoyed a work of fiction as much as I did his tales and jokes.

We children looked forward to the days when he would come to work on our land. We used to crowd round him when he took a break from digging the land, putting away the mattock to sit on his haunches and open his packet of paan.

'Mathai! Mathai! How come you are so dark?'

'People say you are a sahib. Where is your memsahib?' The questions piled upon him.

'That's right, young master. Mathai was born in Parith. Mind you, in Parith. I couldn't stand the cold so I came over. On my way here, the ship sank in the Black Sea. For two days Mathai floated in that water. It was then that I got so dark. I tried scrubbing myself with coconut husk and *incha*. But the colour doesn't come back.'

How many times did we listen to this! Yet it never seemed to pall on us.

He would deliver speeches in the French language. That is, he would make gibbering noises and would stop only when we collapsed with laughter. Come the rains and Mathai would present himself in a straw hat and a *swadeshi* slipper fashioned out of the leaf sheath of areca palm. He would have a whole lot to say about them too.

'There's this man, Gandhi. He says we shouldn't touch imported stuff. That's why Mathai doesn't go in for an umbrella and a pair of slippers.'

The yarns he used to spin!

Every year on the day of *Uthradam*, he would change out of his workaday clothes into a clean *mundu* and would come to get his share of rice and *koppu*. He would bring a bushel of long beans too. His pride wouldn't allow him to present himself empty-handed, with no 'offerings' to make. He used to take food at our house on the second day of Onam. Amma would hand out the dishes and we would take them out to him. We used to fight among ourselves for the privilege. When everything had been served, he would seat himself before the leaf, and we would present ourselves to watch. How interesting it was to watch the food disappearing in large mouthfuls!

As, one after the other, we started school and graduated to higher classes, we grew out of the habit of trailing Mathai to listen to his talk. Still, Mathai's tall tales continued to be one topic of conversation that all of us found equally entertaining.

Then the war came. Most of the young people began to leave home to enlist in the army and to swell the labour force in Assam. Prices rose. Still people had money. Even round the necks of pulaya girls, dark skinned as the sky at dusk, delicate gold chains glittered, proclaiming, as it were, the girls' pride in their men who risked their lives in far off lands to send home money.

Once the young men left, the older ones who stayed back had a good time. Since there were fewer men available to work on the land, wages increased.

Mathai refused to leave the place. He stayed home. With what airs and graces he used to come for work in those days! It would be eight or nine in the morning by the time he turned up. Well before sundown he would get in, putting the mattock away.

'It isn't four yet and he's stopped work. By the time he turns up it's nearly noon. And then he is in a hurry to leave. Nice of you! Being our old hand, is this how you should carry on here?' Amma tried to reason with him.

'What do you know, Kochamma? Wasn't that the five o'clock train that you heard just now? They need work only from nine to four in the harbour. And they also get a noon interval. Get someone else to work on the land. You'll see.'

So that too was tried. A new labourer was called in to build the fence that year. After having him and his friend work hard on it for two days, Mathai had to be called in to finish it.

It was during one of those days that a dark, strapping woman came, bringing Mathai his lunch.

My younger brother came running in and called: 'Amma, Mathai's memsahib has come!'

'Oh, come on! Mathai's wife has been dead for ages.'

'Okay then, ask him yourself.'

What he said was perfectly true. Amma could not help laughing.

'Why did you bring this upon yourself in your old age, Mathai? Do you have no other way to spend your money?'

'It is easy for you to say that, kochamma. I have married off my two daughters. There is no one at home. You really can't expect me to cook my food after a hard day's work, can you?'

A few months later, one day, when the young woman brought him lunch, she was seen carrying a small baby, a cute little thing as dark as his mother.

Mathai hauled him on to his shoulder as soon as he set eyes on him.

There was something oddly touching about the picture they presented – the man who had toiled through life to the sunset of his days and his child perched on his shoulder.

His life centred round the child. 'It's been forty years since I set eyes on a male child, master. It's been years since the one from my first marriage died.'

The days went by. The war came to an end. Those who had enlisted in the army were being sent back home. Assam too did not offer any more jobs. Those who had left home in high spirits returned, crestfallen. There was surplus labour in the country but the demand for labour did not increase. Wages began to come down. The prices of rice and victuals did not drop. Everybody was happy as long as the money brought in from outside lasted. Then they sold whatever they could and stood staring at starvation in the face.

The young and sturdy somehow pulled on. The older men who had not bothered to leave home in order to strike gold – either because they could not or did not want to – were pushed to the wall. They were the ones who had not forsaken the land. But nobody cared for them now. Whom do you employ if not those who can put in more work for the same wages? Who wants the old when young men are available?

Mathai aged very fast. His old vim and vigour disappeared without a trace. Finding work every day became an old tale. He had a couple of regular houses that had not started hiring others.

It was the month of *Edavam*. The rains were slowly setting in. One morning Mathai came to our house. He changed into a *kachamundu* and started to dig the coconut bed.

'Did you ask him to come? And why does he start digging so early in the season?' Amma inquired of Achan.

'I didn't ask him.'

Amma went out into the yard.

'Hey! What are you up to, Mathai? The rain hasn't reached the ground yet. Shouldn't you wait for the *njattuvela* before you start to make beds for the coconut trees?'

'What do you know, kochamma? Have you seen the sun shine for two days? It has been raining all the time, hasn't it? It's late as it is. It's been two weeks since the Thekke Madom people started work on their land.' Mathai's tongue had lost none of its sharpness.

'If you can't find work anywhere else you just turn up here. After all, no questions are asked here. We keep an open house,' Amma went back in, muttering.

One evening I was sitting on the porch, reading. Achan was sitting out in the courtyard. I heard the gate open. Someone was coming in. I could not make out the person at first. It was only when he came out of the shade of the mango tree and approached us that I saw him clearly. I was shocked. It was Mathai.

No, it was a corpse that had once been Mathai. He had changed so much.

His limbs had shrivelled up and hung limply, as if suspended from his body. The smooth skin, once drawn tightly over his powerful muscles, hung in loose folds. His face and head were mottled with grey bristles. His eyes, which used to look everyone fearlessly in the face, were two hollows. And for the first time ever, I saw him dressed in a shabby, torn mundu.

Mathai moved into the yard and stood before my father. I didn't hear either of them speak for a while.

They stood, silently facing each other. Two men who tried to make a living on their own, one with his brains, the other with his brawn. And the difference between the two! 'Have you been ill, Mathai?' Achan spoke in the end.

'Only ill with not having enough to eat.' Achan fell silent. What could he say, after all?

'My child is starving, master. It has been three days since the hearth has been lit. I'll repay you somehow, please, master ...' He bit his lips. How could he frame that sentence, he who was used to only demanding his due and not begging? It seemed as though blood would spurt from his eyes.

Achan rose to his feet quickly and went in. He came out and placed something in Mathai's hands.

Without bothering to find out how much it was, he turned and walked away, as though he had been dealt a blow. He went out staring at the earth that he had nurtured with his lifeblood.

It must have been a couple of months later. His wife came to our house. She brought the child along too, now reduced to a swollen belly and skin and bones.

Mathai was laid up. It began as rheumatic fever and now he was bed-ridden. It had been more than a month since he went to work.

'Why don't you take him to the hospital, Rosa? They'll look after him. You'll get rice gruel too,' Amma advised her.

'There is no point in going to the hospital, kochamma. He spent two weeks there. They sent him away, saying he's been cured and that he only has to be fed properly. He couldn't get up when he got home. What's the point in their saying he's been cured? They always send people away to make room for those who arrive newly. Mathai says he won't set foot inside a hospital even if he were to starve to death.'

'Why don't you find some work, Rosa?'

'What work can I ever do with this kid, kochamma? If I leave him home, he will cry and Mathai will get angry. He'd rather starve than have the child cry. Even otherwise, what work can I do now?' She glanced meaningfully at her own big tummy.

'It's been four days since Mathai touched food. If I could get a handful of rice ...'

She came for broken rice for a couple of times. Then she was not seen for a few days.

It was a holiday for my college. I was helping Amma slice vegetables. My younger brother came in and said, 'Amma, there's a woman waiting in the porch.'

'Who's that, Aniya?'

'Go and find out for yourself.' He ran away.

I went to the porch along with Amma.

'Well, isn't it Rosa? What's the—'

Amma did not have to finish the question. Rosa began to cry.

'Mathai's gone, Kochamma.'

She somehow got it out between weeping.

Amma offered her the usual platitudes.

She stopped crying. It did not seem as though it was on hearing Amma's philosophising that she stopped.

People like her had no time to mourn the dead. Their primary concern was with burying the dead.

'What do you need now, Rosa?' Amma asked her.

'*Nadan mundu* for a winding sheet.'

Every time I think of my childhood, it is his picture that comes before me.

('A Winding Sheet for Mathai' first appeared
in *Samyukta* Vol III. No. 2. pp. 132–137)

NINE

In the Abode of God

All that I had striven to build through the years lay shattered around me.

My pride would not let me bend and pick up the bits and pieces.

Pride – what a meaningless word!

My sandcastle, which I had fashioned with my hands and set out in beautiful hues – my sandcastle – where I sat on a straw mat spread in the middle. My sandcastle, where I could call myself, in pride and glory, the empress of a starry kingdom. Was it because I couldn't bear to see it crumble that I refuse to bend down? What if I found fragments of my own blood-stained heart among the pieces that I would see if I bent down to look?

What was the power that brought me here? I had begun to feel that it would be a relief to give myself over to the darkness that beckoned, hadn't I? What is this power?

Does this mean that the instincts and intuitions acquired in myriad births down the ages had remained essentially unchanged in the unconscious mind? Primeval instincts ...

Does this mean that this feeling – which my forebears had considered a part of their lives which lay beyond the pale of reason – had mingled with my blood and lain unnoticed under the pall of material knowledge?

Like a hurt child who runs to his mother to hug her and cry its pain out, – am I a child who seeks the succour of a power considered omnipotent?

God is the procrastinator's last refuge! I remember having said that to someone a long time ago. Did I flee to this place because I am a coward who doesn't have the guts to sort the pieces, pick those that are intact and build anew on a stronger base?

She stood bewildered in front of the door of that famous temple's *gopuram*.

Do the sad eyes of those who love me follow me here?

It is a sea of strange faces that is behind me.

Are they all heart-sore, like I am?

Seekers of material wealth!

Wouldn't there be a few who came to seek the truth?

The god stood smiling, adding to the dazzle of the lamps inside the sanctum sanctorum.

She stood with folded palms, trying to give herself up to that smile.

What did I expect?

There is only disinterestedness here. The disinterested god of the land of Upanishads.

You stupid woman, your heart and your pain – what is special about them?

Men in their thousands bring their sorrows to me. You are like the rest of them. Aren't you?

I am graven on stone. Stone that smiles!

Are you just that Lord, nothing more?

In that case ...

'Move! Hmm. Offer your prayers and move! Please don't block the view. Come on, move!'

A man wearing a yellow strip of cloth over his dhoti stood holding on to the *mandapam* and the steps to the sanctum.

It was he who had spoken.

She moved away from the door.

Holding on to the door frame, he was repeating the same words like a machine every five minutes.

A young man with a homely face and a stocky figure, he had a sore throat from raising his voice every now and then to exhort the people to move on.

'Either move this way or that. It's difficult if you stay put right here in front of the sanctum.'

It was a grandmother with two kids in tow.

'If people refuse to budge ...'

It was only then that she realised that the old woman meant her.

A pretty young woman too moved on to the sanctum through the space cleared by the old woman.

The sanctum was closed.

People crowded onto the two sides of the door. It was auspicious to be caught in the shower of holy water sprinkled on the devotees as soon as the door to the sanctum was opened.

One's body.

The drum beats started suddenly. From somewhere close by.

She moved a little away.

A song rose amidst the beat of the *edakka*. A sweet voice. Clear too.

Jayadeva's songs.

The rush was growing.

'*Haririti haririti japati sakamam.*' The disinterested god.

'*Hare*!' the cry rose in unison.

From where she stood, she folded her palms together.

Oh Lord! Are you still smiling?

'Move, please move a little off, please. Don't touch me! For pity's sake, don't pollute me please!'

Nampoothiri women in damp clothes and palm-leaf umbrellas.

Virtuous mothers, I have no desire to touch you. Neither do I have a desire to annoy you, you unfortunate mothers, still compelled to confine your lives behind these old palm-leaf umbrellas.

She pressed herself against the wall to make room for them.

When they had moved to the sanctum one after the other, leaving enough room, she moved out of the inner courtyard.

What a rush!

You foolish woman – who seeks refuge in a man-made god to escape from men – how can you go round the sanctum without brushing against someone?

Oh Lord! Are you smiling?

'Give me a receipt. A receipt please!'

A plump little boy stood there, holding out his hand.

'I don't have one with me, child.'

He went away, muttering something under his breath.

He joined a bunch of boys dressed in everything from a kachamundu to a mere loincloth. When he reached them, a guffaw went up from them.

She joined the crowd on their way to the outer courtyard.

Are the song and music moving this way? She turned to look.

Behind the *nagaswaram* and *maddalam* walked a man and a woman wearing garlands.

'Must be out of the top drawer. They've got music and all.' An old woman who was walking beside her spoke to her friend.

'How much do you have to pay for this?'

'Twenty-five?'

'Hey, no! For that you'd get an elephant too.' A third one put in.

Lord! Have you been turned into a business?

She moved behind a banyan tree.

A middle-aged woman came along. Her forehead bore holy ash and sandal paste marks.

'Please give me the ticket. Let me get some rice to eat. God will bless you. I didn't have a bite of supper yesterday.'

'I don't have a ticket.'

'You haven't got a receipt for the *vellanedyam* in the morning?'

'No.'

'What about *payasam*?'

'I don't have that either.'

'Oh!' She pulled a long face and left.

God, do you encourage the tribe of beggars—

'Have they put on the silk, dear?'

An old woman who was lying curled up on a mundu near the wall hastily scrambled to her feet and came up to her.

'Put the silk on?

'Did they take out the nedyam in procession?'

'I don't know.'

The old woman shook out the mundu and moved hurriedly away. She moved to the sanctum.

Three or four men wearing a yellow strip of cloth over their mundu stood guard at the door.

Inside the temple, the Brahmins were partaking of food along with the Lord.

Men, women and children milled around like termites near the door. They were all in a hurry to occupy the front.

The door opened. It could hardly admit three people abreast.

What a rush!

'Ouch! My leg—'

'What cheek! How dare you push me back when I try to go in?'

'Don't push.'

God! Do you smile when you see the antics of these human beings, your children? Did you look on with the same smile when fratricide was committed on the battlefield of Kurukshetra?

Is your heart really made of stone?

The stone that smiles!

She went round the sanctum once. The poor were being fed sacred rice outside the gopuram.

The haves extend their charity towards the have-nots.

Giving out rice to the needy is auspicious. That too on the temple premises. The old and the infirm.

They say Gautama once saw the sick and the dead.

They doled out what was there. There wasn't enough to go by.

Pushing and pulling and fighting. Oh, God!

Somehow, everything died down.

Only a handful of people remained: a young woman who gave her blind mate the rice that she'd fought tooth and nail to procure, along with a crushed chilly that she'd got out of the folds of her mundu, and now sated her hunger happily watching him eat greedily. And the small boy trying to console his little sister who was weeping, since the rice that he could get for her wasn't enough to satisfy her hunger.

'Come back, as a shower of mercy.'

Shower of mercy, Oh God!

For that, should there not be rain clouds that stole your hue and turned dark? Will it be possible for fleecy clouds that dazzle your eyes in the blazing sun to do that?

She walked on, past the last pillar. She reached the intersection. Whither now? God, are you sending me away empty-handed?

You had granted everything to that poor Brahmin who once came to see you with a handful of *avil* and who returned, lost in you, oh, eternally beautiful one, without seeking whatever he had come to seek.

Oh Lord! When I reach where I have to, will I too gain what I never sought of you? Without ever realising it, shall I have been cured of this pain that's become part of me? Oh God! Will this dust that lies thick over the barren land of my soul be swept away and fresh green sprouts emerge?

For that, you are not my beloved coeval. And you did not grab what I had brought you. To love you – To believe in you – Oh God!

('In the Abode of God' first appeared in *Samyukta* Vol III. No. 2. pp. 138–143)

TEN

History Did Not Repeat Itself

'Someone wants to meet you, Sir. He's been waiting for some time now,' Raman Nair said, while sorting out the day's mail and placing it before me.

'Tell him I can't.'

'I did. I told him he ought to have fixed it all up beforehand. Then he gave me this note. The poor man has been waiting for a long time.'

Oh, since when did Raman Nair begin to feel sorry for people who waited to meet me?

Money must have changed hands. That must be it. He placed the note along with the mail and went away. 'I wish to discuss something personal with you. Could you please spare me a few moments? If you can't make it today, tell me when I can meet you tomorrow. It's something urgent. I hope I am not troubling you.'

Very polite!

What exactly did he want? So urgently too! There was a PSC interview scheduled for next week. He must have come to know that I was on the board. If I were to set my mind to it, I could give him a leg up.

For which, polite notes won't suffice, sonny! It takes blue currency notes.

Things have come to such a pass that I can hardly drive past Victor's porch. Didn't they ring up to say that it was to be yesterday? It must have run up to quite a bit. How did that rascally Jew have the gall to ring me up at my office? His son's bridge-construction and the contracts – I'll show him.

Ringing me up at my office!

Raman Nair's expression when he came in to inform me about it – that grin of his—! I wanted to slap him across his face. But there was no go. Times have changed, haven't they?

In any case, let this polite person turn up in the morning tomorrow. Let's see whether he has anything more than politeness in stock.

I was about to make a note in the margin and set it aside when I noticed the address given at the bottom of the page.

Hey, this man is an MBBS. Not an engineer. So this has nothing to do with the PSC interview. I have nothing to do with the doctors' interview.

Then who the hell can this blighter be?

What do I gain by meeting him?

Nothing.

Still, why should an absolute stranger write to me like this?

I kept staring at the name for a while.

Will this be him?

Ah, yes. He's the person.

The man whom they have snared in advance for Su!

Let's meet him. Isn't he about to become my son-in-law? Let's see what he is like.

But why should he feel this sudden urge to meet his prospective father-in-law, just like that, out of the blue? And very respectfully too. Maybe he wants to touch me for money. What else? Maybe he's not satisfied with what he's already got.

If that is the case, you have come to the wrong person, sonny! Here am I, searching every avenue for repaying Victor's loan. I have no idea where my salary disappears before the fifteenth of the month!

Raman Nair came in, bringing a bundle of files to be signed. 'The man who gave you this note, is he still there? Send him in.'

He went back quietly.

He heard a knock at the door.

'Come in,' he said without raising his head.

That is a ruse. When the person comes up to you, raise your head and look straight into his eyes. If he's the nervous sort, he's sure to get more so. Then it becomes very easy to get him round.

But I don't think it'll wash with this chap. He isn't in the least bit nervous.

Good. Their choice isn't bad. At any rate, he's good-looking.

'Take your seat.' I put my pen away.

'Are you very busy? I thought it would be more convenient if I came over here. Hope I'm not troubling you.'

'No, it doesn't matter.'

'Maybe you haven't placed me.'

'No, I haven't.'

'I completed my medical studies last year.'

'How nice! You are not practicing?'

'Yes, I'm working here in the General Hospital.'

'Where do you stay?'

'My house is close by.'

'I see.'

He did not speak for a while.

'Is there anything I can do for you?'

'Don't you recognise me? It was your father-in-law who financed my studies.'

Ah, yes. It was he who had given me money to continue my studies too. That was their standard technique. Put a noose round your neck and catch you.

'Oh, I see!'

'My father had promised him that he'd get me to marry your daughter when I finished my course.'

'Did he pay you on that assurance alone?'

'Not on that alone. We'd mortgaged our house to him.'

The same old trick. The selfsame one that had been tried on me. If you mortgage the roof over your head, you don't run away.

'Hm ...'

'I heard that you too had come up the hard way. That's why I came to meet you.'

'You haven't told me why you came to call on me.'

'There's something that I'd—' he paused.

Was the earlier hunch correct? Does he want more money?

'Tell me.'

'Can I speak to you frankly?'

'Why not? Isn't that what you came for?'

'Yes, but still ...'

'Don't waste my time, please.'

'Well, your people insist on an early marriage.'

'So?'

'I'm in love with another girl, sir.'

Oh! That made me sit up. The same old story again.

Leela and I ...

Now this young man—

'What did you say? I didn't get you.'

'I am in love with another girl. She was my classmate in medical college.'

Leela had never been my classmate. She was my *murapennu*, my uncle's daughter.

No, we had never been in the same class. She was younger than me by a couple of years. She came to stay in my house when she joined college. That was all.

Unniarcha, the brave. Jhansi Rani Lakshmi Bai – the names I used to call her!

Why should I be reminded of all that now?

I have forgotten all that, haven't I? After all these years—

Those interminable spats with Leela—

It was a pleasure to annoy her.

Feminist – Women's Champion Against Male Chauvinism—

Unniarcha, the brave. Brave, my foot!

How she used to burst into tears at the least provocation! The bravado never went deep enough.

Laughter, tears and tantrums – how easy everything was for her!

Leela, who started singing the moment she heard raindrops pattering on the tiled roof!

Leela, who stood in the courtyard to watch lightning streak the sky!

My Leela, who loved sunshine, flowers, frost, rain and all. My Leela, who loved everything and everyone.

Leela, the brave—

'There is no place in my life for another woman, Sir.' The young man was speaking.

'If I were to marry somebody else, life would have no meaning. It would be a hollow thing, Sir.'

Isn't my life hollow? Does it mean anything at all?

This lad—

Still he shouldn't be allowed to get away with it.

'All this is melodrama, pure and simple. You are saying by rote something that you got out of a book.'

'Melodrama, Sir? Something out of a book! Do you think your daughter would be happy with me? With a man who has another woman in his heart?'

I'd never thought about that. Not until now. Is life happy for Lakshmikutty? Happiness and sorrow ...

She finds happiness in a fat bank balance, a motor car and diamond earrings, doesn't she?

But I never gave her a fat bank balance. All that I ever acquired was Victor as a creditor.

'You are getting angry. Think about it, please. You too were young once, weren't you? This will destroy three persons. I would like to live happily. I have a lot of ambitions, Sir. I would like to do something worthwhile with my life. Please give me a chance. If I don't have my girl by my side, I'll be shattered.'

I too had them. Plans and principles.

And the desire to do many things. Leela and I were planning to serve the country. We were even prepared to go to jail.

And he's asking me whether I too had not been young once!

Of course, I was. Just like this tall, slim young man in front of me.

Looking at me now, who'd guess that I too used to read poetry and be moved by the speeches of Subhash and Jawharlal?

The poetry and the zeal in me died out. They died out on the painted lips of Anglo-Indian women and in the frothing liquor that bubbled out of the bottles in Victor's back room.

The door to my downfall lay through Victor's back door. It was when my salary did not suffice to meet Victor's bills that I began to explore other avenues, wasn't it? What have I not done for a handful of silver? Handed out contracts that should never have been. Turned a blind eye while people siphoned off government money!

It was that devil Subramonya Iyer who led me down, rung by rung, to damnation.

In a weak moment, I signed a paper which I should never have. When I was hard-pressed for money, I did something I should never have, under that fiend's instigation. After that, I have been a pawn in his hands, haven't I? And followed it up all with other misdeeds under the menace in his eyes.

I am finished and Leela too—

Leela – falling at the feet of every visiting godman. Telling prayers incessantly on her beads. Taking ritualistic dips in the water. Offering pooja and visiting temples – My Leela who was as colourful as a rainbow.

They say she has the Lord's name, 'Rama,' worked into the hem of her shawl. And makes the students write out 'Rama' time and again in her class. And she got into trouble over that, didn't she? There was a complaint from a guardian and the Headmistress demanded an explanation from her. A report had been sent and the whole affair resulted in a lot of unpleasantness.

Twenty years—

I haven't met her since then. No, I did see her once after that. When I had been to attend the funeral rites of my uncle, I just had a glimpse of her. I shouldn't have. The old memories of her would have sufficed. My Leela would have remained forever eighteen, fresh and blooming as a rose in my mind and not this gaunt, withered stranger.

Three lives have been ruined.

Lakshmikutty – has she been ruined too?

Perhaps, she too had started her life with me with a clean slate.

Was it this loveless conjugal life that made her like this?

That day she interrupted the talk to say—

I had given her reason enough to feel unsure of my fidelity, hadn't I?

Still, while her father had millions salted away, when I wanted him to finance my studies abroad—

Instead of pressing my case, she—

Her father did not pay up because she had not wanted him to.

Was it solely her fault?

She might have feared that once I left the place I might never come back.

Afraid of losing their grip on the capital – that was the interpretation I had placed on it.

Has that house ever been a home since then?

After that, I have regarded her simply as a machine that ensured that I got my food on time and freshly-ironed clothes filled the cupboard without fail, haven't I?

I have never really been the head of the family, a husband and a father again after that, have I?

A father!

A son who would whimper if I so much as looked at him. A daughter whom I happened to describe when not in my full senses as having inherited her mother's brains and father's looks.

Everything utterly wrong!

I knew that this marriage was all wrong to begin with, didn't I? But never – not to this extent—

A mistake – one that ruined three lives.

When I had taken leave of her for the last time, Leela did not cry. Her eyes had not filled with tears till I came away.

'You shouldn't worry, Kutettan. Take it easy. This is fate. Think about Santha and Rema.'

It was she – whom I used to call forget-me-not – who consoled me.

Santha and Rema—

'Do you want me to take to the road? With these two girls in tow?'

It was that question from father that disarmed me.

There was no other way to repay the debt.

Santha and Rema – I don't think I have faced them after that.

Rema – the motherless child who was my darling. I haven't spoken even to her after that. I didn't even call on her when her husband died.

Sisters!

Doesn't this young man have any sisters younger than him?

Forgetting even his presence, I had been lost in my thoughts.

He was sitting there, staring at my face. What was he trying to read on my face?

'Don't you have any sisters?'

'Yes, a younger one. That's why I've come to you. She's doing her final year BSc. Once she is through college and lands a job somewhere, I wouldn't care if the house were to go.'

His sister is studying. She doesn't have to barter her brother to live. She can stand on her own feet.

'Please don't think that I have no integrity. I'll repay your money to the last paisa. My only request is that you should give me time. My Vimala isn't rich either. Her people spent their last paisa on her education. Otherwise she'd have given me the money to get out of this trap. Both of us are willing to work. Only, please give us an opportunity, I'll repay every paisa. I'll account for everything, the principal and the interest. In spite of everything I'd have sold the house and paid you. But my father tells me that he'd given his word to your father-in-law before he died. The son is supposed to honour his father's word, isn't he? Only you can save me. If you promise not to insist on this, I'll talk my father into agreeing. Say the word and please release me. If you do me this good turn, it will earn your daughter someone who is in full possession of his heart.'

'A good turn—'

'So you mean to turn me away?'

'What if I refuse? You'd still have to agree to this proposal, wouldn't you?'

'No, Sir. This wedding will never take place. You want to know what I'd do if you were to refuse? I'll do this: I will go to your daughter, whom I think of as a sister, and plead with her not to destroy me and herself into the bargain.'

Leela's son would have possessed the same spirit and guts. He would not have quaked at a glance from me.

Leela's son—

Leela doesn't have children, she spends her time chanting the name of God who'd proved himself merciless, doesn't she? Leela does not have children.

The children she never had.

The children she might have had.

The children she does not have—

They are nonexistent or even less than that—

Like Lamb's dream children, they are not destined to acquire a body and soul, even if they wait for a millennium upon the shores of oblivion.

My boy, you may go. My daughter has money, which will surely get her another man. Just as you said, someone who is in full possession of his heart.

You may go.

'Well, I'll not insist on your keeping your father's word. You may go and - what's her name?

'Vimala, Sir'.

'Ah! Find happiness with your Vimala. You may return the money in your own time.'

'Sir—'

('History Did Not Repeat Itself' first appeared in *Samyukta* Vol III. No. 2. pp. 144–152)

ELEVEN

Mistakes

She had expected the manager to be alone in his room. Flanking the table and facing each other, sat two other men.

'Take your seat, please.'

She sat facing the manager.

'I had meant to come as soon as I got your letter, but I couldn't make it yesterday.'

'You mean about that bill? That has not been entered as paid here. We have been going through the accounts.'

'What happened to the money then? It's been three months since I paid.'

'Did you pay cash? Got a temporary receipt or something like that?'

'I sent a cheque. I don't have a receipt.'

'In that case, it would be easy to trace it. Maybe they forgot to enter it here. We'll make enquiries. All we need is the cheque number and date. There's no problem.'

'The cheque—'

'There is nothing to worry. We'll get the date of encashment from the bank. Did you make it out in favour of our company?'

'No. That's why—'

'Then whom did you make it out to?'

'I gave a cash cheque. I wrote "pay cash".'

'Oh—'

'Your man told me a cash cheque needn't be disclosed for income tax reckoning and so it would be a favour to you.'

'Now, did he really? There's no way he could have said that.'

'Yes, he did. I've given him a cash cheque earlier too. I even got a receipt very promptly.'

'Do you remember the cheque number and date?'

'I don't remember the date. I didn't enter it in the counterfoil. I must have forgotten to. The cheque number—'

She got her diary out of her bag and opened it. '34851.'

'How much did you say it was?' It was the fat man, who sat on the right side, who spoke.

'Nine hundred and eighty-two.'

'Oh, nearly a thousand.'

'Yes, it was the payment for two or three consignments. They were paid at one go.'

'You don't even remember roughly when it was paid?'

Was there a tinge of condescension in his voice? An insinuation that you can expect no better from women? The airs that the three gave themselves! She bit on her lips and sat quietly for a moment. No, there's no point in losing your temper, she told herself, It's your mistake.

'I made out this cheque at home. I didn't go to the dispensary that day. It was only three or four days later that I recalled it and made the entry in my book as on that day. I can give you the date of entry in my book.' She took out her diary again. '17 April.'

'Who was it that insisted on a cash cheque?'

'Mr Gopinathan Nair. It was he who came there every time representing your company.'

Yes, Gopinathan Nair. It was because of him that I made this foolish mistake.

His fair skin and straight hair.

'Gopinathan Nair? Nair's on tour. It's obstacles all the way.' Was the fat chap laughing up his sleeve?

'I don't care what the obstacle is. I won't stop till I get to the bottom of this. To cheat one deliberately!'

'Sure that's what we want too. We must get to the bottom of this. Please don't think that we are not helpful. Let's proceed systematically.'

Don't get angry, doctor. We—'

'I'm not angry.'

This one's worse than the stocky chap. Talks as if he were talking to a child—

'Was it Nair who took the cheque from you?'

The bald man, who sat quietly twirling a pencil in his hands and staring at it, suddenly asked.

'No. It was a peon.'

His gaze returned to the pencil.

'He came with a note from Mr Nair. He wrote, I was to send the cheque through the peon.'

'Have you kept that note?'

'I did but I can't find it now.'

This time the fat person really did laugh.

'I can identify the peon if I see him.'

'Peons work on shifts. All of them won't be here now. We'll make enquiries.'

Shift, my foot!

'So you – well, I'll find a way to deal with this.'

'Doctor, let us not part on a bad note. Don't get it wrong. We'll let you know in a couple of days.

'All right. Thanks.'

The manager saw her to the door. As if, accompanying her to the door would set everything right. I'll show them all, she thought, I'll show them I'm every bit my father's daughter.

The blighters! The airs they put on!

Back in the moving car, the wind cooled her head. No point in blaming them. If you behave without sense, as though you were a mere woman – they had been pretty serious, till they got to know the whole story.

She had really been foolish.

That Gopinathan Nair—

Serves you right.

When someone came and smiled at you once and said this or that, you agreed to whatever he said.

You could have spoken to Thomas or Miss Kurien who're old hands. It never occurred to you.

They had been purchasing medicines from this company for years, even from the time when father had been looking after everything. Instead of finding out how cheques were issued—

Till her father was confined to bed, she had never bothered about anything except the patients.

That's why she got into this fix. Still, she reminded herself, you don't make out a cash cheque just like that.

Fool!

Better not tell anyone. That after all this while, you still do not know how to make out a cheque.

Or, don't I?

Gopinathan Nair—

When he walked into the consulting room with his file case, you always felt he brought the sunshine in with him.

The pungent smell of carbolic soap and lotion that wafted in from the inner room. Posters on the wall, courtesy Parke-Davis.

The poster that depicted the primitiveness of the first surgery had never appealed to her aesthetic senses.

There was no place for aesthetics in a doctor's consulting room, after all.

There were pictures – compliments from various companies – under the glass top of the table too.

Never paused to ask why they were placed there. Father used to do so. The practice was kept up.

Pregnant women, sallow with anaemia, and children who'd start to bawl at her sight (oh, are there so many bawling kids in this world?).

Hysteric young girls: 'I'm not well, doctor, I can't read, the moment I look at a book, my head starts to ache.'

Only the delivery cases and these people ever came to her; the serious cases went to the men.

Back pain. Headache. Pains and aches all over. Grouches.

I can't stand this, doctor, I really can't – only complaints.

The doctor's consulting room is a place where you could slip out of the garb of self-control, which is considered one of the signs of culture.

Into that world of aches and pains when he came smiling, untouched by any of those—

Dressed in well-ironed pants and shirts and ties that went beautifully with them.

How entertainingly he used to talk! However bored she was, she would perk up when he came in.

It was only when she set eyes on him that she smiled.

And that man—

Deliberately talked her into—

Realising her weakness—

He sent her a proper receipt the first time. That had been a small sum. And when it came to a really big amount ...

She had the car stopped when it reached the State Bank building and got out. She had to wait in the agent's room for fifteen minutes. In the meantime, they went through the old accounts and located the relevant details. The cheque had been cashed by one Raphael three months back on 11 April.

Once back home, she sent this piece of information to the company in a note. The messenger came back in an hour with a reply.

There was no peon of the name of Raphael in that place. Nair will be back in a week. They'll ask him. In the meanwhile, she might lodge a formal complaint with the company.

There was nothing to do except wait for him to come back. And was there any point in waiting for him? Would he own up?

At any rate, she made a formal complaint, carefully noting the date and the number.

She had not been expecting them to make a move for yet another week when a peon brought her a note from the company.

Could you please say whether the bearer of the note was the person who took that cheque from you?

That was the gist of the note.

It was the same person. She recalled his face with great difficulty.

His name was Raghavan.

The employees at the bank might have got it wrong then.

At the company they might have got some other lead. So the fellow has been traced. Maybe they'd take it seriously now.

Five or six days went by. There was no move from their side. Are they done with their enquiry or what? Why not remind them one more time?

One busy Thursday afternoon, as she got up to leave after disposing of the last patient, Thomas came in and informed her that there was someone to meet her.

He finds time to call only at noon? Why don't these people keep in mind that she too has a home? She had left home before eight in the morning.

She couldn't place the man for a moment when he entered the room. Then she recognised him as the bald man who had kept staring at his pencil in the manger's room.

'I wonder if you remember me.'

He spoke after a brief silence.

'Yes, I do.'

He lapsed into silence again.

'I came to talk to you about that case.'

'Ah, how did it turn out?'

'Nair has returned from his tour.'

'Has he?'

'Yes. He was back day before yesterday.'

'Oh.'

'We spoke to him about that money.'

'What did he say?'

'He agreed to having taken the money from you. He sort of borrowed it because he was badly in need of money. He had no intention of cheating you.'

'It's been three months. All this while—'

'He meant to replace the amount before you came to know of it, doctor.'

'Then why didn't he?'

'Now he is ready to. He couldn't till now.'

'Now? Now that everything's out and he can no longer hush it up. Isn't that so?'

'At least he owned up to it as soon as he was questioned. Suppose he hadn't? If he had denied it, you couldn't have proven it in any court of law, doctor. Raghavan did cash the cheque, but that hardly proves anything. You say he took the cheque. Even that's not a piece of evidence that will stand cross-examination. Raghavan said he couldn't recall whether he had cashed it or not. In any case, if you were to prove that the cheque had been given to Gopinathan Nair, it doesn't prove anything beyond the fact that you gave Nair a thousand rupees. Is there anything to prove that he was paid in his capacity as the company's representative? Nair could very well claim that the thousand rupees wasn't money due to the company.'

'After having cheated me, he must also lie—'

'No, doctor, I was only trying to present how it would have been if, as you say, cheating had really been his intention.'

'He owned it up since he knew I've got the note he sent me that day. That's it.'

He wouldn't know that I have misplaced it, she told herself. These people wouldn't have told him.

'Oh, you've got it? Does it say that you must send the amount due to the company?'

'In the note - that is—'

'Leave it. No need to go into all that. Nair has agreed that it was the amount due to the company that you paid him. And he's willing to repay the money.'

'This is not just about a thousand rupees. Repaying the money wouldn't be the end of it either. After deliberately taking the money, now when he doesn't have a leg to stand on ...'

'You are saying the same thing again, doctor. There's nothing deliberate about this. There is nothing more to it than having made use of the money in an emergency.'

'What emergency? A very convenient kind of emergency!'

'His mother has cancer.'

She did not speak.

'She's been under treatment for a while. It was on the day he got the thousand rupees that the doctor who'd been treating her here told him that she should be taken to Madras for Cobalt treatment.'

She sat listening to him but made no reply.

'You must believe me, doctor. It was on the 11th that your cheque was cashed, wasn't it? He went on leave for two weeks from 18th. He'd been to Madras with his mother. I don't have to tell you how expensive it is to give a person Cobalt treatment at a private nursing home in Madras, do I? Since he had no money with him at the time ...'

'Well, how is his mother now?'

'She's worse and has been brought back.'

'Where did he manage to get the money now?'

'Since there was no other go, he had to find it.'

'He might have conned somebody else.'

'Miss Malati, I'm not in the habit of intervening on behalf of others. I knew he was in a real fix. That's why I came here to trouble you. He made a mistake he shouldn't have. Okay, but there was nothing deliberate or pre-planned, no, nothing like that behind all this.'

'Had he just asked me for a loan ...' She didn't finish the sentence.

Had he come to her just once and said, my mother is ill and I need money for her treatment.

Not a thousand ...

Oh, if only he had said, I need a thousand rupees, Malati, giving no reason ...

Smiled his dazzling smile revealing all his teeth ...

Damn!

'There'll be a directors' board meeting in two days to discuss this case. Most probably they'd decide to dismiss him. This is a serious offence. Some of us might feel sympathetic towards him. But leniency wouldn't be shown. He's got a good record. No complaints so far. Still, with a written complaint from someone of your social position ...'

He paused. She kept quiet.

'If you were to withdraw your complaint, people like me who're on the board might talk the others into going easy on the punishment.'

He paused, as if he wanted her to say something at least then. He kept staring at her face for a while.

'His career would be finished if he were to be dismissed from a company like ours for a misdemeanour like this. This will finish him. Please don't think I have a special interest in his case. I am only sorry to see a nice young chap like him go to the dogs.'

'Why did he get me to make out a cash cheque, saying that it was to hoodwink the income tax people?'

Taken in by his fair skin – he'd have sensed it – he might have known that I'd agree to anything, that he could get away with anything—

'I did make enquiries about that too. It was a practical joke got up by him and some other youngsters to beat an Income Tax officer who thinks a bit too highly of himself.'

She laughed.

His face grew red.

'So you insist on your pound of flesh.' He spoke in English.

'One who eats salt must drink water.'

'In that case, let me take leave of you.'

She'd have been home long since but for his advocate. She followed him out. That must be his car in the front. Leaning on the bonnet ...

Gopinathan Nair!

So, he had been waiting at her doorstep all this time after sending the other man in to plead his case.

The car moved away. He didn't see her. Her own car moved forward.

She ransacked her house that very evening.

His note must be lying somewhere. She had never been in the habit of throwing anything away.

She looked everywhere. She came upon it at last in the cupboard under her sarees and blouses.

The note he sent.

Kept it secure among your clothes, you fool!

'Please send the cheque per bearer. Thanks.' Just that!

An epistle of love, kept perfumed and secure in the closet ...

Will this prove that she'd paid him? Or won't it? No one would claim that they gave someone a thousand rupees just like that?

Why not send this along too?

For the next three or four days she went about, unable to decide whether to send it on or not.

In Monday's mail, there was a letter for her, in an envelope that bore the company seal.

The meaning sank in only on reading it a second time. Since he was unable to continue to serve the company due to reasons of health, he was resigning from his job. A copy of Gopinathan Nair's letter to the company manager.

Copy to Dr (Miss) Malati Nair

was typed below.

So he has lost his job.

When he stood leaning on the bonnet, a shock of his straight hair had fallen on to his forehead.

Even in the midst of her wrath, she hadn't failed to notice it.

Gopi ...

('Mistakes' first appeared in *Samyukta*
Vol III. No. 2. pp. 153–161)

TWELVE

Handkerchief

I have never seen him. I'm not going to either. He was my brother's friend. All I know of him is from what I have been told by Rajettan.

Early teens are an age when girls hero-worship their elder brothers.

Before that, the main occupation is fighting. Especially if the age gap between them isn't more than two or three years. At that time brothers are bullies, always poking fun at whatever you say and teasing you.

'Amma! Ettan ...'

'Why do you make her cry?'

'Amma, come and see what she's been up to here.'

'Don't you go and vex him, girl. Mind your own business.' Brothers had to have some means of killing time, hadn't they? What better one than teasing your younger sister who hangs around you once you reach home?

When the brothers outgrow the teasing stage and the sisters outgrow the hanging-around one, there comes the age of hero-worship.

It's a beautiful age. There will never be the same kind of intimacy between them at a later age. Once they grow into young men and women, they have their own lives to lead. Then there will only be growing apart.

Yes, before that, it's a beautiful age.

I was fourteen when my brother went away to Madras to study.

I have been talking about the person who was his friend at the time.

I shouldn't say friend. Rajettan was a student and he was a teacher. I am not sure how to put it. It won't be enough if I just say that he was his teacher.

Let me call him Madhava Menon. That was not his name. But let's call him that.

He was a teacher in Rajettan's college. He never taught my brother. My brother studied a different subject.

I only knew him from what my brother used to tell me when he was home during the vacation.

Whatever he said was taken to be the gospel truth in those days. I used to wait for him to be home.

He was my window to a world outside – one that I didn't understand, that I hadn't seen, that I longed to see in those days.

The world of men.

How varied were the hues that a young girl's imagination imparted to that world!

A world where a woman could never hope to enter, even if it hadn't been walled in by aristocracy and propriety.

Cigarettes, bicycles and heroics – the world of power.

A world which a woman can never fully fathom.

(I happen to be acquainted now with a woman who can whistle beautifully.)

It was to me that Rajettan would narrate his yarns. As soon as he was home, everyone would hang around him for a couple of days. Then they went about their business and he would get nobody but me to listen patiently to everything.

News from college, idiosyncrasies of his teachers, pranks that the students got up to in the class – he would describe everything in detail. It was his descriptions that started my craze for English movies. I made the acquaintance of Stuart Granger, Audrey Hepburn and Gregory Peck.

Only through hearsay. I could see a movie only if either of my parents condescended to accompany me. And neither of them was interested.

My two elder brothers were working in distant places. My elder sister was also away.

If I insisted too much on seeing a movie—

'Your sister never threw tantrums like this.'

That was it.

It was a great disadvantage having such a well-behaved elder sister. It was also her shadow that loomed large in front of me, when I demanded costly, colourful dresses.

My beloved sister doesn't know that I used to curse her in my mind.

Rajettan and I were friends. It was between us too that most of the fights used to take place.

'Bhadrakali!'

'Chudalamadan!' I wasn't the sort of little sister who'd give in.

I still remember the tears I shed the day Rajettan left for Madras.

My brother never used to write to me. When he came home during the vacation – how fast those days used to fly!

Now I don't think that everything he told me in those days was true.

When you find that you can get away with any old fib, you'd naturally ...

The new-fangled custom that Rajettan brought from Madras was this – he must have a cup of coffee first thing in the morning.

Now, the custom in our house was that nobody should have a morsel of food before having their bath. Earlier, Amma used to insist not only on the bath but also on a visit to the temple.

The very first thing that Rajettan gave up on reaching Madras was this bath.

He was loath to give up his morning cup of coffee when he was home. So it fell to my lot to procure him this coffee. By the time Amma came back from her bath and the visit to the temple, even the coffee mug would have been washed clean.

Both of us were under the impression that Amma didn't know.

But I am sure she knew. She wouldn't have been displeased had she been told that her darling son didn't even wash himself. If her son broke the rules, she would only pretend not to have noticed and turn a blind eye to it, rather than go against his will.

We weren't old enough to know that then. We considered this coffee-making a pretty serious conspiracy or a subversive activity. How awfully funny the whole thing was! And the smoky brews that I got my brother to drink in the name of coffee!

It was when he came for the second time that we got to know Madhavan Master well. Rajettan went down with typhoid over there. It was Madhava Menon who sat by him and nursed him, that too disregarding his own ill-health. He went back with permission to shift his residence from the hostel to Master's house. The students were extremely fond of him. He had company every evening. When he joined them, to laugh and make merry like they did, he never gave one the impression that he was a man of great intelligence and erudition.

Someone with a serious heart ailment at that. A life lived in the knowledge that death, which might come to claim it unannounced, was right behind.

He spoke only to Rajettan about his illness. He hated to talk about it.

My brother was against his joining in the loud chatter.

I think my brother wanted him to talk to him only.

Once he even tried telling him that he found it hard to study with all this racket going on around him.

'I am sorry that you find it difficult to study here, Rajan. In that case, you must shift to the hostel.'

My brother never mentioned the difficulty again.

Madhavan Master used to write in the magazines. Humorous pieces that would make you hold your sides with laughter. He never wrote anything that didn't have a smile in it.

The doctor had advised him against exerting himself but he never shied away from cricket matches with the boys in the blazing sun.

After making a day of it, he would have to endure pain throughout the night but that never deterred him.

My brother had tried to get him to be careful.

'Careful of what? Will you be quiet? You've got to die someday.'

You have to die some day. Laugh through life till then.

We used to worry a lot about him. We even made elaborate plans to make him live more cautiously.

I never saw him. I do not even know what he looked like. All I know is that he was slender, tall and of wheatish complexion.

Did he have curly hair? Large eyes?

I like noses that are slightly hooked at the tip. Did he have one?

There were a hundred things that I wanted to find out about him.

How do you ask your brother all this?

He hated to pose for photographs. So I never even got to see a photo.

'I told you he's not handsome. But he's got personality.' Ettan had nothing more to tell me.

However much a man cared for another, he'd perhaps notice nothing more than this about him.

I came to know of the time when they went swimming much later.

They often went swimming. This time they had been to a different beach. And went in a bit farther than usual.

'Come on, let's go back,' he said suddenly. My brother turned back, even though he didn't fully grasp what the matter was. He had nearly made it back when he turned back to see him lagging very far behind.

When my brother started back in confusion, he called to him.

'Go on Rajan! I won't be long.'

Rajettan waited for him. They walked back together. 'Why didn't you keep up with me?'

'The sea here is shark-infested. I remembered that only later. I don't usually go for a swim here. I thought I saw something moving in the water.'

'If you saw a shark, shouldn't you get out of the water fast enough?'

'You are young, Rajan. I wanted you to get out first.'

It was when he was home during the long April vacation that he told me about this. He'd been home a couple of times before that, but hadn't told me about it.

It was during that particular April vacation that I started to work on a handkerchief for him. To begin with, I wanted to knit him a muffler. But I didn't know how to knit. I didn't have the needles either. Even if I were to learn to knit, everybody would come to know about it as soon as I started buying the accessories. Buying silk thread without anyone's knowledge posed no problems. And no questions would be asked if somebody happened to see me working on a piece of white cloth. It was a muffler that he really wanted. But what could I do?

I settled for the handkerchief. (Somebody told me the other day that it was unlucky to present someone you love with a handkerchief.)

I cut the cloth into four square pieces, made a broad hem at the edges. A flower in one corner. His initials in the opposite corner.

I was not an expert at needlework then, nor am I one now.

Still I plodded on. I didn't know that you were supposed to stretch the cloth on a hoop if you didn't want it to wrinkle.

When I had done, I thought they looked a bit soiled from too much handling. So I washed them with perfumed toilet soap. The yellow colour ran a bit.

Never mind. It was just a little bit. I folded them neatly and placed a couple of heavy books over them to make them look as if they were ironed. I managed to get a piece of gilt paper from somewhere and wrapped them in it. I opened the packet and showed them to my brother before handing the packet over to him to be given to his friend.

Rajettan was to leave the next day. When Amma came with big tins of banana chips and fritters coated with jaggery, there wasn't enough room in the case.

(He was supposed to bring these tins back but he never did.) He offered to pack them in the hold-all.

Amma didn't like the idea. She was afraid that the chips might lose their crispness.

'Come on, move! Let me see. You take these things every time. Why shouldn't there be room this time? You must have packed everything in a disorderly fashion. Let me pack.'

Amma pulled everything out. She started to repack. There was room. But her eyes fell on my paper packet. 'What's this?' We stood quietly.

'Where did you get this from?'

'I made it, Amma,' I said preparing myself to face the worst.

She was about to wrap it up again when – till then I had been proud of the fact that my mother could read English.

'Whose initials are these?

Rajettan did not speak.

And I did not even raise my head.

I got told off in the evening for having dared to embroider handkerchiefs and to send them to a strange young man without consulting anyone.

It seems Rajettan got his share before he left. So the handkerchiefs that I spent sleepless nights to finish never reached where they were meant to.

I cried a lot that day.

By the time my brother came home for the vacation, Madhava Menon's condition had become worse. He had stopped playing cricket. During their evening walks, he would put his hand companionably around my brother's shoulder. Quite often, my brother served as a prop. Every half furlong or so he had to stop.

'There's such a nice breeze here, isn't there? Let's stop here. There's no hurry. After all, we came out for air.'

Rajettan, who knew the reason only too well, would stop.

When the boys kicked up a racket in the room, he never joined them.

'Rajan, will you open that window? Isn't it a bit too stuffy here?'

My brother lacked the guts to scream, 'Oh, you scoundrels! You're killing this great man who's gasping for every breath. Get out!'

He returned home in Rajettan's company. His mother, who'd come to the railway station to receive him, fainted when she saw him stepping out of the compartment.

He died during that vacation. The numbing pain wore off after a while. It turned into a deep resentment towards everything and everybody, especially towards myself. I couldn't laugh for a long time after that.

Did I fancy that he wouldn't have died had my handkerchiefs reached him – carrying all the prayers and wishes of my young life ...

Those handkerchiefs that I had taken so much pains to work, whose yellow threads were stained with all the tenderness there was in me – did I believe that they would protect him like a talisman into which the mantra to defeat death was invoked?

I never made handkerchiefs after that.

Today is my birthday. The birthday present of a dozen handkerchiefs, which came by post in a box, lies before me.

Folded neatly from corner to corner to reveal the hems neatly done in green, they are not handmade.

The person who sent me these gossamer-thin ladies' hankies does not know that when I receive them they'd revive painful memories in me. Memories that haven't lost their bitter sting for me.

These delicate beauties must have been chosen, keeping in mind the fact that I love green.

There's a world of love behind them. Still – what happened to those on which I embroidered yellow flowers with tiny violet centres?

Do they still lie, yellowed and faded in Amma's clothes chest which gave out the smell of dried kaithapoo when you opened it, among the old 703 *mul onnara*s and upper clothes with jari, waiting to be bartered for steel dishes?

('Handkerchief' first appeared in *Samyukta*
Vol III. No. 2. pp. 162–168)

A PATH AND MANY SHADOWS

Chapter 1

There was a small bamboo gate that allowed access to the top of the hill from the *thodi* on the eastern side of the house. It was through this that the little girl came out, pushing the bamboo pole aside. With one hand she pressed a bundle of books close to her chest. In the other she carried a lunch box. After climbing over to the other side, she placed the box and the bundle of books on the ground and pulled the bamboo pole back in place.

The bamboo gate was on the fence at the back of the house. After the morning milking, the gate would be opened and the cows driven out to pasture. It was a makeshift gate: two bamboo poles driven into the ground with holes bored into them, then yet more poles inserted crosswise into the holes. That was all. There were steps leading to the house and a *padippura* too in the front. If you went that way, you would have to climb over two stiles in the fence to reach the hilltop. It was longer too. Going through the gate at the back was shorter and easier.

To reach the road from the house, you had to go up the hill and then down it. There was no other route.

It was not a big hill. It was actually more like high ground.

Dry stalks of gingelly lined both its slopes.

Every year for a couple of months the barren hill would wear green. Once the rains were over, some crop or the other was always grown on the slopes. Every year different people would lease the land.

The gingelly had been harvested before the *vela* in the *kaavu*. Only their stalks stood about, drying in the sun.

The girl flitted among the dry gingelly stalks. A little further, wild chrysanthemum was in bloom. Clutching her books and the box in one hand, she plucked a couple of the yellow button-like flowers with the other and pushed them into her hair.

A little to the south, there was a white oleander bush with a couple of granite blocks at its base. It was said to be the haunt of *bhoota*s. A *yakshi* had been invoked in the granite. You were not supposed to go near the place. She picked a few flowers lying on the ground at a distance. They also went into her thick curly hair.

A dragonfly alighted on the stalk of some wild plant. She stalked it for a while.

There were two crevices running diagonally across the hilltop, looking as though the body of the earth had cleaved again. She jumped carelessly over both and continued on her way.

The kaavu was on the other side of the hill. There was no inner sanctum or even a roof. Right in the middle of the four outer walls was a huge banyan tree. Beneath it sat the vengeful Vanadurga, exposed to rain and sun.

After lingering here and there, she finally reached the kaavu. A little way off from the temple there was a small house thatched with hay. Velichappadu, the oracle, lived in the house. He and his brown-and-white dog, scrawny and shrivelled like him.

Walking up to the front door and pushing the gunny sack screen aside, she poked her head in and hollered.

She had strict instructions to make her obeisance at the temple inside the kaavu. She never quite managed to remember to do that every day but never forgot to shove her head into Velichappadu's house and hail him.

The owner of the house and his dog emerged. He was an old man with a couple of worn out canines in his betel-stained mouth. The front of his head was bald and shiny like a mirror. At the back was his silvery hair flowing past his shoulders.

Goddess Bhagavati's hair!

The old man came out and silently held out a packet toward her. The girl did not speak either. She opened the packet and put a small lump of jaggery in her mouth.

The old man stood watching her.

He never forgot to keep something for her: a piece of coconut, a small lump of jaggery and, if there happened to be a *paattu* the previous day, even an *appam*. Something.

When she finished the jaggery, she smiled and turned to go.

Once she reached the road, she took to her feet like the wind. Wasn't she supposed to reach school by ten? And she had to make up for time lost in dawdling, didn't she? ...

The school got over in the evening at the right time. She had company till the market where the four paths met. Her friends bid her goodbye there. They had to go eastward.

As soon as she was alone she started to run and stopped only when she reached the kaavu. At the back of the house, Velichappadu was sitting on the wall of the well, leaning on the pillar that supported the pulley beam. The old dog lay stretched to its length at his feet.

She stopped in front of him.

The old man raised his head.

She gave him a smile, revealing even teeth.

'Would you tell me a story today?'

Velichappadu nodded.

The little girl was excited. She threw the books and the lunch box to one side. On some days Velichappadu would refuse. And he wouldn't relent no matter how much she begged him. Sometimes in the evening he wouldn't even be outside. On such days she never called him.

There was a single chethi shrub full of ripe berries – next to the well. She collected a few in her lap and seated herself on a flat stone right next to Velichappadu.

'Tell me a story. Not about the demon Darika. Tell me some other story.'

Velichappadu liked to tell stories of Bhagavati. He never tired of repeating them. When she wanted to listen to some other story she would say that beforehand. Sometimes Velichappadu would not oblige her. He would start on the same old Bhagavati tale. Then she would keep quiet ...

'Which other story do you want?' came a sudden query.

She thought for some time. 'Lord Ayyappa's story will do.'

Velichappadu started narrating the story. The little girl sat listening, throwing a berry into her mouth now and then. As the story unfolded in his gravelly voice, the barren hill and the gingelly stalks and the distant cashew grove and the even more distant line of the blue mountains disappeared from the girl's sight. A big forest. Hunters, hounds and hunting calls and noises. And the darling baby lying alone at the foot of a tree, laughing and playing by itself.

She wasn't fond of listening to the petty squabbles and jealousies of the court. When he described them in detail, the berries would disappear rapidly.

Finally came the point at which the young boy went in search of leopard's milk. The little girl's hands stopped moving. The young prince, mounted on the she-leopard and herding the cubs, was before her eyes.

As the voice trailed off, she came to her senses and realised it was time. She scrambled to her feet and, picking up her books and the lunch box, started for home. The old man sat where he was, looking at her hurrying away.

She walked straight, never glancing toward this side or that, along the narrow path that led through the gingelly stalks. She reached the bamboo gate to find it secured from inside.

The cows had come home. There was no other way but to go through the front gate. She followed the fence to the front. Climbing over the stile on the lane, she reached the front yard through the padippura, only to find her father pacing up and down it. She broke out in a sweat.

'Mani, where have you been all this while?' The cold voice reached her just as she was climbing the steps to the front porch. Silently, she turned toward him. She could not even bring herself to look up.

'I am asking you, Mani. Where have you been after school was over?'

She still could not find anything to say.

'Don't you understand Malayalam? I am asking you, what have you been doing till now?'

'I ... I ...' she began, giving in to that cold compulsion, but could not continue.

'She must have had games practice at school. She wouldn't stay back otherwise, would she?'

When she turned toward the voice, her Cheriyamma was standing on the front porch.

Oh, she's here to butt in, she thought, with a brief on my behalf. That was the only thing she lacked – Cheriyamma's assistance.

Achan did not speak for a short while. She knew even without looking up that the piercing look was fixed on her.

'You may go in, Mani,' he finally said, 'Just wait till you do this again. If you are not here by five in the evening, you'll have it.'

She went in without saying a word. Throwing the books on the table in the eastern room, she ran to the kitchen. As per her grandmother's dictum, she had to remove the dress she wore to school and wash her hands and feet before her evening coffee. If she bothered with all that, coffee would be even later. She was extremely hungry. If no one else was around in the kitchen, Kunjiamma would give her coffee. In that case, she would have it sooner.

Cheriyamma had not returned to the kitchen. Thank God.

'Kunjiamme, give me coffee, please.'

She was busy slicing vegetables.

'Manikkutti, did you wash your face and feet?'

'Please hurry, Kunjiamme. I am dying of hunger.'

'If you are so hungry, why don't you come straight home from school?'

'Are you giving me the coffee or not?'

She took the coffee from near the stove and gave it to her. Also an *ada* from some stored on the wooden ledge.

What was special about this day?

'When did Achan come, Kunjiamme?'

'He came early. He was here for lunch.'

Oh, that explains the sweet dish.

Before she was finished, Cheriyamma came into the kitchen.

'Have you not been told not to go straight from school to the kitchen? And Kunjiamme, you are even worse. You don't bother to check whether she has washed her hands and feet before giving her coffee. How many times does one have to say these things? You seem to think that one must do the exact opposite of whatever one is told. Then how can this not happen?'

She slipped out through the other door.

Let her blab. When she was tired of talking she'd stop.

When she went to the paved floor near the well to rinse her hands after eating, grandmother was giving Gopu his bath. Before grandmother could see her and start a ruckus about not washing, she slipped out. She couldn't put off changing her dress any more. Wasn't she supposed to wear the same dress to school the next day as well?

Her usual practice was to run to the *thodi* immediately after having her coffee. Make a round of the cow shed too. Since Achan was home today, that would not be possible. It would be dangerous if she ran into him.

After changing her dress, she dawdled about in the eastern room moving her books this way and that.

Grandmother came in.

'Go wash yourself, girl, before it's dark. Gopu is finished. There's some water drawn from the well left in the pot. Hurry! Here's your towel.'

She took the towel from her and walked to the bathroom.

'Why lock yourself into the bathroom? Can't you wash yourself near the well, girl?'

She pretended not to hear grandmother's shout.

Cheriyamma was cleaning broken rice, sitting on the verandah.

'Mani, are you going to wash yourself? There's a cake of soap on the corner shelf in the bathroom. Scrub yourself well. The girl's body has become dark like coal. I had better come and help you scrub. At least for a day, I'll make you clean.'

'No, I don't need anybody's help. I can manage on my own.'

Cheriyamma returned to the sieve that she had placed on the ground. Just let her come to scrub me clean, I'd show her. Become dark indeed! May be I have, but what's that to her?

She was combing her hair in front of the mirror after her bath when grandmother started calling to her.

'Aren't you done with primping, Mani?'

But it was Gopu who came into the room and not grandmother.

'Oppole, please come. Don't you know that Achan is home?'

With the grandmother leading, the children walked to the northern room near the stair.

The brother and sister walked into the room, pushing the door open. The grandmother just stayed near the door.

On the cot by the window, their mother lay in her usual place.

'Gopukutta,' she called softly.

He went up to her. As on every other day, she pulled him to her and started touching and patting his body and head.

Mani hung back. Her turn always came second.

While she was standing there with nothing to do, she ran her eyes round the room.

There was no change.

On the window sill, in the middle, a picture of Lord Guruvayoorappan. There were two smaller pictures flanking it. One of Krishna as a cowherd playing his flute to his cows and calves. The other was Krishna again, but seated on a tree with the clothes of the bathing Gopikas in a bundle by his side.

There was only Krishna in Amma's room.

An elephant-shaped incense-stick holder stood on the window sill, leaving room for the lamp to be placed in front of the picture of Guruvayoorappan. Next to it there was the earthern money pot for coin offerings to the temple. A little way off to the other side was an old tin, containing sacred ash, with dry sandal-paste balls sticking to its lid.

Nothing had changed.

The spittoon was under the cot. They had not forgotten to place it there.

Now his pride would not allow him to demand anything. And even if he did, what was there to be got? The children were all afraid of him. The young men ignored him. And not many of his generation were left.

And it was when the feeling that he was entirely dispensable had begun to eat into his soul that she came into his life.

He was walking along the western side of the ground where *koothu* was performed when he saw a girl slip and fall into the crevice. The place had become extremely slippery after the rains. He had gone to her and pulled her out.

She had thick hair that reached below her shoulders and large eyes.

He thought she'd also take to her heels like the others. But she showed no fear of him. She wiped the mud off her hands and picked up her books.

'My pencil is at the bottom of the crevice. Can you get it for me?'

Still not entirely free from astonishment, he climbed down into the crevice one more time. She showed him where it lay from above. He picked it up and climbed back.

She took the pencil, which had by then lost its lead point, with her left hand and with a smile that revealed small pearly white teeth said, 'It's late. I have to go.'

He had waited for her by his door in the evening.

The girl who could not bond with her kin and the old man who had no kin to bond with. Though she lived surrounded by next of kin in the two-storey house by the hillside, she was essentially alone. It was the northern room at the foot of the stairs smelling of ayurvedic liniments and incense that the word 'mother' brought to her mind. She was unable to visualise her mother separately from the old bed in the ill-lit room. Ever since she could remember, she had thought of her mother as part of that room.

She watched milk, coffee, rice gruel, cooked rice, pickled mango, buttermilk curry, all disappear into the room one after the other and empty glasses and dishes come out. She didn't know what went on in that room. She had never felt the least desire to know either. She had never even wondered why someone should spend their days lying abed like this.

She would make the daily trip to the room because there was no getting away from it. If those lifeless eyes fell on her, or those bony hands with their knotted tracery of veins touched her, a numbness would creep up from somewhere at the bottom of her mind. She could be at peace only when she got out of the room. It was only at dusk, when it was time to light the lamp, that the individual who was her mother consciously crept into her mind. And that too as a chore that had to be finished quickly. Her thought processes always skirted round the airless room and the individual who inhabited it. It was an unconscious urge to exclude whatever was uncomfortable.

She had listened to Kunjiamma hinting darkly at many things after one of her spats with Cheriyamma. She had come to understand in bits and pieces something about the time when her mother had been a woman with blood flowing through her veins. But she never gave the matter much thought. In fact, she hardly ever paid any attention to the talk. She realised only years later that those bits of information had been accumulating slowly at the bottom of her mind to assume mountainous proportions.

Only a year separated the brother from the sister, but the difference in their nature was more than a whole world. He had no problem doing as he was told. His tendency was to conform rather than to oppose.

Everybody liked him better, including their grandmother and even their bedridden mother.

The only thing she and Gopu did with one mind was the trip to the northern room at dusk. They had never discussed it but she knew he also found it difficult.

They hardly ever saw Achan. He was never home half the time. And if he happened to be home, even a leaf was supposed to move only with the consciousness that he was home. She had never seen him talk or laugh loudly. She had also never seen him get angry or lose his temper. He always maintained the same facial expression and the same tone of voice.

She too was afraid of Achan. Her only thought was to avoid, at all costs, running into him.

It had been only a couple of months since he caught her climbing an areca palm. She had climbed it because Kunjiamma had asked her to pluck areca nuts. Before she could climb down, Achan had seen her. She had started out thinking that Achan was not home. But he came and saw her at the most inopportune moment. He called her in and told her to sit in a corner of the porch. She had to spend the whole day sitting there. It was only after everybody had gone to bed that she had been allowed to get up and leave.

Till then she had not moved. Cheriyamma had come and peeped at her. Even pretended to be sorry for her, the wretched woman.

She hated Cheriyamma. She had been given to understand that her mother hated Cheriyamma even though she was her only sister. Even if Kunjiamma was unable to carry the rice gruel and other things inside, Cheriyamma would never take her place. She wouldn't even enter the room. Once, when Kunjiamma hadn't been there and grandmother had not been keeping well, Cheriyamma had carried rice gruel and the chutney to the door and it was she who had then carried them in. Cheriyamma would not face Amma.

'How would she? One's conscience should be clear, shouldn't it?' she heard Kunjiamma mutter one day when she was in a bad mood.

Grandmother was harmless. The only thought she had was about Gopu: bathe him, feed him, send him off to school, all these constituted a full time occupation for her. She had no other thought. It was because she had no sons of her own that she loved Gopu so much.

It was Kunjiamma who told her that.

If you wanted to ask something there was only Kunjiamma. Only she ever explained things to her. But Cheriyamma disapproved of her talking to her. If she happened to see her talking to Kunjiamma she'd be angry with her.

Chapter 3

One day on her way to school, when she stopped at Velichappadu's place, she did not find him at the door. When she called to him, he told her to come in from within.

He was lying curled up in a ball on the old coir-string cot with a blanket drawn up to his chin. She did not ask him why he was lying down. Even on that day, he took out a packet from under the tattered pillow and held it out to her.

She called on him in the evening too. He was lying in the same position. The brown-and-white dog was sitting at his feet.

The next morning, the old man did not open his eyes even when she went and stood near him. There was only a peculiar wheezing sound. She tried calling him once. There was no response. After waiting for some time she left. It was time for the bell to go.

On her way back from school in the evening, she found two young men standing in front of the house. She slipped in through the back door. This time when she went near him and cleared her throat, he opened his eyes. But there was no twinkle of recognition in his eyes. His lips did not even twitch. She was astonished. In the morning she had thought that Velichappadu was sleeping. Why was he pretending not to see her? What was wrong?

When she saw one of those men who had been standing in front of the house come in, she slipped out the same way she came in, through the back door.

As soon as she got home, she rushed to the kitchen.

'What's wrong with Velichappadu, Kunjiamme?' God was on her side for once. Only Kunjiamma was in the kitchen.

'It seems his game's up.'

'What's up, Kunjiamme, what game?'

'Isn't he pretty old? During the paattu on Friday, he did the ritual dance in the rain. Will the old man listen if you tell him not to? Well, if in your seventy-fifth year you danced in the rain, even if you are Bhagavati's own man, you will catch a fever. They say his chest is full of phlegm. I heard Chettichiyar say that he won't last till morning.'

'Does that mean that Velichappadu will die tonight?'

'Go, change your dress and come, Manikkutti. You don't drink your coffee, you go asking after Velichappadu. This is your turn for the day! What queer news to harp on!'

There was no point in hanging about there. It was one of those days on which rice would be de-husked. Chettichiyar must be around still.

She ran straight there. Chettichiyar was separating the broken grains from the whole ones after rice was pounded and winnowed.

'What's wrong with Velichappadu, Chettichiyare?'

'The mischief of *chinnan.*'

'Who's that?' A fine time to joke!

'God, whatever do you want to know? There's nothing she doesn't want to know! His *Kaalan* is about to arrive. This is the illness for that. Everybody thought that even Kaalan had forgotten him.'

'Is Velichappadu going to die?

'Why should children know about these things?'

'It's not that, Chettichiyare. Who were those people I saw on the porch of his house?'

'Now how do I know? Are there people on his porch?'

'Yes, I saw two men standing there.'

'Oh, so they must have come. The old man had two nephews by relation, staying on the other side of the river. I heard people say that someone had been sent during the day to fetch them.'

'So it must be them.'

Chettichiyar said nothing. The cleaning of paddy went on uninterrupted.

'Now that they have come, won't they bring the doctor to him and give him medicines and then won't Velichappadu be okay?'

'Oh, yes, of course! Medicines, my foot! They have come to cut the firewood and burn his body when he's dead. Who needs the doctor in one's nineties?'

'Achan brought in the doctor when grandmother was ill.'

'Are you going to scoot or not? I can't winnow the rice with you getting under my foot. And you got bran all over your frock. I am going to call and tell them.'

Thus, she had to exit the place. After that, she did not bother asking anyone.

At night, she couldn't sleep for a long time. The unseeing look in his eyes and those lips that refused to smile stayed in front of her eyes even after she fell asleep.

She started out earlier than usual the next day. When Cheriyamma asked her what the hurry was about, she ran away, muttering something.

On this day, there were not just two but many more at the temple in the kaavu and around the house. There was no way she could go in and see him without being seen herself. She moved near a grey-haired old man. She waited near him for some time but he paid her no attention.

'What happened?' at last she asked softly.

It was then that he noticed the little girl standing near him with a troubled look in her eyes.

'Aren't you going to school, my child? Don't stay here. Go.'

'Velichappadu ...'

'There's nothing to be afraid. Go. There are all these people here.'

'I am not scared. Is Velichappadu dead?'

'Yes, he's dead. They are about to take the body for cremation. That's why I told you not to stay here. Go quickly. Run.'

Won't let me stay, she thought.

She went away.

On her way back in the evening, there was nothing there.

Not a single person.

She slowly went in. The coir cot lay empty.

There was nothing in the room. The pots and pans that used to lie here and there, the blanket that used to be spread on the cot, the pillow: everything was gone.

There was the cot in the empty room. At the foot of the cot, only the dog lay stretched to its full length. She slowly crept near it and placed her hand on its head.

Cold.

She was startled and drew back.

She understood what death meant. She stood for some time looking back and forth at the empty cot and the dead dog. Then she ran out.

She did not go in for her usual coffee. Nobody even noticed it. She shut herself up in the eastern room for some time. When Gopu came, she left the room and went and sat in the thodi for some time. When she grew restless there, she slowly climbed to the top of the hill.

She was experiencing, for the first time, the pain of losing some cherished thing. Her heart was aching without knowing the whys and wherefores of something. The very first wound to the heart. She never fully comprehended what was happening around her. She hardly ever got anything she longed for. Yet to lose something she had was something that had never happened to her. She couldn't even make out what was happening to her.

She didn't feel like crying. She didn't know how to cry.

She walked up through the gingelly stalks.

She could clearly see the road, the temple by the side of the road and the areca palm trunk that was the flag post of the temple.

Beyond the gingelly stalks lay a grove of cashew trees. And in the distance lay the line of blue mountains almost brushing the horizon.

She could not see the trees and the woods clearly, only blue lines. They floated like a chain, up and down, up and down.

She stood gazing at them. The wind which came whistling by danced among the strands of her thick hair. Her unruly hair flew into her eyes and face. She stood still, not bothering to brush them off her face.

Blue mountains, which have never yielded to human presence, were whispering consoling words in her ears. The hillside seemed to fold the grieving child in its embrace.

The western sky suddenly turned red. In a short while, the outline of the mountains became hazy. Everything was red.

Some more time crept by. Darkness blanketed the hillside.

She stood thus, alone on the deserted hillside.

Stars were beginning to open their eyes.

The soft wind was still playing in her hair.

Its merciful caress was smoothing her pain away.

'Mani ... Mani ... Mani ...'

Grandmother was coming in search of her.

'Where has this girl been all this time? She goes and stands alone on the hilltop at dusk! Has she no fear? A girl standing alone next to the edge of the kaavu! What kind is she? I have cracked my throat calling to her. Instead of washing herself and taking a couple of the Lord's names, she goes strolling on the hillside!'

Even before she drew near, she heard grandmother scolding her.

She ran ahead so as not to let her grandmother catch her.

Chapter 4

It took quite a few days for the wound to heal.

She could never walk past the kaavu without going into the hut and looking around. It wasn't as though she expected something. She simply could not break the old habit.

Being chided for climbing up the hill at untimely hours became a regular happening at home. But she could not stop it. It had become a necessity.

On the barren hilltop, she was experiencing, in the stroke of the dry wind, the consolation of unfamiliar caresses.

Days passed.

One Sunday afternoon, she was hanging around in front of the kitchen with nothing to do.

Kunjiamma was trying to de-husk a coconut using a chopper, all the while cursing Chettichiyar, who had broken the handle of the axe. Since she didn't have the knack to do the job with the chopper, it was the name-calling that was getting done. The husk was getting pounded into fibre but there was no sign of the coconut actually emerging from within. On the hilltop, at a distance, Mani saw strangers walking up, and she moved to the fence. It was Mammali and another coolie with a box and a bed in front. Just behind them was a boy wearing blue trousers and a white shirt. Then, a lady, who seemed to be Cheriyamma's age. There was also a man. They were coming from the railway station.

'Who are they, Kunjiamme?' she called down.

Kunjiamma hadn't finished her struggle with the coconut.

'How do I know everyone who passes this way? You are funny!'

The newcomers had turned into the lane and were almost level with the fence.

'Uh ... Ah, isn't this Ammukutti Amma? When did she come back?' Giving a break to her toil with the coconut, Kunjiamma joined her at the fence.

'Can't you see she's coming back now? And just who is this Ammukutti Amma?'

'Ammukutti Amma? She's your aunt. Ammu Cheriyamma.'

'You mean this Cheriyamma's sister?'

'No, this is your Achan's sister. There is just the two of them, brother and sister.'

'Who's the other person?'

'He must be her son. How the boy's grown! The last time I saw him he was just taking baby steps. How beautiful he was to look at!'

'Then who's that?'

'He's the boy's father.'

'Will they call on us, Kunjiamme? What do I call Ammu Cheriyamma's son?'

'You should call him *Etta*, what else? I don't know whether they'd come visiting, the last time they did ... that was eight or ten years ago.'

Their conversation at the fence must have been loud.

Cheriyamma turned to look at them.

Her face made you pity her.

Neither was she tall nor well-rounded.

Seeing her pause, her son did too. So did her husband. The husband gave her a smile that lit up the whole of his dark, unattractive face.

Kunjiamma hurried away when someone hailed her from inside. They walked away. She stood near the fence, watching them till they disappeared beyond the *palliyal*.

After that, she saw Kochachan and his son going for evening walks every day.

Kunjiamma had told her that their house was beyond the stream and the paddy fields.

She would climb to the thodi on the western side of her house and watch the father and son going for a walk holding hands, talking and laughing.

As soon as he saw her the father would give her a bright smile. She took to waiting in the thodi for the smile. Sometimes, when he passed by he would ask her something.

Two or three weeks after their return to the village, Ammu Cheriyamma unexpectedly came into the house on her way back from the kaavu, after a bath and prayer. Her son was also with her.

She and Gopu were in the front yard. Their Achan was not home.

Leaving Ettan with them, Ammu Cheriyamma went in. Even though she saw him every day at school, she was hardly acquainted with him.

After a few minutes of dithering, she invited him to inspect their grounds. He agreed and they set off.

She took him straight to the verandah in front of the kitchen.

Kunjiamma was coming in after milking the cow. 'Who do we have here?' she started immediately, 'Are you on your own? Didn't your mother come?'

'Yes, she's inside.'

'You must be on your way back from the kaavu.'

'Yes.'

'What's your name?'

'Vikraman.'

Vikraman. She liked the name.

Vikramettan – good. She heard Ammu Cheriyamma calling him Appa.

Appettan would be easier.

Kunjiamma placed the milk pail on the verandah and stood them together.

'Nice pair. You look very much alike.'

She thought that was true. Ettan had the same forehead, eyes and nose that she saw in the mirror every morning.

'You take after your mother's family.'

Ettan smiled and did not say anything.

'This is your murapennu, *kutta*.' She did not quite know what that meant. Did Appettan know? Just as she was about to ask Kunjiamma for an explanation, Ammu Cheiryamma's low voice was heard from the front porch: 'Appe, let's go.'

She didn't stay for even fifteen minutes. What was the hurry? After that, she used to meet Appettan once in a while on her way to school or back. They did not visit them after that. Nor did anyone return the visit.

And finally the month of *Makara* arrived. It was time for *chuttuvilakku* and vela in the kaavu.

In the evenings, Cheriyamma would take them to the temple. They were thus able to watch the vilakku and *niramala* for some time.

Finally, the day of the vela arrived. Achan was not home. He had not been home for over a week. Had Achan been home, he would have taken them at least to the top of Vaniyan's shop, if not actually to the festival ground. He'd leave them there and go. Early in the morning, he'd come back to fetch them back home. She and Gopu would stay there. Sometimes, there would be other children and their mothers. From there, you could see the effigies of bulls being brought in and the play. You wouldn't be able to see the koothu, for which you need to be really close. Still you could watch the bulls play. If nothing else, at least that was possible. This year it seemed as though even that would not happen. If Achan did not come, who would take them?

Cheriyamma was heard saying that Achan was extremely busy and that was the reason for his non-appearance. If only he would take leave for just this day and come—

It was noon.

People dressed as *poothan* and *thira* came to the house, performed and left.

How terrified Gopu was of them! She had once seen poothan go in and ask Kunjiamma for water, which he then drank after removing the mask.

Time passed. The sun had gone down. The bull effigy belonging to the Puthenkalathil family was taken in a procession through the path in front of her house. It was a big bull. It would not pass through the palliyal. The fence had to be pulled down. It was Appettan's father who did that. The palliyal belonged to them anyway. It was a big bull, a handsome one, its whole body covered in red silk and a lot of bells hanging round its neck.

When her grandfather was alive, they used to take their own bull effigy in procession. And that too in a grand manner. That was what Kunjiamma had told her. At that time, it came third, after the ones belonging to the *nampoothiri* and the *thampuran*. When it became Achan's responsibility, he opted out one year saying he could not be bothered and they lost their place. Now even if someone in their family wanted to, they would have to take the last place.

Oh, Achan is not yet home.

It was seven. She and Gopu managed to have their supper early and took their places near the fence.

People had started making their way to the temple: men, women and children. Leaving almost no one home, they were all setting out. The kaavu was actually within hailing distance. So, if you had to sit like this at home when all this was happening there—

Having to watch people making their way to the kaavu was becoming almost unbearable.

It was then that Kochachan appeared, holding Appettan by the hand.

'Mani, aren't you going to watch the vela? Why are you waiting here?'

'There's nobody to take us. Achan is not home.'

'So have you made up your mind not to watch the vela because there's no one to take you?'

'Cheriyamma won't let us go on our own.'

Kochachan turned toward Appettan.

'Won't it be a pity, son, if just these two did not get to see anything?'

He stood thinking for a short while.

'Mani, go and ask your Cheriyamma if you might go with me. If she says yes, I will take you.'

She started toward the house without even waiting for him to finish. Gopu followed her.

Cheriyamma was just sitting down to her supper after her evening bath.

'Appettan's father is going to the kaavu. He offered to take us. We are going.'

They did not wait around to hear the response. Finishing what she had to say in one breath she ran out. Gopu was right behind her.

Instead of walking across their property, she made straight for the front gate and reached the other side of the fence.

Kochachan was still standing there.

When they reached him, he asked, 'Did you tell her?'

'Hm,' she said.

Going with Kochachan was not at all like going with Achan. Instead of taking them to the top floor of a building, he took them right to the middle of everything.

It was time for the bull to be taken out. The procession always began at the foot of the banyan tree that stood where the four roads met. They moved there. The effigies were being positioned. Appettan was holding the lamp for the bull of the Puthenkalathil people, since they had no boys old enough to do the job. Actually, it took two to do it but now there was only Ettan. He was excited. And she was getting to see everything for the first time. The way you rose in public esteem when you stepped up on to the platform holding the *kuthuvilakku* and held the bull close to you with your free arm around its neck! To keep himself from falling asleep, he had filled the corner of his *mundu* with puffed rice.

Around eight or ten people lifted the bull.

'Appa, be careful. Don't fall off. Hold on tight,' Kochachan called out to him. Appettan stood there, smiling down at his father with a grown-up air.

The effigies of bulls, red and white, mingled and moved forward in a line. There was Parangottu Nair's double bull. It was the most handsome among the lot. Kochachan walked forward, holding them both by the hand and never losing sight of the bull on whose platform Appettan was standing.

Now and again Appettan would throw puffed rice at her.

'Kochacha, will you get me also up on the bull?' she asked him when she could no longer suppress her envy.

'Whoever heard of girls holding the lamp for the bull? Shame! I am hearing this for the first time.' She did not say anything after that. To Kochachan everything was a joke.

Bangles, ribbons and balloons were displayed for sale by the side of the road. Kochachan moved toward the bangle sellers. He bought four pairs of bangles. She herself chose four bangles each to her liking for both wrists. When he bought balloons for

Ettan and Gopu, one was bought for her also. Kochachan slipped Ettan's balloon into his pocket. The bull effigies lined up before the temple. The fireworks began.

She had never had an opportunity to watch rockets and sparklers go off at close quarters. When the crackers began to go off en masse, Kochachan asked her, 'Are you scared?'

She said no. Gopu said nothing.

Kochachan hoisted him on his shoulders till the crackers stopped going off. It was very late when the fireworks were over.

They were getting ready to take the bulls inside for the performance. All the boys were brought down from the platforms.

Along with Ettan, they climbed the wall of the *gopuram*.

Oh, for what a long time the bulls played, jumping and prancing about and competing with one another!

They watched till the end. Then they moved slowly toward the *koothumadam* where the *koothu*, a shadow puppet show, was being performed.

They were watching koothu at close quarters for the first time.

You can never have enough of watching dark shadows dancing on a white cloth. She liked everything – the song which she could not quite make out, the 'aaah' sound made in a peculiar humming tune by the second performer, Hanuman and Ravana.

It had never been so much fun before. When they started for home, dawn was breaking in the east. When they reached Kochachan's house, the door was locked. When she and Appettan hollered, a light started moving inside the house.

'Who told you to take my children?' She turned back at the sound of the familiar voice. Achan. She recalled seeing his face among the crowd.

Gopu was no longer sleepy. He let go of Kochachan's hand and moved away.

'Nobody,' Kochachan answered with a slow smile.

'Then why did you take them?'

'I did not take your children. When I was passing this way, I saw two children standing hopefully by the fence. I took them. I did not take them because they were your children.'

'So you go about taking other people's children to the fair?'

'If the children have no one to take them – if they are willing to come with me – after all it doesn't cost me anything,' Kochachan smiled.

Cheriyamma came and opened the door. In the faint light of the oil lamp in her hand the faces of the speakers could be seen: one was angry, the other serene.

'You can't take my children without my permission.' Achan's voice had never risen so much before.

'Then you should take them yourself.'

The more irate Achan became, the more amused Kochachan became.

'That's for me to decide. If I feel like it I will take them. If I see them standing here looking out like this, I will take them along again.'

'You will not.'

Kochachan smiled his slow smile once again. Then looking toward where Cheriyamma stood just inside the house, he pushed Gopu forward.

'This boy is half asleep. Please take him inside.'

'So goodbye,' he said to everyone in general. Taking his son by the hand he walked away.

Chapter 5

It was after that that she and Appettan started going to school together.

Ettan would wait beyond the fence till she was ready. He never went to school without her. He would wait for her in the evening too.

He waited beyond the fence but never came into the house.

She would meet Kochachan once in a while on the hilltop.

Ettan's conversation always centred around Kochachan. He kept talking about going to this place or that with his father. They went out for walks every day. They returned only very late in the evening. They would just stroll about, climbing uphill and down paddy fields. To the town-bred Appettan everything was new.

One day their school closed early. For some reason, the students were told to go home.

They started for home in the sweltering sun at noon. At the market junction, her friends bid her goodbye, leaving her and Appettan alone. When they were walking past the kaavu,

Appettan said, 'Mani, would you like to come home with me? There's time today.'

It seemed like a good idea. No one at home knew that school had closed before time that day. She had to be home only by four. Till then, she could visit Appettan's house. She had taken lunch to school. Since she had started from school after having it, she was not hungry either.

She made up her mind to go. When they reached the lane, she walked softly but swiftly so that no one in her house would know. She relaxed only when they were past the palliyal.

A single slab of granite formed a bridge across the stream. Now there were only puddles of water here and there. They had to cross the bridge and walk along the narrow bank bordering the stream for some distance. Lush green paddy fields lay below. The rice saplings were about nine inches high. They nodded their heads in the gentle wind and smiled. For quite some distance, there were only paddy fields: its green crisscrossed here and there by the narrow boundary ridge overgrown with wild adakkamaniyan weeds.

The stream went round the paddy. The road was beyond that at a distance. You could not see it clearly because the banks of the stream were overgrown with aattuvanchi trees. And they were the only things you could see.

They crossed the paddy fields and climbed the incline opposite.

Appettan's house stood on high ground. It had no padippura, only a wooden beam barring the way. There was no one on the front porch. Placing their books in the porch, they went in. Ammu Cheriyamma was sleeping on a mat. Appettan woke her up.

Cheriyamma hugged her as soon as she saw her. Since she was not in the habit of receiving hugs, she felt only a kind of uneasiness.

'Thank God you felt like dropping in on me today. Do you know how long it's been since we came to stay here?'

She did not say anything. She wanted to avoid having to tell her that she had not told anyone at home about her visit.

Cheriyamma turned toward her son. 'Why Appa, don't you have school today? Why are you early?'

'We had classes only till the afternoon. We were let off at noon.'

'You have come straight from school? Aren't you hungry?'

'We had our lunch, Amma.'

'But I must give her something to eat.'

'You may get her something. We'll be right back. Come, Mani.' They ran out.

At the entrance to the eastern ground, there stood a huge mango tree full of flowers and small mangoes. They walked, picking up a few tender mangoes from the ground and eating them.

They also ate some of the tender leaves of a tamarind sapling. A cinnamon tree stood at a little distance. Its leaves were sweet. On the other side lay a veritable forest of the wild creeper njottanjotiyan.

Its seeds were like yellow pearls inside a papery envelope.

They walked on, eating whatever took their fancy. There was a proper path just beyond. Instead of going that way, they made their way through the ground overgrown with wild plants. The farm lay beyond the grounds. Coconut and plantain groves were watered using oxen. Instead of human beings circling with the pulley, the ox does it. Moving back and forth, back and forth, along the same rut: how amazingly patient it was! You would think it was dreaming.

Cheruman Sankaran was standing near to take hold of the pail of water as it came up. He also worked for her family. 'Kochambidi, why are you here?' He made small talk.

'Just visiting.'

After that he said nothing. She stood watching the water gush forth through the channels made in the earth and circle every coconut tree trunk and pass by, laughing.

'Ask Koru to get up off the rope, Sankara. Let's sit for some time,' said Appettan when he had had enough of watching the water.

The rope attached to the halter of the ox had to be weighted. Only then would it work.

Koru immediately got up.

She was acquainted with him because he accompanied Sankaran whenever he came to work.

Both of them sat on the rope, lifting their legs off the ground. The trip on the rope was fun.

They got up only when Cheriyamma sent someone to fetch them.

Some time must have passed.

Cheriyamma had been waiting for them with raw jackfruit fritters and coffee. She sent for them when the coffee had started to grow cold.

She was eating jackfruit fritters for the first time that year. After drinking coffee they ran to the porch, carrying handfuls of fritters.

If you went to the gate and looked out, you could see till the very end. They sat on the bamboo crossbeam. Appettan brought her books to her.

They saw Kochachan walking along the ridge bordering the paddy field at a distance.

Before he drew any nearer, Appettan got out and ran to him. He relieved his father of his newspaper and umbrella. Kochachan placed his hand round Ettan's shoulder and drew him closer. She sat unmoving on the bamboo beam, looking at both of them walking close to each other along the narrow ridge.

She felt a sudden ache somewhere inside and grew listless.

Envy—

Kochachan came up to her. He tossed her in the air, caught her and put her down.

'When did you come, Mani?'

'Some time ago.'

'The school closed early, didn't it?'

'Hm.'

'Did you offer her coffee?' he turned towards Appettan.

'Oh, yes. We were sitting here eating jackfruit fritters.'

'And you didn't keep any for me?'

Appettan felt in his pocket and came up with a small, sorry-looking piece.

Kochachan took it and put in his mouth.

'I am going,' she announced suddenly.

Kochachan looked at his watch on his wrist.

'Hm. It's half past five. Hurry, don't you have to be home before dark?'

She flushed.

Don't dawdle here, go home: was that not what Kochachan said?

'Don't go on your own, Mani. It's almost dusk. I will go with you.' She heard Kochachan's voice from behind.

'No, I don't need an escort.' She said without stopping.

'Wait,' a heavy hand fell on her shoulder. She stopped.

'Appa, you go in and tell your mother that I am taking Mani home and will be right back.'

'I am coming too.'

'Come with us then. Take my umbrella in and tell your mother. Then come running to join us. We are setting off.'

Kochachan climbed down to the narrow ridge, still holding her close. He did not speak. Nor did she. When the ridge became too narrow for two to walk abreast, he made her walk in front. His hand still lay on her shoulder.

Appettan joined them when they had covered some distance. The he started talking about school.

She climbed into the palliyal laughing at some foolish thing uttered by a boy in Appettan's class. Kochachan accompanied her to the steps. He left only when she went in.

'Where has this girl been?' That was what grandmother wanted to know as soon as she saw her.

She made no reply. After all, her questions did not mean much.

Achan came home when she and Gopu were sitting down to supper. She was neither called nor questioned. The next day happened to be a Sunday. Nothing happened till evening.

Achan went out after his evening coffee. He came back by around six. As soon as he was back he summoned her.

Now her case was up for examination.

'Mani, when did you get home yesterday?'

'Half past five.'

Cheriyamma must have told him. The wretch!

'When did school get over?'

So it was not Cheriyamma who told him? How would she know the school got over early?

'At one.'

'Then where did you go?'

She said nothing.

'Where were you till half past five after school got over at one?'

'At Appettan's house.' There was nothing else to do but confess.

'Who is this Appettan?'

'Vikramettan. Kochachan's ...'

'Ah, you are on Ettan–Kochachan terms already? Who taught you all this?'

Again she said nothing.

'Haven't I told you not to linger here and there after school, that you are to come home straight?'

She made no reply to that too.

'You don't understand plain speaking, do you? Let me see whether I can make you obey?'

He opened the drawer of the table and took out a thin cane. Had it been lying there all this while? She had never seen it.

'Hold out your hand!'

She held out her right hand.

With the first blow, the palpitation of her heart stilled.

The sixth was also over. The skin on her palm broke and drops of blood started to ooze.

She held out the left hand.

One ... two ... three ...

Don't cry ... Don't cry ...

Six, and he stopped.

She did not cry.

'Now perhaps you won't forget. Remember this: if ever you set foot in that house, this will be nothing compared to what will happen then. You have no Appettan or Kunjettan. Do you understand? I don't want to have you following in her footsteps.'

She stood unmoving.

'Go, don't stand here.'

Her legs were shaking. What if she fell trying to walk?

Fall down before Achan? She walked away, keeping her hands straight by her side.

Gopu was standing in the corridor, his face as white as a sheet of paper.

She ran straight to the open ground. The makeshift gate was open. She was in luck. She climbed to the top of the hill.

She held out both her hands and stood looking at her palms with red welts.

How her palms stung! The pain was excruciating. But it was a lightness that she felt in her heart. Her father was inflicting physical pain on her for the first time. Somewhere inside a chain broke.

She spoke to no one about the day's happenings at home. Somehow, Appettan came to understand. After that he never waited for her near the fence. He would stand a little further up, but wait till she joined him.

When the school closed for the vacation, all these trips to school and back stopped. If at all they met, which was very rare, they met on the hilltop. When Kochachan and Ettan went for their walk on the hilltop, on days when Achan was not home, she would climb through the back gate to join them. They always stopped to talk to her for a while.

One day, when she was coming down after meeting them, Kunjiamma saw her.

'Have you not been told not to speak to them? Then why go and make trouble?'

She started as soon as she saw her.

'No one has told me not to speak to them, only never to go to Kochachan's house.'

Kunjiamma made no reply to that. A few minutes passed.

'Kunjiamme, what did Kochachan do to make Achan so angry?'

She had been meaning to ask her this for many days.

'Can't you just listen to what you have been told? Why do you want to know more?'

'Please, Kunjiamme, just tell me.'

'These are things not meant for children's ears.'

'That doesn't matter. Tell me.'

'How stubborn you are!'

'I won't let you go if you don't tell me.'

'Oh, let's not have you tormented by not knowing. I will tell you. Manikkutti, your father had chosen another alliance for your Ammu Cheriyamma. The date had been fixed, people invited and even the *pandal* put up. The huge vessels for cooking the wedding feast had been brought. That was when Kuttisankaran Nair availed of leave, arrived in a hurry and took away the bride. He did not breathe a word of it to anyone either. What a hullabaloo there was that day!'

Kunjiamma stopped. She waited for some time. The woman gave no sign of continuing.

'Why did he take her away without telling anyone?'

'You want to know why he took her away without telling anyone? Well, otherwise he'd never have been able to take her away. That's why.' She had only then woken up from her reverie.

'It seems as though all this happened only yesterday. How many years to this day, I wonder. I wasn't working for anyone then. My mother was alive at that time. Someone had to look after her. She was bedridden with rheumatism. How could one leave her and go to work? I used to de-husk paddy for people. That was how we managed to pull on. I used to work at Ammukutti

Amma's house too. I even helped de-husk the paddy, which was boiled for preparing the wedding feast. Some rich person from somewhere down south was supposed to marry her. Ammukkutti Amma was crying all the time. She and Kuttisankaran Nair had been in love for some time. He was her brother's friend and used to visit now and then. Slowly they grew to like each other. Kuttisankaran Nair had approached them with a proposal. Her family had rejected him, saying he wasn't good enough for them. By then, he had got employment in the postal department and had left this place too. It was then that the other proposal came. The family was well-known and owned paddy fields and landed property. Do you think Ammukutti Amma had the guts to say no to her brother's face? She kept mum. She nearly died of weeping. How Kuttisankaran Nair got wind of everything and arrived here I have no idea. Whether Ammukutti Amma herself wrote to him also I do not know. I wonder whether she was capable of such things. Anyway, he came a couple of days before the wedding was to take place. Ammukutti Amma used to go to the kaavu every day early in the morning after her bath. Who else did she have to share sorrows with if not the deity? Her parents were both dead. She was afraid to look her only brother in the eye. She went as usual to the kaavu early in the morning the day after Kuttisankaran Nair arrived. She never returned home. They say Kuttisankaran Nair was waiting on the hilltop. He took her away. From where she picked up the courage to leave I don't know. You won't find a gentler person in the whole place. He must have carried her off or something. Anyway, they left by train the same day. They set foot in this place only after a couple of years. By then they had had this boy. I think they have just this one child. Anyway, after that day the brother and sister have not been on talking terms. But one must say this – the brother gave her a share of everything, even before they asked him to. If he hadn't wanted to, he could very well have kept everything to himself. That Kuttisankaran Nair certainly wasn't the type who bothered with settling accounts. Even then everything was divided equally, to the last grain of rice. After the partition of property, she visited the house with her child. He ignored her. She came away weeping loudly. After that, she never again paid her brother a visit. And you can't blame the brother either. What terrible shame she had brought on the family! They say even some relatives from afar had set out to take part in the wedding.'

She fell silent again.

'Kunjiamme!'

'Hm. What now? Now you can't say you haven't been told. Don't have anything more to do with them. A repeat of what happened the other day—'

'Shut up, Kunjiamme.' She ran away from there. She couldn't bear any references to the punishment meted out to her that day.

It was on the hilltop that she finally stopped.

It must have been somewhere near the outer wall of the kaavu that Kochachan had waited that day. He must have carried Cheriyamma when she came out, after bowing before the deity and wearing a turmeric mark on her forehead, as lightly as one would carry a flower.

Chapter 6

'Could you please throw me a tender cucumber over here please?'

The girl who stood beyond the thorny fence round the palliyal asked the man who was inside, drawing water.

'I don't grow cucumbers, watering them and all, so I can give them to some girl. You have to pay. You just might get them then.'

'As if somebody would pay for tender cucumbers not yet broken from the bud. Who wants your tender cucumber?'

'Okay, fine.'

A little time passed.

'Appetta,' rose the voice again from the other side, 'Please give me some. I will not run away as I did yesterday. I will definitely learn the whole.'

'Promise me?'

'I do.'

He walked the length of the plank to empty the pail. Then, taking his hands off the *etham,* he stepped out.

The trousers and the half-sleeved shirts were gone. He was wearing a mundu, hitched up, and a singlet.

A white shirt, its sleeves carefully rolled up, was hanging by the fence.

He went looking here and there for tender cucumbers among the vines planted in lines and spreading in circles. When he had gathered five or six, he went to the fence.

A fair, rounded hand reached up over the fence. He placed the cucumbers on her palm.

She had also changed somewhat. The frock reaching barely up to her knees was gone. The unkempt hair no longer got into her eyes and nose. The polka-dot skirt reached up to her ankles and the blouse was open in the front, fastened with safety pins. The hair, if let loose, would cover her back but it was pulled into a tight plait.

For some time there was only munching: he on this side and she on the other side of the fence.

When she was finished, she moved toward the etham.

'Enough. Let me listen to what you learnt yesterday.'

'I have one more left. Let me finish it.'

'Eat it later. Now start.'

You goddess of bliss, where have you disappeared,
Unexpectedly, in half a moment?

She began reciting with the cucumber pieces still in her mouth.

'You are reciting with your mouth full. Recite when you are finished.'

'Well, you said I should recite now.'

She took some time to finish munching. Then she started again.

She got through four or five lines.

'I have learnt only up to this.'

He started from where she left off:

Sitting on a golden chariot of clouds
I was playing the veena
And singing a lullaby I ...

Changampuzha's lines came floating by in his clear voice.

She was supposed to sing along with him. She sang a couple of lines and slowly stopped.

He was so fully immersed in the singing that he hardly noticed it.

She always preferred to listen. And, to ultimately to lose herself in dreams. She leaned on the fence, biting on a tender sprig.

Had she been questioned as to what she was thinking, she would never have been able to answer. They were warm thoughts, full of light. They were about nothing in particular. Pleasant thoughts that couldn't be given a form.

It was only when he stopped that he would realise that she was lost in a world of her own.

This was a regular happening.

On some days, he would be cross with her over this. He wouldn't speak to her for some time. She really had to try hard to get him to speak to her. The tiff always ended with a promise not to repeat the behaviour. Sometimes, she would be chided. In which case she only had to listen to his words with a smile. His anger would cool.

This poetry-teaching and recital session was a daily occurrence. Whenever her father happened not to be home, she would present herself on this side of the fence and he on the other side.

She never took pains to learn the music in the lines that he sang. She had no desire to learn to sing.

The poetry, full of life, she learnt ardently. At that age everything one heard stuck to one's memory. The words, powerful with a kind of magnetism, went straight to her heart and danced.

Words ...

Words that sang, swayed, were tremulous with tears, floated with rising laughter.

A universe of words.

She was waking up into that new world.

He imparted whatever poetry he had imbibed from here and there to her. It was not enough to slake her thirst. And she found no way other than through him.

He began to go in search of books for her: *Remanan*, *Bashpanjali* and *Asthimadam*.

She wasn't so much reading books as devouring them: each and every line. She would put down a book of poems only when she had learnt the contents by heart. And she didn't have to try very hard for that. She only had to read a poem twice. It stayed in her heart. Only the poetry of tears was good. Edappalli and Changampuzha. They were the poets.

Her nature did not permit the indulgence of tears. She could only break, never bend.

The sprightly child had been forced by circumstances to look inward.

Was it any wonder that only the poetry of failure and melancholy appealed to her?

She never gave much thought to meaning. It was the emotion that appealed to her heart. And also, the honey-sweet form.

On evenings, when the west wind came howling by, she would climb to the top of the hill and recite aloud the lines ringing in her heart. It was difficult for her to do it in the presence of anyone, not just Appettan. It was like laying bare a part of her heart.

She experienced no difficulty when only the blue mountains were listening to her recital. There was nothing she wanted to hide from them. They had been witness to every emotional change in her.

Thus, on the hilltop, where there was none to listen, she would recite the lines, going deep into the emotions beyond mere words. There was no music, no rhythm, only words that came to life on her lips.

Chapter 7

When she wrote her first poem, Appettan was not home to read it.

The time was when she had been reading Changampuzha's poems again and again and dreaming of mellifluous sounds.

Are there apsaras dancing behind the door and in the corner of the room?

Mellifluous sounds.

Were they swaying in front of her very eyes?

She caught their exhilaration. Rhyming words ...

They filled a notebook.

That was how she came to write her first poem.

It made no sense. Seven or eight lines made up of sweet-sounding words.

She did not show it to anyone. She dared not. She didn't write it so she could show it to someone.

Anyway, by that time there was no one to show it to. How could she share it with anybody but Appettan? There was Kochachan, but this was not good enough to be shown to him. She really had to write something worthwhile and then take it to him. He must read it and say, with the smile that lighted up his dark face, 'Ah, did our Mani really write this? This is no child's play. Whoever would have imagined that she had it in her? Smart girl!' Then he would place his heavy, rough hand on her shoulder.

If ever in the world she wanted someone's good opinion, it was his. How could she show this to him? What if he said, 'This is no good, Ammu, try again'?

She couldn't take that from Kochachan.

She might have shown it to Appettan and asked for his opinion. But he was not in station. Why not mail it to him? Oh, his friends might come to read it. Moreover, of late, there have been no letters from that quarter. What could be wrong? He was in a new place and had made new friends. Perhaps he could not be bothered to write. Oh, that could not be the reason. Poor Appettan, he had written three letters in the very first week, describing everything about the place in detail. In fact, he had written them without even waiting to receive replies to the previous ones.

On the eve of leaving the place to join college ...

He had taken her to the cashew grove at the bottom of the hill to take leave of her. His eyes and his whole face were a sight to see.

He stood looking silently at her. And tears slowly welled up in his eyes.

He was going to see the world that lay beyond this place for the first time. Should he not show some enthusiasm at the prospect?

You would naturally be upset when you left home, but you could always come home if you wanted to. It was only an hour or an hour-and-a-half by bus. It was not all that far.

They stood looking at each other a long time.

'Mani,' there was only this cry at the end.

'Appetta ...' How would she know to console him?

'Please do not forget me, Mani.' It seemed as though he would break into tears.

'No, Appetta. Will I ever forget you?'

She had to say only that. Appettan did not wait for her to say more. He turned and ran into the cashew grove.

Should she go after him? She hesitated for some time.

What if he was crying?

She hated to watch people cry.

She did not follow. She stood where she was.

Appettan didn't return. When it grew really dark, she went home.

She was waiting near the fence when he left the next day to catch the bus. Kochachan was with him. They were accompanied by Mammali, carrying the luggage.

Appettan only smiled when he saw her.

He mailed her a letter the day he reached. She got four or five letters in succession at her school address. She sent a reply to one of them. She had to curry favour with Gopu to get the postal envelope.

After that there had been absolute silence at that end.

The headmaster must be withholding his letters. What else could be wrong? Appettan was not ill. He has been writing regularly to Kochachan. It was only yesterday or so that he mentioned receiving a letter.

How depressed she was for a couple of days after he left! Gopu never waited for her on his way to school or back. Appettan had never gone to school without waiting for her.

Radha and Thankom waited near where the four paths met. They would wait for her even if she was late. They would be standing near the junction. Even when Appettan was with her, she would join them there. Now she had to walk alone. It was the same story in the evening too. She would be on her own when the others turned into the other path. When Ettan had been there, he would catch up with her by then. Before reaching home, they invariably had a fight. Appettan had a really short temper. What fun it had been to incite him!

Now she had to walk alone when she had climbed the hill.

It had become a habit with her to go and stand near the fence talking to him when he visited the palliyal in the evening. Her evening would be tedious if she did not stand near the fence. Many a time, she had been told off by Cheriyamma for doing that. She never did that when Achan was home. But then Achan came home that early only once or twice a month.

The day after Appettan left, she went and stood near the fence looking in till it grew really dark. Cucumber and bottle gourd were ripening. Only the gardener was not home.

Full-throated snatches of songs would never come floating from near the beam of the etham, would they?

Cheruman Sankaran's son came in and sauntered among the plants for some time. He plucked a few cucumbers from here and there. Throwing them into a basket, he left.

She stood leaning on an ayani tree near the fence watching him come and go.

It was growing dark.

Another person came into the palliyal.

Kochachan.

It was almost the time when father and son usually went for a walk. They used to go for long rambling walks and returned only when it was really dark.

He had come out when it was time for their walk.

He went in and walked the length of the palliyal from one end to the other. He did not see her. His whole attention was on the plants. What was he looking for, inspecting every plant so carefully?

When he was finished, he moved to the frame in the centre on which the bottle gourd vine was trained, and stood stock still.

She silently circled the fence and entered the palliyal from the other end. Kochachan was still standing in the same place. He became aware of her presence only when she went and stood near him.

Without uttering a sound he drew her close to him, just as he used to do when she had been a little girl in a frock.

They stood looking at the ageing bottle gourd vine for some time.

'He must be thinking about this there,' he said suddenly.

She did not speak for some time. Her mind was searching for an answer.

The nice man was aching inside. She had to console him.

'Two or three gourds need to be weighted with stones, Kochacha.' That was what she said in the end.

She pointed to a small gourd that was beginning to curl at one end.

He recovered from his awkward immobility.

They went searching for small stones. She fashioned small pieces of string from a rope tied to a pole at one end of the frame. They crawled in among the plants, found four or five young gourds and weighted them with the stones. One weighted them so they would grow straight and long. The job was finished. They stood watching for some more time.

Beyond the fence, two *cheruma*s passed by, talking to each other.

'It's dark, Ammu. Come on out,' Kochachan said.

They came out together. After closing up, Kochachan walked her home.

They reached her gate. She went in. Kochachan returned to the hill.

After that they met every day: at the palliyal till the work there was over, then on the hillside.

Chapter 8

It was soon after Onam. Appettan had been home for the holidays and gone back. It was fun when he was home. He had many, may be a hundred, things to talk about. He never tired of talking about life in his college. It was fun listening to him.

When he left life returned to its old rhythm.

Of late there had been some changes in Amma. She was still confined to bed as she had been all these years. But something had changed. When she and Gopu paid their routine visits, she did not pat them or ask them questions as before. She had the air of someone lost in thought.

She and Gopu still presented themselves in the northern room before the lamp was lit in the evening. Sometimes, Amma would speak a few words to them. At other times, she wouldn't do even that. She'd behave as though she hadn't seen them at all. Sometimes, when she had her face to the wall, she wouldn't even turn and look at them.

One day when there was no school, Gopu had gone to the paddy fields to supervise the farmhands. He did not return even after it was dark. When she was tired of waiting for him, she went to the northern room alone. For the past couple of years she had been given the chore of lighting a lamp there. Kunjiamma had taken to going home in the evenings. Her elder sister had a son. She was staying the night at his house these days.

She found it difficult to go into the room without Gopu. Since there was no other go she went. If she didn't light the lamp on time, her mother would tell her off.

The door was half closed. She heard voices from inside. She hesitated before the door. The voices were heard again.

Someone was sobbing loudly.

Was it Amma?

She peered in through the gap in the door.

Cheriyamma was sitting on her haunches on the floor at the foot of the bed. She was crying.

Amma was sitting on the bed. Cheriyamma was hugging her legs and crying.

Cheriyamma had never been seen to enter the room. What happened this day?

She pushed the door a little more open.

Now Amma's face could be seen clearly. Her face wore its usual look of abstraction.

Her long thin fingers were moving mechanically over the head of her younger sister, who was sitting at her feet crying. But for the movement of the hand, there was nothing to indicate that she was even aware of the presence of another person in the room.

She felt she could not stand the look of incomprehension on Amma's face.

She could not see Cheriyamma's face. She had buried her face against Amma's legs. Each sob racked her whole body. There was not much resemblance between them. Cheriyamma was not as small-built as Amma. She was taller and heavier than Amma. Still, she had the feeling that there was some shared resemblance between the two women. Looking at both from where she stood, she wondered whether the younger sister was growing more like the elder.

Her thick dark tresses, which she herself used to envy and which reminded one of the flower stalks of the palm – how did they become the rat's tails that straggled at Amma's feet? No one had seen her weep like this even on the day grandmother died. She had not gone and sat near her elder sister either.

What happened to her this day? Was her mental strength declining too?

Had it been wrong to nurse a grudge against her all this time? Was she also just another victim?

Had the two women been broken by the same man's demands?

Cheriyamma, fair and luscious, has shrivelled up like a piece of rind.

What happened to her?

She closed the door quietly and turned back. She did not find out what had happened. She did not ask anyone either. The younger sister crying her heart out and the older, drained of all emotions, looking at her with incomprehension – the picture stayed fresh in her mind for many days.

Five or six months passed. Kunjiamma stopped going home in the evenings. She didn't know why. Achan was also home most of the time. He never failed to be home, however late he was.

One day an old woman of the family of *mooppan*s staying by the stream came asking for some butter for some purpose. She was around when Kunjiamma and the woman were talking.

As soon as the woman left, she asked, 'Kunjiamme, what's wrong with Amma?'

She did not speak for a while.

'Manikutti, you are going to have another brother,' she said, wiping her hand on a piece of paper to remove the butter.

It took some time to sink in.

'Do you mean to say that Amma is going to have a baby?'

She nodded.

She did not stay there after that. Amma is going to have a baby. It was only last year that Radha had a sister. Radha's mother had gone to her house to give birth to the baby. She had returned only after a couple of months. Till then Radha had managed the house. Radha had been frisking about for a couple of days after her mother's return. It seems her mother had come back home toward evening. When Radha and her brothers started to paw the child, her mother spread a small mat near the lamp and laid the baby down on that for them to play with. Even when they milled around it, the child apparently had not cried. Radha used to recount everything with great pride. How many times had she come to school carrying the child! – this plump and fair baby with curly hair. Radha did everything, including giving the baby her bath. Once she got home from school, she wouldn't put the baby down. The child would wait for her to be home. How was Radha's mother to spare time for the child? Did she not have to do every chore in the house? It was she who did all the cooking and serving of food in the house.

There was no Cheriyamma in the house. And Radha's mother did not spend her days lying in a closed room.

A dingy room smelling of ayurvedic liniments and incense sticks. A coir cot with tins and bottles lined up underneath.

Amma—

One more child for her.

One more child in the house.

One more child for Amma.

Will she bathe it and breastfeed it? Something was wrong somewhere.

Will the child be laid on a mat in front of the lamp and will she and Gopu play with it?

No, nothing of that sort would happen. This was wrong. There was no need for such a child. It was unwanted.

From inside the house, Cheriyamma was heard calling Kunjiamma.

Suddenly the sight of her sobbing at her sister's feet came to mind.

What a hellish place. She walked out into the thodi in the midday sun.

Chapter 9

One Saturday evening, when they reached home from school the house was in a bustle. As soon as they got home, Gopu was sent to the *vilakkathrol*'s house. Achan got home only when it was really late. He immediately hired Madhavan Nair's car and left to bring the doctor.

With a flushed face and red eyes, Cheriyamma was running laps between the northern room and the kitchen. A pan of water, a glass of coffee: she had something to fetch and carry. Kunjiamma was constantly in attendance. Mani was in charge of the kitchen. In between boiling water and brewing coffee, she managed to cook rice and curry. When called, Gopi declined to eat, saying he wasn't hungry. No one had a bite of food.

There was light everywhere: on the porch, in the kitchen, the corridor. The kerosene lamps being deemed insufficient, the *nilavilakku* was also lit. Cheriyamma had done with her running around. She wasn't moving from the front porch. She was looking out for Achan and the doctor. Wouldn't they need anything more in that room? Cheriyamma stood there weeping, without wiping her face or trying to hide her tears. Tears filled her eyes and just flowed down.

It was past eleven when Achan got home with the doctor. When she heard their voices in the lane, Cheriyamma went out into the yard with a lamp. The doctor was a short man in grey trousers and a coat of the same colour. Achan was carrying his leather case. Cheriyamma went in with the doctor. She went back to the kitchen and remained there.

Cheriyamma came into the kitchen once or twice for hot water.

Every now and then, a groan would be heard from inside.

There was no other sound.

She went back to the porch. In the hall, Gopu lay fast asleep in a corner on the floor. He had gone to sleep on an empty stomach. He had been running around till dark. It was he who had gone to fetch the midwife and the ayurvedic physician. Achan had got home only very late.

Achan ...

What was he doing now?

She tiptoed to the porch to see.

He was pacing, in the pale moonlight, from one end of the yard to the other and then back to where he started from.

Never breaking the line, treading the same path that he traced first, never raising his head. He walked with his eyes downcast. What was passing through his mind, she wondered.

Was he recalling the girl he married by giving her a mundu, in a pandal hung with jasmine in the presence of people on a moonlit night just like this?

What did she look like at the time?

Short, fair and slim, she might have draped a silk mundu round herself. She might have worn her hair in a low knot with a too-heavy string of jasmine wound round it. She might have sat down in front of the *nirapara* right in the middle of this yard.

Would this night not bring all that to his mind?

A louder groan was heard from within.

Oh, did she go through all this for me too? Did she groan in pain like this?

After that she had been down with a fever for two or three months.

Nuggets of information gleaned from Kunjiamma at various points of time raced through her mind.

Her mother lay in the grip of the fever. Cheriyamma had come because grandmother could not manage on her own. It was the beginning of every trouble.

Whatever had happened by the time Amma rose from the sick bed, weak in mind and body?

May be there was nothing at the time. May be there were only doubts in the beginning.

At any rate, Cheriyamma had not gone back after that. The man who had been her husband had left the place to evade his creditors. Everything had fallen pat into place. By the time the elder sister recovered from her illness, the younger one had nowhere to go. The house belonged to her also. She too had a right to it, didn't she? Where would she stay if not here? To grandmother there could be no difference between her two daughters. Thus by the time one sister had recovered from the trauma of giving birth, the other sister had become a permanent fixture in the house.

Seeds of suspicion must have been sown in the wife's mind right at that moment.

She had not been mentally strong to begin with. After a long convalescence which nearly broke her, this poison also entered her system. The spark smouldered in some recess of her mind. When it was past bearing, she lost balance and toppled over.

With the second delivery, everything was complete.

Had she loved her husband so much? To the extent that she lost her equanimity when something like this happened on his part.

After all that, now ...

Achan was pacing up and down in the front yard. Somewhere on the hillside a jackal started to howl. A cold wind was blowing. Suddenly it started to rain.

She went into the corridor. A muffled conversation was heard from inside. The lamp placed on the door stoop so it would also light the hall, was burning low. It should not go out, that was a bad omen. She ran to the kitchen and fetching the bottle of oil, filled the lamp. Had grandmother been alive she would have raised hell for using coconut oil from the kitchen for the lamp. Who would bother with that now? By the time one located the bottle of oil meant for the lamp the flame would have gone out.

After adjusting the wick, she sat on the floor, in a corner of the corridor.

It must have been close to dawn.

It was still drizzling outside. She heard the sound of raindrops falling on dry leaves. The first shower of the season released the scent of dry soil. The snakes, it is said, are fond of the scent. With the first rain, every one of them would supposedly come out to take in the scent. To her it had always seemed a nice scent. Her friends told her that she was like the snake.

Hearing a sound on the porch, she craned her neck to see.

It was Achan. He must have come in because it was beginning to rain harder. The sound was his leg knocking down a stool in his way. Instead of sitting still somewhere, he was pacing about the room. The room was only big enough to take eight or ten steps. A canvas chair, two or three stools, a table, a broad bench, all lay in the room. The restless pacing continued amidst all these inside the room.

Cheriyamma came out from the room with a pan and went into the kitchen.

She did not go with her.

Cheriyamma returned to the room in a couple of minutes.

What was happening inside? Did Radha's mother go through this much pain for her cute and plump sister to be born?

Resting her back against the wall, she stretched her legs.

On the porch, the same pacing was going on. There was no sound from inside.

Somewhere in the distance, a rooster crowed. Other roosters took up the call. The birds were all up.

A new day.

She got up and went into the kitchen.

The rice lay untouched in the pot. She moved the pot aside and, carrying the rest of the pots and pans out, poured water into them. Then she swept the kitchen floor in a hurry and sprinkled water all over. She put a pan of water to boil on the earthen stove, in which the fire had still not gone out. Let it boil.

What was now to be done? Sitting still was out of the question. She went into the bathroom and let the pail down into the well. Some water would not come amiss. The copper pot also became full. Suddenly, through the hard grinding noise of the pulley, a faint cry was heard.

Abandoning the pail she ran into the hall.

Yes, the cry, faint and weak, came from inside the room.

Poor thing, was it crying, I can't, I won't?

Or was it pleading, look out for me, please?

When she felt someone touching her on her arm, she turned round to see. Gopu, startled out of his sleep, stood staring. Holding his hand tightly she stood looking at the closed door ...

The doctor, soaked to the skin in perspiration, came out carrying his leather bag. She moved after him into the corridor.

On the porch, the same pacing was going on. Nothing had changed.

As soon as he saw Achan, the doctor said, 'It's a boy.'

Achan did not speak.

The doctor placed his case on the table and fell into a chair. Achan continued to pace. Holding their breaths, Gopu and she hid behind the door.

What would the doctor think?

The doctor lay in the chair for some time. Since nobody spoke, he got up. Taking a piece of paper from the table, he wrote something on it and held it out to Achan, 'Buy this and keep it ready. I have given her an injection. I'll give another in the evening. There is no cause for concern now. But you have to be careful. She's anaemic. Five or six of this will have to be given. It isn't serious. There's nothing to worry.'

Achan took the piece of paper held out by him. He still did not speak.

'The child is a little before term. You have to keep him warm. I have told them how to go about it.' He waited a little while for a response. 'Let me take leave for now. I'll be back again in the evening.'

Even then Achan was silent. He reached to carry the doctor's bag.

'There's no need. Give it to me. The car is waiting on the road, isn't it? I think I know the way. I will manage. Don't you want to see the baby?' He held his hand out for the case. Achan did not give it to him. After a moment's hesitation, the doctor went out into the yard. Achan followed him.

Chapter 10

The house was in an uproar. The doctor would come every day to administer injections. Even the baby was injected, not just once but twice. Cheriyamma was engaged in an-all out effort to retain the life of the baby within its reed-thin frail body. The child lay in the middle of small cloth bundles filled with bran heated to a particular temperature. Sometimes when it cried, no sound would come out. Cheriyamma hardly ever left its side.

On her rested the onus of running the kitchen. She had to prepare everything for the mother and child. But then the others also had to eat. So she had to cook for them too. There were two cows. Kunjiamma would deal with the milking. She had to manage all the rest. Gopu would join in everything. He couldn't do much but was still a great help.

And on top of all, this there was also the examination at school. She somehow managed everything for a month. The examination was over. She was relieved. She would get through.

The doctor stopped coming. Amma's fever broke. Her body was back to normal but her mind refused to return to normalcy. Whatever little light there had been in her mind also went out.

Amma was always singing: singing the baby to sleep. She insisted that its little wooden cradle be kept in her room.

Once, when she had gone into the room for something, Amma had proudly shown her a piece of string tied to the cradle. It was apparently part of a contraption to rock the baby back to sleep when it woke up.

Cheriyamma would have taken the baby for its bath or something but Amma would lie there, pulling on the string to rock the empty cradle and singing in a faint voice. She would be oblivious of the baby being carried out for its bath and returned afterward. Rocking the cradle and singing: that was the sum total of her baby care. If the baby lay crying in his cradle, she never picked him up or tried to stop his crying. She just went near the cradle to rock it and sing at the top of her voice, but she never did anything else to console the baby.

When she heard the loud wails of the baby and the even louder demented singing from the dark room, she could never stop herself from wringing her hands and grinding her teeth.

There was sympathy but also anger and helplessness.

The vacation was almost over.

The college would also reopen. Appettan would leave. She had not even got to see him properly. Where was the time to wait near the fence for him? She was always busy.

Appettan must have had a lot of things to tell her. He had not finished telling her the news. He must have brought a lot of books. He had even told her that he had brought a couple of them especially for her. How was she to meet him and get them?

Was that really because of a lack of time? Had she a mind to do it, could she not have just run to the fence and got them? How much time would that have taken?

It was not that.

It was a period when she did not want to meet anyone. Even talking to people had become unbearable. Even to Appettan. His very first question would be about the baby. She could not bear it. She could not talk about her brother.

The vacation was almost over and school was about to reopen.

The very first day on her way back, she met Appettan on the hilltop. He was waiting for her. She wished he had not. Yet, she stopped for him. 'I don't even get to see you, Mani.'

'I have a lot of things to do at home. There's no time.'

'Where's Kunjiamma?'

'She used to work for us. But now she's gone back to her family. She's not feeling well. She's gone for a treatment. Said she'd be back when she's well.'

'The baby ...'

'He's doing fine. I have to go, Appetta. I have a lot of things to do at home.'

She replied as she started to walk away. Appettan did not go with her. They met every day: on the hilltop at the same time. She did not wait to talk to him. She would speak a couple of sentences to him and leave in a hurry. She would feel bad when she saw his face fall. Yet she could not find it in her heart to stay talking to him.

Even her behaviour at school was changing. She who was always laughing was gradually becoming quiet and subdued. Her friends began to wonder what had come over her. A reluctance to share personal problems and an unconscious fear that she might have to talk about them – were these things at work?

The Saturday before he left, Appettan came to her.

He was waiting in the same place that he usually did.

'I am leaving tomorrow,' he said after a few moments of silence.

'Hm. If you write to me, the headmaster won't give me the letter. Doesn't matter. I get to know everything from Kochachan.'

He did not say anything for a while.

'Mani, please remember me also sometimes. Make a little room for me too in your heart.'

She had the feeling that his voice was breaking with emotion.

'This is not all. I wanted to say a whole lot of things to you, Mani,' he broke off abruptly.

She was confused about her response. 'There's hardly any day when Kochachan and I don't talk about you. I meet him every day when he comes to the palliyal. He gives me all the news.'

He had begun to talk like a man.

And she?

Gopu, who had been straggling, caught up with her.

Appettan turned away so Gopu would not see his face. She too hesitated for a while. Then, slowly, she walked away.

Chapter 11

Months passed.

She used to meet Kochachan every day, either on the hilltop or somewhere else. He was always glad to meet her. And he was the only person with whom she had no difficulty in talking. He never asked any questions that she would hate to answer. And she never experienced any difficulty answering his questions. He never let on that he knew about the birth of her brother. It seemed he understood what was passing through her mind without being told.

Kunjiamma did not recover from her illness. There was no let up in her condition. She was staying home. Even if she made a recovery, she was not going to come back. Her brother's wife had died. There was nobody to look after the children.

Chettichiyar, who did odd jobs around the house, could not manage anything. She knew nothing. So Mani had to do a lot of chores in the house. She went to school after finishing most of the cooking in the morning. Cheriyamma had time only for the child. He had to be carried all the time; he refused to stand on his own feet even for five minutes. He started to crawl and walk only very late. And he was a child who never smiled.

The Christmas season came and went. She was in the sixth form. There was a lot to study. There was also very little time left once she finished all the chores. She was forever busy. If she were to apply herself to her studies and score good marks, she just might be able to go to college like Appettan. But she had no idea what her father's plans for her were. Her only salvation lay in scoring well. And the only way to do that was to turn night into day and study.

One evening, she was on her way back from school. She was alone. These days Gopu stayed back to play with his friends. As she turned into the lane near her house, she came up against Mammali carrying a bottle. He was everybody's odd-jobs man.

An exchange of casual pleasantries revealed that Kochachan was running a temperature. It was nothing serious. Since the fever did not let up, Cheriyamma was sending Mammali to the doctor to buy medicines for him. She recalled that she had not seen Kochachan for five or six days. Since she sometimes missed meeting him for a couple of days – because she was busy with a lot of things – she had not noticed this till then.

There was no way she could see him in person, because her father was home that day. If he came to know about it, there would be hell to pay.

She came away only after she had closely questioned Mammali to reassure herself that there was no cause for concern.

The next day on her way back from school, she looked everywhere for Mammali to see whether he had more news, but he was nowhere to be seen.

Achan had left early in the morning. There was nothing to fear that day.

She went straight toward the paddy field. She did not even bother to leave her books at home. If she were to go in, Cheriyamma would not let her leave.

There was not even a drop of water in the stream. The paddy field was dry and cracked. She walked quickly up to the front yard. There was no one outside. She heard someone talking inside.

Ammu Cheriyamma came out of a room with a glass in her hand. Her face looked drawn.

She went near.

'How's Kochachan doing?'

'His condition remains the same. There's no let up, Ammu.'

'Did you take him to a doctor?'

'I sent a car to bring him over. He prescribed some medicines. Mammali has gone to get them. There's only Mammali for everything. Who else is here?'

'Ammukkutti, who are you talking to? Who's there? Is that Mani?' Kochachan called out on hearing their voices.

She accompanied Cheriyamma into the room. Kochachan lay on the bed with a blanket drawn up to his chin. There was no sign of tiredness on his face. It was flushed.

'Mani, haven't you come straight from school?'

She made no reply. She should have left her books on the front porch of her house and come. It had not occurred to her.

'Give her something to eat, she must be hungry,' he said, turning towards Ammu Cheriyamma.

She went to the kitchen.

'When do the examinations start?'

'In a month.'

'I think Appa will also have them around the same time; or a month or two later. At any rate, by the month of *Medam* everything would be over and he'd be here.'

'Appettan must be busy with his studies. Does he write often?'

'There was a letter from him the day before yesterday. It seems he's going on an excursion. An excursion when the examinations are near! Well, it might provide some fun after studying so hard.'

She stood staring at Kochachan's face, because she did not know the meaning of the word 'excursion'.

'It means teachers and students together go to some place, do a bit of sightseeing, have fun and come back. These people are being taken to Madras. Let him go and see. I wrote to him, giving him permission.'

Cheriyamma came into the room.

'Don't talk much. That itself is enough to spike the fever. The doctor told you to be careful, didn't he?'

'Oh, my jailer is here,' Kochachan laughed.

'Mani, come. I have made tea for you. It's growing cold.'

'Go, have your tea, Mani,' Kochachan urged her.

She sat in the kitchen drinking tea. Since she had no snacks to offer her, Cheriyamma had fried rice *kontattam*.

She finished everything in a hurry and went back in.

'Finished so soon? Was there nothing to eat?'

'Of course there was.' By then Cheriyamma also joined them.

'How's the child doing?' Cheriyamma was only warming to her topic.

'Fine.'

'Beginning to walk?'

'A little.'

'What's his name? Did he complete a year? Did you give him the first offering of rice?'

'No.'

'It's almost half past five,' Kochachan said, looking at the timepiece on the table. 'Don't be too late, Mani. You have to be home before dark. It won't be safe walking through the paddy field alone after dark.'

Was Kochachan rescuing her from the barrage of questions? Even when he was so unwell ...

'Of course, Ammu, don't be late,' Cheriyamma also chimed in.

She bid them both goodbye.

It was almost time to light the evening lamp when she got home. Cheriyamma did not ask her where she had been.

Chapter 12

By the time she got home from school the next day, Achan was home. So she could not make enquiries about Kochachan's health that day. She was not able to meet anyone from whom she could elicit information either. The next day was a Saturday. There was no school. How to manage a visit: that was what she was worrying over as she went to bed that day.

She got up early in the morning. She carried the pots and pans outside and swept the kitchen. Chettichiyar had not come yet. The woman must come and wash the dishes before she can start making coffee. She thought she would finish her bath in the meanwhile. She went into the bathroom and closed the door. After washing her clothes, she had poured water over head when she heard the sound of pots and pans outside.

'Chettichiyare, how can you be so late? Don't you know we have an invalid in the house? Wash the coffee pot quickly.'

Cheriyamma.

'Lakshmikuttiamme, have you heard?'

'What?'

'Kuttisankaran Nair.'

'Which Kuttisankaran Nair?'

'The postmaster. Your Ammukkutti Amma's ...'

'What happened to him?'

'He's no more.'

'Oh, I saw him passing this way only the other day.'

'Isn't today Saturday? He had gone with his wife to the kaavu on Tuesday. There was nothing much wrong with him. He had a mild temperature. They thought it was a cold, didn't pay much attention.'

'How healthy he used to look! When did he pass away, Chettichiyare?'

'Oh, early this morning. There's no one there. The lady's fate! Their only son is away somewhere. She only has Mammali and Cheruman Sankaran to do her bidding. When I was on my way here, the neighbours were beginning to arrive.'

'Oh God, who does she have now? Did they not inform the boy, Chettichiyare?'

'They thought it wasn't serious. When she asked him permission to write to him about his illness, he himself stopped her. He didn't want to upset his son. Now that everything is over, they say a telegram has been sent to the boy.'

The conversation outside came to a halt.

This cannot be true. They must be wrong. They must have heard something and misunderstood.

Tying her half-dry hair into a knot, she climbed on the washing stone and sat on her haunches.

It cannot be true. There was no way it could be true.

Kochachan to die?

She would believe it if it were someone else.

Kochachan—

That strong body and the strong mind within: she felt he was more full of life than anyone she had ever met.

Has the radiance gone completely? And so soon?

No, that is not possible.

She sat on the stone for a long time, her hair dripping water and body wet.

Somebody knocked on the door.

'Mani, aren't you finished yet? Achan is about to go to the thodi. Don't you know that you have to leave the bathroom by the time he comes back?'

She rose.

Achan takes a bath every morning.

She washed her towel in a hurry.

She had not taken a change of dress to the bathroom. She got into the skirt and blouse and under garments she had been wearing, still wet from being washed, and got out in a hurry.

'Who takes so long over a bath?' Cheriyamma was waiting on the verandah.

'Now there won't be any water left.'

Cheriyamma went in to draw water from the well.

Without waiting to answer her, she took her skirt and other clothes from the clothesline in the hall and went in. She hurriedly changed out of the wet clothes and then parting her hair in the middle and throwing it back, made a small knot at the end.

When she was hanging the washing-out to dry in the clothesline in the front yard, Achan walked past, to the northern side of the house. Was he going to take his bath? If so, there was hope.

She went to the spot on the verandah where burnt rice husk and water for brushing his teeth would be kept. The *kindi* was empty and there was water in the yard. So, he has brushed his teeth. So, it was to his bath that he was going.

That would take some time.

By which time she would make it there.

She looked around.

Slowly, she went down the steps. She walked soundlessly. There were a few stragglers in the paddy field. She felt it was taking longer than usual, that she would never cover the distance.

A woman, fresh from her bath and dressed in wet clothes, came up against her. She had to stop and make way for her on the narrow ledge.

Couldn't the woman find some other time for this?

Somehow, she managed to cross the paddy. She climbed over the stile into the yard. It was full of people.

So what they said was true?

People were talking softly, without raising their voices.

She went in. It was quiet inside. No sound at all.

Devaki Mistress of Palekkalam house came out from the eastern room. Seeing her, she stared at her for a moment and passed her.

She moved to the door and stood there. About five to eight people were in the room. Cheriyamma was standing in a corner, leaning on the wall for support.

Why couldn't somebody make her sit down?

Her cheeks were still wet with tears but she was not crying.

She looked like helplessness incarnate.

She was standing still in a corner of the room, neither moving nor speaking. Oh, why did this have to happen to her? Would the poor woman be able to deal with this?

Does she even fully comprehend the turn of events?

That the hands that supported her through life ...

Somebody came up from behind. It was Devaki Mistress.

She went into the room with her.

Ammu Cheriyamma saw her only when she drew near.

She held her close to her. She stood resting her face on her emaciated body.

She felt warm drops of tears on her body.

'My son did not come, Ammu, my son did not come.'

She felt she could not bear to listen to her sobs.

'Ammu, Mani, my son ...'

Her son – that was the only word intelligible through her sobs.

She supported her till she was exhausted from crying.

Somehow, finally, she managed to make Cheriyamma sit on the floor. She slid to the floor and lay curled up there. Placing Cheriyamma's head on her lap, Mani sat next to her.

She would lie quiet for while, then as if reminded of something suddenly, jerk up and start to sob. This happened every now and then.

Someone came and stood at the door. The women made way for the person.

Appettan's Krishnankutty Ettan, Kochachan's nephew.

He came near and spoke.

'Ammayi.'

Cheriyamma lifted her head and sat up.

'A telegram has been sent to Appa. Is that enough or should we send someone?'

'Someone should be sent.'

'I will send someone immediately.'

He went back.

Cheriyamma lay down again.

Time passed. It was noon.

Some of the women in the room left. Some others took their place.

The silence in a place where so many had gathered seemed unbearable.

Kochachan's younger sister came in. She must have reached only then.

She came and sat at Cheriyamma's head. They hugged each other and started to cry.

She slowly got up and went out.

She walked along the deserted corridor to the room where Kochachan had lain ill with fever. The door was closed.

Could she open it?

She hesitated.

She wanted to see him once. She had to.

She opened the door quietly.

His body was laid out on the floor, covered in a white mundu. Small cloth bundles of rice were kept within coconut shells filled with oil, and lit and placed at the head and the foot of the body.

He had spoken to her the day before yesterday, lying on his bed.

Slowly, she moved closer.

There was no disfigurement in death. The face looked tranquil.

'Kochacha,' she called softly, 'Kochacha.' He did not open his eye. Nor did the smile that lighted up his whole face appear.

She stood there, looking at him, never taking her eyes off his face.

She turned her head only when she heard voices at the door.

She must have been standing there for some time. A couple of people came in.

'Oh, what's this girl doing here?'

They were surprised at seeing her alone in the room.

She went out silently.

People were milling about on the porch. They were hurrying here and there with something or the other in their hands. No one spoke.

Four men carried Kochachan to the front porch. So they were not waiting for Appettan. Was it time for the person who was sent to fetch him to return?

Some ceremonies were performed. She had watched them all being performed when grandmother had passed away.

She could not bear to watch him being stitched up in the winding sheet.

They carried him aloft for the last and final time.

Some unrecognisable thing stitched up in a piece of cloth.

Krishnankutty Ettan was at the head: the nephew.

The only son was not home.

When the son arrived ...

The crowd moved to the southern side of the yard with their burden.

She went to the front porch and stood watching.

Slowly, black smoke curled up over the trees. Finished. Everything was over.

She went back in.

After one final heart-wrenching cry, Cheriyamma lay exhausted. Only Kochachan's sister was sitting beside her. The other women hung about the room. Everybody's eyes were fixed on the window opening on to the southern side of the yard.

Time crawled by. One by one, people began to come in from the yard.

Somebody was heard to talk loudly. It was followed by laughter. With that the air seemed to lighten. The journey into the unknown was only this serious. When the body lay inside, it weighed on everybody's minds. Now that it has been burnt to a cinder you can laugh, can't you?

Even on the faces of the people standing within there was the look which said they have done all that possibly could be done.

A look which said we have waited so long, now let's get back to our business.

All of them would leave. The poor woman would be alone.

Look, Devaki Mistress is beginning to stir. Getting ready to leave.

Ammu Cheriyamma lay with her face to the wall. Devaki Mistress was taking leave of Kochachan's sister. 'Meenakshi Amme, let me take leave of you now. You are all here. I have a lot of things to do at home. My elder sister is having her time of the month and can't touch anything. Amma will start coughing if she goes anywhere near the hearth. I have to go.'

She only nodded her head in reply.

Devaki Mistress left.

A couple of people followed her.

She stood near the window looking out.

Time was advancing. The sun had really gone down.

Someone came into the room. She turned at the sound.

Cheriyamma—

From her house.

Has she come to take her home?

Or to pay her condolences?

She came in and sat down on the floor. Ammu Cheriyamma did not see her. She did not lift her head.

Cheriyamma and Kochachan's sister sat, silently facing each other.

Slowly, one by one, the women took their leave. Only the four of them were left in the room.

Finally Cheriyamma also stood up to leave.

'Mani, let's go.'

She nodded her assent.

Going to the door, Cheriyamma said, 'Meenakshi, I would like to ask you something. Would you please come here?'

Meenakshi Amma rose and went into the corridor.

'Why didn't the boy come, Meenakshi? Was he not told?'

'Yes, apart from a telegram, someone was sent in person by car to fetch him. He's not there it seems. He's been taken somewhere from the college. He'd be back either tomorrow or the day after tomorrow. No one knows where they are staying. This is what's written in his fate. The only son wasn't able to take his position at the head of his father's body. Oh Devi, what will it be like when he gets here? How will he deal with this pain?'

When she had called the other day, Kochachan had mentioned Appettan going somewhere.

He went on a fun trip.

Just at this time of all others.

Cheriyamma was talking. The usual platitudes.

'It's fate. Whoever would have thought something like this would happen? You have to bear it, there's no other go.'

The others made no reply.

'Make her drink some milk or something, Meenakshi. If she doesn't take anything ... If only the boy came, that would be a relief to her.'

'We have to make a move, Meenakshi,' Cheriyamma continued after a short silence, 'I saw your son when I came in. He's grown. Bye.'

Chapter 13

It was Sunday. Achan was home. He had been sitting on the porch right from the morning. There was no way she could go out.

What was Ammu Cheriyamma doing? Was Appettan home?

She could not go – in fact, yesterday Cheriyamma had delivered herself of a speech while crossing the paddy field: mainly about leaving without asking first. Had she asked would she have allowed her to go? She must have turned up as part of a ruse to take her home without letting Achan know. Would such a person let her go if she asked nicely?

Achan did not go anywhere till dusk. He went out for a walk only after the lamp was lit and it was dark. Then it was impossible to go there.

She simply could not keep still inside the house.

If she looked down, it was the palliyal that she saw. It was around this time that Kochachan used to come there. She opened the makeshift gate at the back and walked up to the top of the hill.

The last ray of the sun had disappeared. She stood still, looking at the dim outline of the mountains in the darkness.

On her way back from school on Monday, she learnt that Appettan was home. It was Mammali who told her. She had run into him on the way.

That day, instead of going straight home, she went there.

Appettan's room was the one next to the front porch. He was lying face down on the cot. He did not become aware of her presence even after she drew near. She cleared her throat softly. Even then, he did not raise his head. She moved to the cot and called,

'Appetta.'

'Mani,' the cry seemed to be torn from his heart. Sobs racked his chest.

She knelt on the floor next to the cot.

Still lying in the same position, he felt for her hand and held it.

Dry sobs untouched by the dampness of tears emerged, seemingly crushing his heart.

'Appetta ... Appetta,' she called, softly.

'Now I have only you. I have no one but you,' his voice emerged, faltering over sobs.

'I will be there for you, Appetta. You have me, Etta.'

Only the grip on her hand tightened.

Ammu Cheriyamma came and stood near the door.

When she made to rise, Cheriyamma stopped her with a gesture. She stood there, tears streaming down from her eyes.

Her son went on sobbing.

Voices were heard inside. Cheriyamma left. Someone must have turned up to pay their condolences.

She felt she could not bear to listen to his dry grating sobs.

She had never seen men cry.

What was she to say?

She felt it would be a sin even to try to console him.

She went on kneeling beside him on the floor.

She did know how much time had passed. The room had grown dark. At last those disturbing sobs died out.

'Appetta,' she called once again.

'Mani, don't leave me. Don't go. I can't bear that.'

'No, I won't go, Appetta.'

Cheriyamma came in with a glass.

'He has not had even a drink of water. Ask him to drink this, Ammu.'

She rose to her feet. Her legs had gone to sleep with kneeling in the same position for long.

'Please drink this before you lie down again. You didn't even drink water the whole day.'

She sat on the cot with the glass.

'Amma, your son isn't going to die because he didn't drink water. That's for the dutiful. When my father lay dying ...' he got only thus far, the rest was lost in sobs.

The mother sat at her son's feet and wept silently.

She took the glass from Cheriyamma's hands and placed it on the table. A young girl, the maid – sent specially by Meenakshi Amma to help out for a few days – came and asked whether anybody wanted to eat.

'You go and have something,' Cheriyamma said turning toward Mani. She did not have the courage to ask her son to eat.

She gestured no to the girl. Stepping out, she told the girl to go to sleep after closing the door and returned to the room.

'Are you also going without food, Ammu?' Cheriyamma asked her, weeping.

Have not her tears run dry yet?

Appettan drifted off to sleep, exhausted. She, along with Cheriyamma, lay down on the floor. Holding her close, Cheriyamma closed her eyes.

Appettan kept groaning in his sleep. He also kept saying something indistinctly. Every now and then, he would jerk up out of sleep, and call out 'Mani.'

When she answered him, he would not say anything.

Turning and tossing till he dozed off: this went on till dawn.

Every time the son woke, the mother would also wake up. Even though she never spoke, she knew that Cheriyamma had woken up.

When it began to grow light, Mani got up. The other two were still asleep.

Last day's glass of milk was still on the table, with a dead insect floating on the top.

A kerosene lamp was still burning in the corner. She lowered the wick and snuffed it out.

Morning light streamed in through the window, laughing.

She went out, walking softly. She wanted to go and see the funeral pyre on the southern side of the compound. She stepped out into the yard.

Gopu was coming in, climbing over the stile.

Trouble must be brewing at home.

'You are to go home at once.'

'Is Achan there, Gopu?'

'Yes, he came last night.'

'I am coming. Let me take leave of Ammu Cheriyamma.'

'I will also come. Appettan is also inside, isn't he?'

When they went in, Cheriyamma had got up and left.

Appettan was awake and was staring vacantly with eyes wide open.

He looked toward the door. She thought he understood everything as soon as he saw Gopu. His face became even more drawn.

'Appetta, Gopu has come to take me home. Let me go.'

He did not speak. Neither did he turn toward her. After waiting for a while, she went out.

Cheriyamma was in the kitchen.

'The water is almost boiling. Ammu, stay for a cup of coffee at least. You went to bed on an empty stomach, didn't you?' Cheriyamma understood the situation without being told.

'No, Cheriyamme. I haven't brushed my teeth. I have to hurry.'

'Appu, have you come to take your sister home?' She did not press her after that. Gopu did not speak.

'In that case you go. Don't stay. We are giving you children also trouble.'

She started out after Gopu.

Achan was sitting on the front porch. Instead of going that way, she made her way in through the kitchen verandah.

On the kitchen floor, Cheriyamma was scraping coconut.

'Where were you yesterday, Mani?' she started as soon as she saw her.

'With Ammu Cheriyamma.'

'What happened for you to go there now? It's been four days since the death. Now what? A girl goes to school and then does a disappearing act without telling anyone and doesn't even return home! Where ever do we go looking for you? What was it that made you go there yesterday like this?'

'Appettan has come.' She had not meant to answer but it slipped out.

'What's that to you? This is weird. His father died. He came home when he learnt about it. Why should you go there for that? To console him? Would you console every boy in the place?'

Before the harangue could last longer Gopu came in.

Achan wanted to talk to Cheriyamma.

By the time she finished brushing her teeth, Cheriyamma was back and making coffee. She stopped stirring it when she saw her.

'Mani, do you know why Achan called me?'

'No.'

'He called me in to say that from now on, should you go to their house or meet him your schooling will be over. You will not be allowed to step out of the house.'

She said nothing.

'You have not properly understood the seriousness of the matter. It is because he is extremely angry that, instead of telling you himself, he told me to tell you. This time you really did cross the limit. When you went there that day I thought I'd let it pass and I covered it up for you. That was why I came to get you before it was dark.'

'Why did you have to keep it a secret? Could not you have told him everything the same day?'

She had always resented Cheriyamma trying to hold a brief on her behalf.

Cheriyamma kept staring at her face for some time. Then she bent down to get the sugar bowl. She started to walk into the house.

'I will never be able to straighten you out, I know that,' Cheriyamma said, as she reached the door.

She did not turn back.

Straighten me out indeed! Who asked her to?

Chapter 14

There was martial law in force at home. She was not supposed to step out of the house without permission. Gopu had strict instructions to stay by her side on the way to school and back.

She could not run to the hilltop whenever she felt like it. Cheriyamma had warned her that if she were to be found anywhere on the path through the barren ground frequented by people, Achan would immediately be told. Come back from school, go in and remain in: this was to be the routine.

The examination was nearing. She had a lot to study. She had stopped writing poetry and cut down on her reading, and was studying all the time.

She must get through somehow.

Appettan also had examinations.

She wondered what he was doing.

He had not gone back. She learnt that from Mammali whom she had met one day.

How did he manage there, the poor thing?

Mother and son must be spending time staring at each other.

'Mani, I have no one but you. Don't leave me ...'

Pity, she couldn't even go there and see how he was doing.

She could have tried telling Gopu to go. If he happened to be in a good mood he might even go. But should they find out about it at home, he would be in deep trouble.

Thus days passed. Had Appettan gone back? If he had not ...

Fence-building was in full swing at home. Cheruman Sankaran was hard at work. She wanted to ask him, but Achan would not leave the grounds when the fence was being put in. After a prolonged wait, she got an opportunity. Achan was called away by a visitor. She grabbed the moment to go down to the thodi.

'Sankara, do you know whether the son of my Cheriyamma at Puthen Kurishi has gone or not?'

'He's in a very bad shape, *imbidi*. Says he's not going back, ever. The young master has become skin and bones. He never comes out of the house. Spends his time in bed, doesn't eat or drink anything. He'd come and sit before the bowl if the old mistress went and fell at his feet, crying. And he would get up and leave without eating anything. He has no thought of continuing his studies. How well they used to live when the master was alive. One's heart would break if one went and stood in front of the house. Nobody lights an evening lamp there these days. Mother and son shut themselves in at dusk and go to sleep on empty stomachs.'

Achan's voice was heard from the other side.

'I have to go, Sankara. I have a lot of things to do.'

She went back in.

She could talk him out of it, if only she could meet him.

Having no one to speak to and then having to nurse his pain alone in that house ...

If he could share his pain with someone and break down and cry, he would get some relief.

Was his mother capable of sharing the son's burden of sorrow?

Did she possess something that she could actually give to her son?

Had she not given away whatever it was that she possessed?

She had given way everything she had to give years ago when she took hold of a strong hand outside the temple wall and stood on the other side, having crossed the river and kicked away the bridge. After that, she had only taken and never given anything. The hand that she had been fortunate enough to hold on to had been so rich that it could give and give yet never grow poorer. That hand had been lost. Everything lay shattered. She is lost and bewildered.

What is the son going to get from her?

'Mani, I have no one but you ...'

When you see someone drowning – see him go down gasping for life, his hand reaching out to you – should you stand watching on the shore without even lifting a finger?

'Don't go, Mani, don't go leaving me alone ...'

She had to do something.

That night she composed a letter to Appettan while pretending to pour over her textbooks. To begin with, she didn't know what to say. But once she started, words came on their own.

Appetta, I heard people say that you are not planning to go back. Don't ever do that. Life is not to be wasted harping on whatever is past and what we cannot change.

Kochachan's only ambition in life had been to see you educated and in a good position. He must be watching from above to see whether his son is taking the path that he himself had intended him to take.

His eyes would surely be watching you with the same love. Don't ever cause that soul any pain.

Don't forget that Cheriyamma has no one left in the world but you. You are her only support.

Believing that you will go back soon,
Mani

She was able to meet Sankaran only in the evening the next day. He agreed to take her letter to Appettan without her father coming to know about it.

The fence building was almost over. Only half-a-day's labour was left. Sankaran had left, saying that he would come only in the afternoon to do it.

She had school the next day. It was the last day of school. She returned home after the photo session and the tea. By the time she got home, Sankaran had finished his work.

Achan and he were standing in the yard settling his wages.

By the time she came out after leaving her books in her room and having coffee, Sankaran was preparing to leave. Achan was not in the yard. She approached him.

Seeing her, he took out a letter from inside a packet of pan and held it out to her. She took it.

At that very moment, Achan came along the southern verandah.

Had she not panicked, he would have suspected nothing.

He stood looking at her for a moment.

She and Sankaran grew pale.

'Mani, what's that? Let me see.'

She only stood still.

She wondered what Appettan had filled the letter with.

'I am asking you to bring it over ...'

She climbed on to the verandah and gave him the letter. What was the point in refusing? Achan would know how to get it out of her, wouldn't he?

He did not read it through; just glanced through it.

Then he turned toward Sankaran.

'From now on, you don't work here.'

Sankaran made no reply.

'And in future if you try to give something like this to my daughter I will break your bones.'

At this point Sankaran raised his head and looked at Achan.

'What happened when you tried to hold in your sister?'

'What did you say? Get out, you!' Achan jumped down the stone step.

By that time Sankaran had made his exit through the gate.

Without even sparing her a glance, Achan went in. She walked slowly toward the kitchen.

What had he poured out into the letter?

The next Sunday she learnt from Chettichiyar that Appettan had gone back.

She could not meet him before he left.

How could she? She was under house arrest. Don't go out, don't talk to anyone outside the family. The injunctions were delivered not directly by Achan but through Cheriyamma.

Since the study holidays were on, there was no way she could get out on the pretext of going to school. Oh, it did not matter. Appettan did go. That was enough. She immersed herself in studies.

She had to pass with good marks. If not – that did not bear thinking about.

If the only way to get out of this cage were to be blocked—

Chapter 15

Somehow she got through the examinations. She managed to put in an average performance and when the last examination was over, it was as if a load had been lifted off her mind. She slept like a log. In fact, she felt relieved when she had dumped all her books in a corner.

The curfew was enforced during the vacations too.

Even a visit to the kaavu entailed Cheriyamma's chaperonage. She spent her days in the kitchen and the open hall attached to the kitchen.

She was forever busy. Achan was almost always home. Breakfast and lunch and everything had to be prepared with special care.

Cheriyamma had time for nothing but the care of the child. He developed a rash all over his body. His chest had become hollow. He'd crawl all over the place. Cheriyamma was forever brewing ayurvedic potions for him and scrubbing oils all over his body and bathing him. She kept saying that he had to be fed ceremonially in front of a lighted lamp with four types of curry and rice. That had not happened. There had to be a day when he was well enough for all that. But he would crawl into the kitchen and stuff his mouth with whatever happened to catch his eye.

She learnt that Appettan's examinations were over. It was Chettichiyar who brought news once in a while. She had not yet been expelled from the house.

She wondered how he had fared in the examinations. He was never seen to take an evening walk. What was he doing shut up in his house?

Days passed. Once in a while, when there was time, she would sit with a pen and paper. Sometimes the words would come. If she managed to write something, she felt a kind of relief that day.

Then the results were published. She was placed in the first class.

Now ...

She did not have the guts to tell her father she wanted to go to college. No one asked her what she wanted to do.

There was no sign of any move. A couple of days passed. She began to panic. If she were not to be sent anywhere to study ...

On Monday, her father called her and giving her a piece of paper, asked her to sign and return it.

An application form for admission to a college.

Everything had been filled in. Only the signature had to be put in.

She read through the form once.

It was not to Appettan's college but to another college about twice the distance away. She had heard of it.

You had to catch a bus first; then board a train for a two- or three-hour journey.

Had Achan deliberately chosen the place? Ignoring a place that could be reached in a one-and-a-half-hour journey – maybe he was hell-bent on not sending her to a place which also contained Appettan.

It did not matter. She really did not mind the distance. She only wanted to study somewhere.

She returned the paper after signing it.

In two weeks' time, she received a card informing her that she had been selected for the course. If she met the Principal the next Monday and paid the fees, she would be admitted. Oh, she was going to finally breathe the air of freedom! She wanted to jump up and down with joy.

But as the day on which she was to leave neared, very slowly her joy at leaving began to ebb.

How intensely she had wished she could get out of this cage.

Now that that wish was about to be granted, she felt a great sadness. Does the attainable lose its charm? Do you feel resentment only when the chains bind you hard? When you are unchained, do you feel only pain?

When she had wished intensely to get away from the suffocating atmosphere, had she not remembered that the sense of duty that she felt toward the lives enclosed within it was something that ran in her blood?

Amma—

She might not be aware that her only daughter was going far away. Still, would she not miss her daughter when she did not turn up with her breakfast and gruel at the appointed hour? If she told her mother to sit up, she would sit up. If she placed food in front of her mother and told her to eat it, she would eat. Things had come to such a pass now.

Her little brother had arrived in the world unwanted. She had never even held him with affection. He was growing up, like the personification of mistakes committed by others, without ever receiving much love.

This is my world, she told herself.

She had to go, leaving this, leaving every loved one behind. Leap into the unknown. No ... No ... Even if it were to choke her, she would rather live here like this ...

Preparations for the journey were going on while misgivings and doubts were fomenting inside her mind.

Nobody asked her whether she wanted to go. One by one, items necessary for her travel were getting ready. A small box was bought. A small bedding was ready. Five or six sarees were bought.

A plank of wood floating on water. It had no will. Her fate was being determined at the hands of others. She had no business with it.

Finally, the day on which she had to leave arrived.

She could not meet Appettan. She was leaving her home. Even then, she could not meet him in person and take leave of him. Were his results out yet? How had he fared? What a long time since she had last seen him! He never went out. Was he still shut up in his house, grieving?

Chettichiyar had stopped coming. Her relative, a naïve girl, had been coming to work in the house for the past few days. Had she been in a position to meet Chettichiyar, she could at least have sent word to him about leaving. If she tried to reach him a message through this girl and if the girl gets caught by Achan—

It was time to leave. Every piece of luggage, securely tied up, had been taken out. Mammali had come to carry them.

For the first time in her life, she wore a sari. She did not feel like calling Cheriyamma for help. And Cheriyamma did not volunteer either. When she had somehow got into it, she felt she would choke.

Achan had had his lunch and was standing, ready to leave.

She walked to the northern room. Amma was lying on her cot, murmuring something to herself. She was counting on her fingers too.

'Amme,' she said, approaching the cot. Amma stopped murmuring to herself. She turned and looked at her face, holding the hand on which she had been counting in the same position.

'I am going away, Amme.'

'Hm' was the only response. And with a look that said, is that all, so that's over, she turned her head and went back to counting and murmuring.

There was no point in waiting. Amma had even forgotten that she was there.

She walked slowly to the door.

Gopu was standing in the hall leaning on the door.

When she saw him standing there looking sad, she felt everything she was holding in check would burst forth. She clasped him close, silently.

He stood close to her, like a child.

'What's holding her up? Isn't she ready to start?' Achan called out. She wiped her face with the end of her sari and started to move.

For a moment, Gopu held tightly to her hand. With that gesture, was the younger sibling imparting strength to the older?

She looked into his red-rimmed eyes once again and turned to go.

Achan called again.

She went out.

Carrying the child, Cheriyamma accompanied them to the gate.

Her tongue refused to form the words of farewell.

She moved behind her father, like his shadow. It was drizzling.

They reached the hilltop. She turned to look westward.

The blue line had vanished and everything was black.

Was the sky showing its dark face on the very day that I am leaving, she wondered.

They waited at the bus stop in front of the kaavu.

When the bus came, Achan waved it to a stop. She got in. Inside the bus, everything was dirty and muddy. There were seats reserved for women. You had to climb over another seat to reach them. The rain had leaked in, soaking everything within.

The bus revved up to go. Had she got a window seat, she could at least have looked out. But she was in the middle.

When the Muslim woman sitting next to her asked her where she was going, she pretended not to hear. Rain water was leaking, drop by drop on her right shoulder. There was no place to move away.

They finally reached the place. Toward the end of the journey, the rain had let up a bit. They hired a coolie to carry the luggage and moved into the railway station. They had to wait another half-an-hour for the train. At last the train came, coughing up smoke. It was her first train ride. But she did not thrill to it.

The compartment was full of people. Achan managed to find room for her in a corner. She sat looking out. Paddy fields, groves, barren hills appeared as if by turn. The train was chugging forth as if it had no time to stand and stare. Coal dust came flying in and got into her eyes. But she did not pull her head in.

By the time they reached their destination, lights had come on in the compartment.

A porter came to carry the luggage. They went out, her father in front and she following him.

The porter placed the bedding covered in a blanket with red and blue stripes and the blue box in a rickshaw. Achan told her to get into the rickshaw and go. A man lifted the handle of the rickshaw. He started to run, pulling the rickshaw through the crowded streets. The road looked like a black ribbon stretching endlessly on. She craned her neck to see. Was Achan following her? Yes, he was right behind her in another rickshaw.

A policeman was gesturing furiously from inside a round cage right in the middle of the junction. The road was flooded by a kind of faded blue light with something artificial about it. When she passed under the blue light, even her sari seemed to change colour.

On the right side of the road, the name of a hotel was written in letters of flame on a board in front of a two-storeyed building.

The emaciated man pulled her along the road, dodging large cars that sped to and fro.

She had only heard of carts that were drawn by human beings instead of animals.

The rickshaw stopped before a gate.

The compound wall was taller than usual by two feet. Something was sticking out along the top edge of the wall.

She moved forward a little and peered closely.

Broken pieces of glass! Broken pieces of glass with their sharp edges sticking up covered the top edge of the wall on all four sides.

Achan also arrived.

It was on to a spacious porch that they entered.

The rickshaw driver brought in the box and the bedding to the porch, took the fare and left.

In a short while, a manservant arrived. Achan sent word through him.

The yard was lined with plants. From somewhere the scent of jasmine floated in. She peered into the darkness. Nothing could be seen in the darkness. In which corner had jasmine flowered in the darkness?

A youngish woman in a white sari came out from inside and spoke to Achan.

'Opting for first group, aren't you? The interview is tomorrow,' she said, finally turning toward her. She answered her only with a yes.

'Raman Nair!' She hailed the man servant who was standing a little away.

'Carry this box to the room at the end. The one on this side of the stairs.'

'Let me take leave of you now. It's very late,' Achan said, and added, 'Mani, I will come tomorrow. I am going now. I will leave only after meeting you again.'

She stood there, gazing at the way her father had left.

'Don't stand here like this. Come, I myself will take you to your room.'

She followed her along the inner verandah. They knocked at the closed door of the room at the end. No one answered from inside. After waiting for a short while, they pushed the door open.

There was no one in the room. The light was on.

'This, Remani, is your room. Another girl is already here. She must have gone somewhere. She will be here soon. Raman Nair has brought your box and all. Just check whether everything is there. You came by train, didn't you? You must be tired. Ah, Lakshmi Amme—' she called, seeing a woman passing along the verandah.

Lakshmi Amma came in. She was very old.

'This is a new girl, Lakshmi Amme. Take her in and give her dinner.'

She left with the air of someone who had done whatever had to be done.

'What's your name, *kutti*?' Lakshmi Amma moved a little closer to her.

'Remani. Is the lady who just left the warden here?'

'Yes, she teaches mathematics or something in the college.'

'What's her name?'

'Saradamma.'

She did not ask her anything after that.

Lakshmi Amma moved closer and inspected her bedding and other things.

'So come now and have some rice first. By now everything would be cold.'

'I don't want rice.'

'Not having dinner? Aren't you hungry? When did you start from home? Where is your home?'

A hundred questions.

She had not meant to go without dinner. It sort of slipped out suddenly. She did not want to listen to the woman's conversation for long. It was better to go without dinner.

'I am not hungry at all. We had snacks on the way.' A white lie was the only way out.

'Okay, don't eat then. You are away from home for the first time, aren't you? It would be difficult for you. Do you have a father and mother at home?'

She had no intention of stopping.

'Yes.'

'Siblings?'

'Yes.'

'Have you stayed anywhere without your parents?'

'No.'

'Poor thing. It's okay. In a couple of days you will make friends here. Then you will feel sad when you have to leave.'

She said nothing.

The woman stood there for some more time.

Is she going to start again?

'The light will be on in the verandah all night. There's nothing to fear.'

She left at last.

She moved to the cot to unpack her bedding.

There were three cots on three sides of the room. Also three tables, three chairs and three shelves.

A bedding had already been spread on a cot. And it had been covered with a blue bed spread. A blue tablecloth covered the table nearest that cot.

She untied the string used to tie up the bedding and rolled it up and threw it into her box. Then she opened the bedding and shook it. Before she spread Cheriyamma's 'Jaganathan' *onnara* on it, she glanced once again at the blue spread on the other cot.

Why did the other girl not put in an appearance?

Somewhere nearby she heard a clock strike nine.

Then there were two bolts of thunder.

Suddenly, it started to rain.

Every drop big enough to fill a pot.

She opened both the windows.

She wanted to sleep before the rain stopped. It was nice to lie down listening to the sound.

Should she close the door? But if she were to latch the door, what will the other person do when she turns up?

She lay down on the bed and pulled the sheet up to her neck. The room was full of light almost as bright as daylight. Had she ever been used to anything other than a kerosene lamp?

Even when she closed them tightly, her eyes were full of a kind of flushed light.

She had never allowed a lamp to be lit in the room, not even when told that little Gopu would be scared of the dark.

Oh, what would everyone be doing?

Gopu must be awake. He would be reading.

Cheriyamma must have put the child to bed.

Amma—

She turned toward the wall and pulled up the sheet a little.

The cold wind was creeping in.

She curled up a little more inside the sheet.

What rain ...

What beautiful rain ...

Over the tired body another sheet was spread.

Chapter 16

She woke up to the sound of bells ringing at some distance.

There was only faint light in the room.

The darkness had not disappeared completely. It took her a couple of minutes to get her bearings.

She got up, moved to the window and stood there, looking out.

Her gaze had to take in the high wall studded with shards of glass and return.

There was only a narrow strip of ground between the wall and the room.

She thought she had seen garden plants on the porch last night. There was nothing on this side. Only a pile of broken pieces of lime plaster, stones and soil.

She turned back to the room.

There was somebody in the other cot.

Someone with a slim body. She was sleeping on her side with a palm pressed to her cheek. The long hair dangled down the side of the cot in a plait.

The blue bed sheet which covered her bed yesterday was folded neatly and kept at the head of the cot. So it was not meant to sleep on but to be spread on the bed once you got up.

She folded her bedding. Then opening her box and taking out her comb, she started to comb her hair.

She heard the sound of water falling into a vessel from somewhere near.

She opened the door. Just as Lakshmi Amma had told her, the lights were on in the verandah.

There was movement near the bathrooms.

Taking burnt rice husk and a coconut spine, she went out.

All the bathrooms were occupied. There were about five to eight girls round the two water taps near the verandah. There was heated conversation. As soon as they saw her, they stopped talking. There was silence for some time.

She had the feeling that they were all looking at her.

She moved to the water tap without raising her head.

The conversation started again. It did not make sense to her at all. It was all about this master or that. She somehow managed to brush her teeth and get back to her room.

Two girls were standing at the door of her room looking in and laughing. The sound of laughter could be heard from inside the room too. Another girl came out dragging the long-haired girl.

'Oh, please let me go. I have to straighten my sari,' the long-haired one was saying. The others must have arrived to drag her out of bed.

'There's no sign of my roommate. When I went to bed last night, she was here. I will close the room but not lock it.' The long-haired one left with the other three.

She went in and sat down on a chair. There was nothing to see outside.

There was a window opening on to the veranda. It might offer a better view if she opened it.

The building surrounded a central courtyard on all four sides. There was a small garden in the middle. She had seen sunflowers in full bloom. She had found other flowers too when she had stepped out.

But she had the feeling that she simply could not open the window and brave the strange faces that passed through the veranda.

She heard the bell one more time.

Why did it ring?

She did not stir. She was not in the mood to go out, find someone and ask for information.

She sat there for some time.

It was not the high wall before her now.

The barren hill dotted with dry gingelly stalks. The road that wound below like a narrow ribbon. The cashew grove on one side. The blue mountains rearing up against the sky in the distance ...

She turned her head at the sound of a cough from behind.

The long-haired girl was standing there, grinning from ear to ear.

A big-toothed smile.

She liked that smile.

'You came last night, didn't you?'

'Yes.'

'You're Remani, aren't you? I learnt that yesterday itself. I am Ammu. Bad name, don't you think? Nobody even gave me a nice name.'

'But Ammu is a nice name.'

'Nice name indeed! Is that a name? Nobody ever named me. That's what happened. I was extremely ill on the twenty-eighth day after I was born. Everybody thought I'd never make it. So nobody bothered with giving me a name. When they saw I was not going to die, they started calling me Ammu. So I really don't have a name. I must pay five rupees and get my name changed to something like Mantaralakshmi.'

She laughed.

'Aren't you going to take a bath, Remani?'

'Yes.'

'What's this "Re" for ? Won't Mani be enough? I will call you only that.'

'That's what everybody calls me.'

'That's it, then. Mani. It's better than Remani. Let's go and take our bath. We have to be in college by ten,' Ammu said, undoing her plaits. As they both got ready for their bath and stepped out, Ammu took a big lock lying on the table.

They were both going out; the room had to be locked.

'The key has to be kept somewhere here. What if you were finished before me, Mani? Do you take long over your bath? I take only five minutes.'

Before she could make a reply, Ammu pushed the window open and kept the key on the sill. She seemed to be the type who did not expect all her questions to be answered.

She started again during their trip to the bathroom. 'I have been here for a week. I have learnt the routine. My elder brother is here. He's doing Economics Honours. Their classes started early. When my brother came over I had to come along so as to save them an extra trip.'

They locked themselves in two bathrooms.

She opened the shower. It was nice standing under running water. The water was not as cold as the water from a well. Even so, it was nice to have water falling in a jet over your body.

When she reached her room after her bath, Ammu was applying talcum powder on her face. 'That was some bath. I kept the key here for nothing. I finished my bath at least half-an-hour ago.'

She just smiled.

By the time she had got out the powder and the *chanthu*, and was trying to do her hair, the bell rang again.

'Hurry up. That's the bell for breakfast,' Ammu was in a hurry.

'What was the earlier bell for?'

'Oh God, that was for the morning coffee. There's just coffee at six. Didn't you know that? So you have had nothing since morning. That's too bad. Come.'

She tied the end of her wet hair into a small knot and hurried along.

Circling the courtyard and passing through the corridor on the far side, they entered the dining room.

'The place is always crowded. And everybody talks at the same time.'

'You haven't bought a plate, have you?'

Even before she could answer no, Ammu continued, 'Doesn't matter, we'll get Raman Nair to buy you one. For now I'll manage. You take mine. I'll get another one.'

Ammu turned toward a group standing near.

'I need a plate.'

'Take the blue one. It belongs to Rajamma. She went to her local guardian's house last evening. She will be back only this evening,' said a short plump girl in a green sari.

'Hey, did you manage to break the one you bought the other day?' a girl with glasses standing at some distance from them called out.

'No, this is for my roommate. She arrived only last night.'

Ammu turned toward her.

'Hey, this is Mani.'

'Mani, these are all your seniors: Indira ... Parvati ... Kamala ...'

Mani stood smiling. She did not feel like noticing their faces. Nor like memorising their names.

They took their places on stools near the dining table.

They were served dosa and chutney. Coffee was poured into glasses.

How did you eat amidst this racket?

She had not eaten last night. She was hungry.

Somehow, she managed to eat a couple of dosas.

Ammu was busy talking to her neighbours on both sides.

Finally, they were finished.

By half past nine, they were both ready.

Mani managed to wear her sari properly. She plaited her hair.

By the time they started, taking the money for the fees and the certificates with them, three or four other girls came to the door. All of them left together.

A central courtyard and buildings surrounding it on all four sides: that was the plan of the college. There was a garden in the college too. It was full of flowers. Right in the middle of the garden was a small pond. Water lilies floated over it.

They went up to the office on the first floor.

A group of students had already taken position there. She moved a little way off. Everyone was talking in hushed voices. And everyone had friends. Those who came from the same school were standing about in groups and talking.

The place seemed to be full of Ammu's acquaintances. Only she, Mani, had no one. No one from her school had come there.

Perhaps no one, hailing as she did from a distant place, was there.

She was tired of waiting. Her feet were beginning to ache. There was no place to sit even if you wanted to.

They were beginning to call the students one by one. A peon would come out and call a name. A student would accompany him in.

Every now and then, boys, in groups of three or four would pass by, turning and looking at them.

Inside the room the clock struck twelve. Finally her name was called.

Ammu had been called in earlier. She went in, hugging the certificate book to herself. She was quaking inside.

It was with a smile that the Principal talked to her.

He read out her address loudly from a piece of paper.

'Are you staying in the hostel?' The question was in English.

'Yes.'

'Do you like the food?'

'I came here only yesterday.' That too she managed to say in English.

He did not ask any more questions.

He took her certificate from her and looked at her marks.

'You have very good marks. You must study well here too. Try to get a first class, okay?'

He smiled and nodded toward the inner door, 'You may go.'

She moved into the next room through the door.

A couple of people sat there with ledgers and receipt books.

Students who had been sent in before her had not left.

She too stood holding out the money.

It took some time to get out of the place with the receipt. Ammu and her friends were still on the verandah. No one had left.

They spent some more time waiting for another girl to turn up. They made their way back only at one o' clock when the bell rang.

Back at the hostel, they went straight to the dining room. It was even more crowded than in the morning. She ate perfunctorily and left.

She spread her bedding on the cot and lay down. She tried to sleep but could not. You could make out the movements of the students on the upper floor. She lay listening to them for some time.

Ammu came with a thin girl of wheatish complexion.

'Haven't you got up yet?' she started immediately, 'This is the third occupant of our room: Nalini. She arrived just now. Miss Sarada entrusted her to me, saying she was to occupy this room.'

The manservant from the day before brought in her box and bedding.

So the third cot had an occupant.

She lay, listening to Ammu and Nalini talking.

The bell for evening tea went. By the time they finished tea, Nalini's elder sister had arrived to take her. She was staying in the same hostel and studying for a BA.

Ammu left with them. She was alone again. She heard the clock on the porch strike five.

Somebody knocked on the door.

'Coming,' she called out.

Raman Nair, the manservant.

'There is a visitor for you.'

She got up. It must be Achan.

Achan stood on the porch talking to Miss Sarada. When she saw her, Miss Sarada smiled and left.

'Didn't you go to college?' Achan asked her when she got near.

'Yes, I did. There are no classes today and tomorrow. They actually begin only the day after tomorrow.'

'Did you pay the fees?'

'Yes.'

'Do you have any money left? I have paid all your dues at the hostel. They said you need to pay only next month now. Do you need money for something else?'

'Not now. I have about twenty rupees with me.'

'Hm. I think that will see you through. Find out how much the textbooks will cost you and write to me. I will send the money. Buy only what's absolutely necessary. You are the eldest. Remember that I have other children to educate.'

She made no reply.

'Okay, I'll leave now. I have not applied for leave for tomorrow. I have to leave by the night train.'

She made no reply to that either.

'If there's anything, write to me. Don't be lazy. Pay attention to your studies.'

Do you need money?

Write to me if there's anything.

Study well.

He was leaving his daughter behind in a distant place for the first time.

Since she had never been in the habit of crying, she didn't cry. But she was smouldering inside.

She wanted to cast away her ego and cry, Acha, I can't do this, take me along with you.

But the words did not come out.

He hesitated for a while.

'Hm. So that's that. Write to me. Bye.'

Chapter 17

The next day had to be spent in utter idleness. There was nothing to do; not even a book to read. There was only the sound of the bell being rung at regular intervals to listen to. She finally learnt what each bell signified: at five in the morning it rang to wake you up, at half past six it meant coffee, at nine breakfast, at one lunch, at four in the evening tea, at seven prayer, at half past seven bed.

You had to eat when the bell rang no matter whether you were hungry or not; you also had to sleep no matter whether you were sleepy or not.

If you were in the habit of eating and sleeping only when you felt like it, would it be possible for you to accustom yourself quickly to this clockwork routine?

That day spent in absolute idleness seemed like an aeon.

Ammu spent very little time in the room. Listening to her endless chatter could sometimes be boring. Nalini spent most of her time with her elder sister. So it was on her own that she spent the day.

It was noon. When the senior students left for college, she went on a tour of the first floor. Just like the rooms on the floor below, the rooms had three cots and three tables each.

She got bored looking at the blue bed spreads through the window. She had also been made to buy one exactly like them yesterday. Every inmate in every room had blue bed spreads. At night, she listened to the clock striking eleven and twelve. She slept fitfully till daybreak. She had classes. She got ready with a couple of notebooks and pens. Ammu had told her that the class was in the large hall near the office. Ammu knew everything.

By the time they reached the class, the boys were already there. One row in the gallery class was kept vacant for the girls. When the bell rang, a completely bald person entered the class. He was a professor of English.

He went up to the platform and sat down. The students also sat down.

'Answer to your numbers please.' His voice was gruff.

606, 607 ... he started to read out the numbers.

Ammu had offered to find out her number.

Each student answered to their number when called: yes sir, present sir, here sir.

649, 650, 651.

She too rose to her feet.

651. I am no longer Mani. I have become 651. Just three digits.

After 650 but before 652.

Once he finished calling out the numbers, he started to say something. She did not feel like listening.

He gave them the names of the books prescribed for study. Everybody noted them down. She did too.

The class was dismissed in half-an-hour.

They walked along the whole length of the verandah before going down. They went to the waiting room, which was a little way off. There were others who had also been let off. How crowded the place was!

At the next bell they started out again. This time the class was in another room.

The roll call and lecture were just as before.

During the third period a notice was read out, informing everyone that there would be no classes in the afternoon. They returned to the hostel to have lunch.

There was nothing to do except shut yourself up in your room.

At dusk, she made another tour of the first floor. Behind the stairs there was a closed window. She wanted to open it. She inched her way along the edge, holding on to the banisters for support, and pushed the window open.

There was hardly space to stand. She stood, holding her breath, her hand gripping the window grill. Standing there, she had a clear view, unobstructed by buildings, of the backwater on the west.

The blue expanse of water lay absolutely still.

A small country boat with a small sail unfurled slowly moved into her line of vision. She followed it with her eyes till it disappeared from her sight with the regal air of a queen.

On the far side there was a small island with leaning coconut palms.

There were huge pillars stretching toward the sky.

She had once seen the picture of cranes in a book.

A bigger country boat loaded with quarry stone sailed up. Two men were rowing it with all their might. Even from this distance she could make out the effort involved in rowing it.

A steam boat sailed by coughing up smoke. Suddenly, lights went on in the island.

Below, the bell rang.

It was time for prayer.

She did not move.

It grew darker as she stood watching.

The coconut palms on the island disappeared. Only the lamps could be seen standing about in a line. The cranes, seemingly holding their heads high, had also disappeared from sight. Only the red lamps at their extremities hung above, as though suspended from air. They reminded you of the blood-shot eyes of a *rakshasa*.

A sliver of light moved slowly into her sight: the kerosene lamp in a small country boat.

There was another right behind. Its white sail could be faintly seen.

For some time, the expanse of water lay empty.

Suddenly, it looked as if someone had poured molten silver over it.

Has the moon risen suddenly? Have the rain clouds drifted away in the twinkling of an eye?

White silk rustled over the slice of water seen through the gap in the window. Small white folds kept forming ... and disappearing ...

'Mani ... Mani ...'

The voice came from the direction of the stairs. Someone turned on the light at the back.

Ammu.

She did not answer.

'Where has she gone? Mani ...'

'Look, she's standing on the window sill.' That sounded like Nalini's voice.

'This is weird. Are you meditating, hanging from the window? After all the shouting we have done – you definitely must have put in some effort to get up there.' Would she ever hear the last of this from Ammu?

Mani slowly moved along the ledge, holding on to the banisters.

'What were you doing up there, not even bothering to answer us?'

She said nothing but stood smiling at them.

Would they understand her if she told them that there was poetry in distant lamps that came suddenly on in the darkness and in moonlight falling over water?

That night she went to bed early. As soon as she lay down, she fell asleep.

Classes began in earnest the next week. She learnt how to get closer to the other residents. They in turn learnt to ignore the peculiarities of her northern slang. And she began to internalise their mannerisms.

Thus she came to terms with the new environs.

College was generally fun. Classes, practicals, everything was interesting. Ammu had the number next to her. They were required to sit next to each other in class. They had to be together for the practicals too. She was drawing closer to the talkative girl.

It was when her mind was slowly healing itself that she received a letter from Appettan.

It ran into six or seven pages. Most of what he had written had no logic and made no sense. He did not pass the examination.

With that blow, he seemed to have completely lost all control over his mind.

'Mani. I can't bear this. I have no one to share my pain with but you.'

The letter was a long cry.

The cry of a fragile heart on the verge of a breakdown.

She lost whatever peace of mind she had achieved by then. She sat down and wrote to him immediately. She posted it without waiting to read it a second time. She wrote him much more than what she would have told him had they met in person.

She waited for a reply to the letter. It did not come. There was no news at all. At the end of a month a letter came.

From Bombay—

He was in Bombay in answer to a call from a friend. He could not think of appearing for the same examination. He could not think of going back and studying again.

He wanted a change from old and familiar things. In the new surroundings he might be able to forget his pain.

His friend had assured him that he was sure to get a job. He had to make some money quickly. He also had to pay off some debts incurred by his father. Reading the letter only made her even more uneasy. She wanted Ettan to study and find a good job. What was he going to gain by loitering in Bombay?

She wondered if he would have really worked hard and sat for the examination this year if she had not sent him to appear for it back then.

He had written that he was planning to write the examination while working somewhere. She wondered how practical that was.

What was the point in harping on all that? He had made it very clear in his letter that he wouldn't go back without getting a job. If Ettan wanted to study, the only way out was a mortgage.

How was poor Cheriyamma fending for herself with her son gone to make money? She replied to him without committing herself on the rightness or otherwise of his actions.

Letters arrived again. Sometimes, she would receive them on a daily basis. Then for a week or two there will be silence. Then they would arrive regularly. He had not found a job yet. The doors on which he knocked never opened.

In some places he would think he was almost in. He would have met the right person and the only thing that remained was to receive the order. It was at this point that they would reject his application, citing some flimsy ground and hire another person.

One letter would say he was about to get a job and that all his troubles were about to be over. The next letter would plumb the depths of despair: there was nothing to hope for, everything was headed toward perdition.

The letters faithfully reflected how his mind swung between light and darkness.

On one side, there was the thought that he was becoming a burden to a good friend, on the other the agony of having to trouble his mother for money. There was also the feeling that nothing would ever be right.

The tone of his letters was getting darker and darker.

Among the shadows that cast a permanent pall over her mind, this also found a place.

But life was on the whole joyful. Her soul, released for the first time from its cage, partook of the free air with zest.

The place was a carnival for those who loved books.

Chapter 18

Just before Onam holidays began, Appettan's letter arrived. He had found a job as a clerk in a company. It involved long hours of hard work. The pay was also not great but at least it was something.

When they returned to the hostel after the vacation, only she and Ammu were left in the room. Nalini was getting married. Everybody was invited. They all pooled in money, bought a wedding present and mailed it to her. Nalini did not return to continue her studies after marriage. Thus, just the two of them were left in the room.

Slowly, they were drawn to each other.

They were poles apart by nature.

One was an extrovert easily moved to laughter and tears. It was difficult for her to hold her tongue. The other was of a serious turn of mind and spent her time poring over books. She never opened up to people.

It was such natures that were drawn together: admiration on one side and affection on the other.

One day, quite by accident, the other girl discovered that Mani wrote poetry. On Appettan's initiative, a poem had been published in a magazine. Ammu happened to see the edition lying in her box. Immediately, she snatched it and ran off with it.

With that everything was complete.

In the beginning, she had been known among the girls as Ammu's Mani. Ammu took to quoting lines written by her. It was always, Mani said this, Mani said that.

To begin with, Mani resented this. She had always been in the habit of hiding her emotions and could not come to terms with someone shouting them to the world at large. It took her some time to realise that all this was actuated by the purest motives and not out of hypocrisy. One day, Ammu returned from her rounds to find her reading something. It was dark. There was no time to study. She was reading something with great enjoyment. As soon as she came in, Ammu started to make a racket, 'Mani, don't read, come out with me, don't you want to see what our friends have brought back after shopping?'

Since she did not feel like putting her book down, she declined. But Ammu would not listen to her. She insisted she went with her. Mani refused to budge. She really was angry when Ammu tried to snatch her book away from her. When she could not get hold of the book, Ammu left the room. She switched off the light on her way out.

Mani got up and locked the door from the inside. Turning on the light, she continued her reading.

After some time, she thought she heard somebody knocking on the door. She ignored it. She did not open the door.

Ammu did not return to the room after that. She looked for her at dinner. She was nowhere. She waited for her till half past ten. She must have slept over in some friend's room. She did not go looking for her.

When she returned from her bath the next day she heard someone moving in the room.

Ammu had come to get her toiletries while she was away.

Her first thought had been to just let her go. But when she saw her leaving the room clutching her things to herself, she felt sorry for her.

She called her softly, 'Ammu.'

Ammu stopped. She did not turn. The tears broke. It took half-an-hour to get her to calm down.

When you inflict pain on somebody, by that very act you bestow on the recipient power over you.

And was it not through pain that the chain of love was forged?

People who were thrown together day and night would naturally come to share personal details. Mani hated sharing them. From whatever she had let slip from time to time, her friend came to grasp the situation to some extent.

Their intimacy was growing stronger.

Ammu introduced Mani to her elder brother, who was studying for an Honours course. He was a well-read young man with a maturity that went beyond his years. Every time her brother, whom she addressed as Chettan, came Ammu would call her. She was reluctant at first. But then she started to like his visits.

It was he who gave direction to her voracious but haphazard reading. He told her about books. She located the books in the library, borrowed and read them. He had laid down the condition that she was to write a couple of pages about every book that she read. She did write two pages each about the first couple of books that she read. Then the practice was dropped. She was in a hurry to read new books. However much she read, she was hungry for more.

She wrote poems. When she read them over, she was dissatisfied with her efforts. She would tear them up and write again: poems that described the blue of the clear sky.

A bird born and bred in bondage was venturing out of its cage for the first time and taking to its wings, drugged with the heady sense of freedom.

Was the sound of its own wings flapping in the air so beautiful?

Listening to the sound of it so much joyful?

It hovered higher and higher in the air so the sound of its wings wouldn't stop.

Higher and higher ...

Still higher ...

There was no destination—

Nowhere to reach—

And no desire to reach anywhere—

How much this moment had been longed for: when a piece of the sky had beckoned through the bars of the cage; when wave after wave of music had floated in from a distance.

If only its seductive beauty lasted forever!

Ammu discovered another one of her poems. She gave it to her brother, who got it published in the college magazine.

Every now and then she would write something. Ammu's Chettan would then arrange for its publication. A couple of her poems appeared in a magazine published from the city. Her fame as a poet spread.

She was beginning to emerge as an individual in her own right among the students. If you are good-looking also into the bargain, would it be really difficult to acquire a fan following?

The teachers and students talked her into taking part in plays. She was scared at first. She started doing them only under compulsion. But very soon she began to enjoy them. There was some joy in living someone else's life. She came on stage as the ascetic's daughter brought up in the company of fawns and as Drupada's daughter complaining to the consort of Goddess Lakshmi. She posed as Mother India with sadness in her eyes and a smile on her lips.

She was part of tableaus and plays. Thus two years of college life was spent joyously. She was part of every activity. She never opted out of anything. She was game for both play and work.

An overriding urge to escape from the shadows that pursued her—

Appettan's letters came for her regularly. Most other were complaints about the humdrum life in the city. Some would contain descriptions of books that he had read or movies that he had seen. She answered most of his letters: letters describing what she had been reading or doing. To the extent possible, she never revealed her troubled side to him. The poor man already had enough troubles of his own.

Among all this, she never forgot to study to score well in the examination. Since the powerful figure of her father always dwelt in a corner of her mind, studies were never neglected.

The final examinations were almost upon them. She turned some nights into day, studying. The hostel rules did not allow anyone to keep the light on after ten. She studied discretely, by the light of a candle, in her room. If she did not score good marks because she was busy with this and that, that would put a period to her education.

She wrote the examinations fairly well. She did not do badly in the practical examinations either.

The last day had come. Gopu was waiting for her. He had joined the same college after high school. Achan must have sent him also there to keep an eye on her. His examinations had been over already. He was waiting to take her home.

It was time to leave. Gopu had started out after the coolie carrying their luggage.

Ammu hugged her and wept.

Chapter 19

The vacation was a particularly difficult one. Her little brother kept falling prey to one illness after another. Cheriyamma also was not keeping well. She suffered from rheumatism. It was she who prepared the ayurvedic potions. She didn't feel like calling Gopu to help her out as she used to do before. He'd grown up. One year of hostel life had changed him completely. His manner had altered. He was hardly ever home during the day.

She waited anxiously for the results. Ammu wrote once in a while. A couple of other friends also wrote to her. That was the only relief. Appettan never sent her letters to her home address.

The results were announced. It was Gopu who brought the newspaper. She had been placed in the first class.

She was on tenterhooks the whole day. Achan was not home. Musn't he come home for the next course of action to be decided?

Achan got home only the next evening.

There was no talk about this that day.

She could barely sleep at night. Would Achan say something? Would he send her again to study?

In the morning, Cheriyamma came to ask her what she wanted to study. For a moment, she stood still in surprise. She was not expecting such a question. Instead of deciding on something himself and asking her to study that, Achan was actually asking her opinion about—

'Now what? Don't you want to study?' Cheriyamma asked seeing her hesitate.

Not study? Oh God! She thought furiously for a moment.

'I would like to do English Honours.'

'Shall I tell him that that's what you want to do?'

'Oh, yes.'

She sent her application in a couple of days.

She received the notification of admission only after Gopu had left. This time Achan saw her off at the railway station. Gopu met her train.

She began her hostel life with mixed feelings.

Ammu would not be joining her. She had ceased studying and her family was busy with proposals of marriage for her.

She would be sharing her room with someone new. The classes were to be conducted in a new mode. No practical classes at all. There would also be fewer students in a class.

It was on the day of the interview that she learnt who her classmates were. There was only one other girl in her class: Vijaya Devi. Though they had been classmates over the past two years, they had never been friends. She never came forward for anything or volunteered to do something. She knew Mani but Mani had to ask her for her name.

Among the boys she was only acquainted with Balachandran. She knew none of the others. A couple of them had studied in the same college but had opted for other groups. The others had come from different colleges. They were seven in all.

She had not expected Balachandran to join this course. When they were intermediate students, they had been assigned practical classes in groups of four. Since there were not enough girls, a boy had been allowed to fill up the numbers in one group: three girls and a boy. Mani, Ammu, a girl called Meenakshi and this Balachandran. Poor boy. They had given him a really tough time. Ammu! Was she the type to spare anyone? Meenakshi was also not bad at all. There were experiments on which the four of them were supposed to collaborate. They would not allow him anywhere near their work. It was often Mani who, taking pity on him, asked him to come and take a peek when they were finished. Otherwise, he would stand somewhere at a distance, quietly. The other boys would look on and laugh.

Ammu always argued that his habit of drawing back was due to a character flaw. Had he been smart, he could have pushed in and done his share of the work.

Only she would take his side and support him. Was it his fault that he landed among girls? How could he butt in among them and do his share? Then he would probably be accused of a more serious character flaw.

Back in the hostel, all of them would sit around abusing him to their heart's content. They had reason. As luck would have it, his seat was next to the row assigned to the girls. He used to sit in class with his head resting on the desk. The girls held that he didn't even have the gumption to hold his head high.

His stiffly-ironed full-sleeved shirt and trousers and his gait, which seemed to hint at some great personal disappointment, always irritated Ammu intensely. Her names for him included 'handsome fool' and 'tepid rice gruel'.

She almost laughed when she met him in front of the Principal's room, thinking that his lot had been thrown once again with hers.

As soon as he saw her, he came up to talk to her. He wanted to know her marks. He then told her his own marks.

That was followed by a long speech: on the reasons which made him miss being placed in the first class – the difficulties involved in doing an Honours course – who all were placed in first class that year and so on. Somehow she managed not to laugh.

After looking at the timetable, she left with Vijaya. Their classes were not regular. Once in a while, they would have a class. The rest they had to read themselves. There was complete freedom.

Vijaya's house was nearby. She did not stay in the hostel. Mani returned to the hostel.

Chettan came to meet her the same evening. Ammu's marriage had been fixed and would probably take place by the end of the month.

During the following days, Chettan came to meet her frequently, mostly to give her the invitation cards to be given to Ammu's friends in the hostel. Their friendship had not been affected by Ammu's departure.

Ammu's wedding took place. The bridegroom was employed in Singapore. He had only a few days of leave left. He took her along almost immediately. Ammu did not have time to visit her friends in the hostel and bid them goodbye.

Ammu's place had been taken by a girl called Indira. Her subject was Chemistry, which involved slogging in the laboratory till five in the evening and after that wrestling with huge tomes on Chemistry. She was a smart girl who found time with all the above to enjoy life with her friends in the hostel.

Classrooms for Honours courses were separate. Mani mostly spent her time in the three or four rooms at the western end of the first floor. And if there happened to be some time left, she'd spend it in the library. She had nothing to do with her classmates. Everybody had been a little in awe of her in the college and the hostel. The alienation was now complete.

There were still some in the hostel who loved her beautiful doe eyes, her long tresses and the poems she wrote: admirers who would place a rose or a packet of sweets on her table and run away. Most of them were young girls who had joined that year. They never dared to approach her.

Actually Indira was the reason why her relationship with the others in the hostel did not fully blossom. It was she who brought the news and the tales circulating there to Mani.

The classes on the whole were interesting. The Professor taught philology, which was the only class she found boring.

Panicker Mash taught Shakespeare. Even during her intermediate days, she had been captivated by his eloquence. If he had to teach an essay, he would talk about the author and his achievements for an hour. He would stop only when he had covered all aspects. She used to note down the names of the books mentioned by him and run straight to the library. He was everybody's idol. He joined the students in all their activities. He was mad about sports. He would be on the grounds when the four o'clock bell sounded. He was also the president of the Arts Club. He was part of everything that happened on campus.

It was he who was teaching them *Macbeth*. When the bard's lines came out in his deep voice, you saw the lady dismayed by the blood stain on her hands that she couldn't wash away and the superhuman Lord unfazed by defeat, who meets his death with his head still held high. Those classes were her ideas of heaven. Forgetting everything, she would sit, lost in that voice.

Chapter 20

Ammu's brother used to come and meet her every Saturday, as he used to do when Ammu had been staying there. He would spend a lot of time talking to her. Gopu never took that long. He would tell her if something happened at home. If he got a letter from home, he would give it to her. Then he had nothing to say.

It was election time in college. It was also the time when boys approached girls en masse on election campaigns. Every evening there would be at least five or six boys hanging about the hostel gate. This had been going on for some time. When she had had enough, Miss Sarada turned away a couple of boys, saying she couldn't give permission to those whose names did not figure in the Visitors' Book. At the time of admission your parent or guardian was supposed to tell the authorities the names of persons who were likely to visit you or who should be allowed to visit you. It was their names that would be found in the Visitors' Book. How would the names of election comrades figure in it? So a group of students was turned away. With that the meetings in the hostel compound came to an end. There was rebellion.

Were only uncles and brothers allowed to visit? How many who do not fit that description come and visit the girls? What is special about some people?

In the melee someone mentioned Mani's name. That was immediately taken up by everyone. What was the justification for Ammu's elder brother being allowed to visit Mani? If Mani could be allowed to meet him, why could the others not meet their friends? What was special about one person? The only person unaware of this hullabaloo was Mani. Most of the hostel inmates were old friends but they had never been in the habit of making small talk with her. It was through Indira that she got to know the gossip. For some reason, Indira chose not to tell her about this.

As she walked along the verandah, she heard certain whispers. She did not know what they signified. Also, she did not give them much thought.

It was a Saturday and she was going in after meeting Chettan. She had just placed her foot on the porch when someone spoke in a loud voice from behind. 'Big people. They write poetry and all. So they can do anything, meet any one. The rules don't apply to them, do they?'

At this, she turned to look. There was a crowd. Nobody she knew well at all. She could not also make out who had spoken. She waited for a short while to see whether something more would be said. There was nothing. She went to her room. Indira was writing her record. It took some time to get the facts out of her. It required a lot of cross-questioning.

The matter involved Chettan's visits. Stories involving her and Chettan had also been concocted.

It was anger that she felt. Should there not be a limit to spreading nonsense? Instead of minding their own business, they ...

But they had a point, didn't they? How could a single person be exempt from the rule?

Actually a fitting answer to their nonsense would be to meet him every day.

Still, Miss Sarada – it might be out of a sense of delicacy that she had not spoken to her about it.

She wished she could let Chettan know about this development. Why make people talk?

The next Saturday her friend came as usual. The small talk was over. She was hardly aware of whatever was said after that. She was wondering how to broach the subject.

After some time, he suddenly asked, 'I heard someone say that somebody came here to meet you people and weren't allowed to do so. Is that true?'

'Yes.' She felt like worshipping him.

'What really happened?'

'Some campaigners came here and Miss Sarada refused them permission saying their names did not figure in the Visitors' Book. Now the students are saying ... I ...'

'Hm. Why don't you say it? What are they doing?'

'They are saying bad things. They are asking whether the rules do not apply to people who come to meet me.'

'They are referring to me, aren't they?'

She nodded. Now what more was there to say?

He was silent for a while. 'I too have heard some of this. Linking our names isn't a recent thing. It has been so for at least a year.'

'I came to know only the other day.'

There was silence for a while.

'Mani,' he spoke at last.

'Hm.'

'Can I ask you something? Can you see me in that light? Is there hope for me?'

She stood staring at him.

He gave her a peculiar smile.

'Are you shocked? Am I not supposed to ask you such a question?'

'No, Chetta, it's not. I – That's – I—'

'Tell me.'

'You should think of me as another Ammu. That's what I'd like.' She paused, 'No, the other thing is impossible.'

He made no reply.

After waiting for a while, she called him.

'Chetta.'

'Hm.'

' Chetta, are you angry with me?'

'No, my little sister. You have done nothing wrong. I am at fault. You have never given me any cause to think of you that way. Still, I kept hoping. That's my fault.'

'I want you, Chetta, to remain my elder brother always. Mine and Gopu's. Don't get me wrong. I want an elder brother's love.'

'I haven't got you wrong, Mani. Please forget what I told you this day. I'll not repeat it. You, my sister, have a big heart. Whoever gets to own it someday will be a very lucky fellow. I won't be envious of him. I will always keep a brother's love toward him.'

He paused for a few minutes. Then he continued speaking.

'North Indian women salute their brothers on Rakhi day by tying a bracelet on their brothers' wrists. We have no such custom. But from this day, I am Mani's brother. Please remember that I am there for you should you need me.'

She stood there mute because she could not speak. A few minutes passed by.

At last he spoke, in his normal voice, 'What they are saying is right, Mani. Why should we break the rules? It isn't right, my coming here to speak to you. If necessary, we can meet in college.'

She did not say anything even then. Just nodded.

'Let me take leave of you now. Don't ever forget one thing: you can tell me anything. I will do whatever it is that you ask me to do.'

'Bye.' Taking leave of her once again, he turned and walked away.

Chapter 21

Vijaya was absent one of those days. When she was going downstairs after classes, Balachandran came calling after her.

'Please read this and tell me what you think,' he said, holding out toward her a little book with a blue cover.

She took it from him and looked at it. It was a collection of short stories.

Since it was inscribed 'With the best compliments of the author' on the title page, she looked at the name.

A. N. Balachandran

Had he written them?

'Balachandran, do you write stories?' she asked, feigning interest.

'This is my first book. I gave a copy each to our teachers. Please read it and tell me what you think, Remani.'

She agreed to do so and came away. The top of the staircase was hardly the place for small talk.

She finished reading it the same day. Seven or eight stories, all equally puerile. Failure in love was the common theme. From start to end, melancholy reigned supreme. But there was nothing that touched one's heart. She put the volume down, thinking: poor man.

Learning that what she had been reading was a collection of stories, Indira too thumbed through it. After scanning through the whole, she said, 'Hasn't he got anything better to do?'

When Mani remained silent, she said, 'If you aren't good at anything else, you should go and dig a pit for plantains, and not write stories that bore people to death. Publish the book himself and go seek the opinion of whoever chances to meet him. He must have a thick skin.'

'That's why he didn't ask for your opinion, Indira. His skin probably hasn't become that thick.'

'So in your view, madam, this is a rare work of art.—'

'Well, he must have taken some pains to write this.'

'You need some guts to publish drivel like this.'

'Will you be able to write a book like this?'

'No, definitely not. My only prayer is that before I feel an urge to commit this dire deed, I may be snatched away to heaven.'

Mani sat quietly with a smile.

'Isn't this fellow Ammu's Ebrasi?'

'Is it his fault that he's very thin?'

'Are all thin people such sissies?'

'All you need is one look at a fellow to decide whether he's smart or not.'

'Why play games? You know very well, Mani, that his book is worthless.'

'Nobody writes *Anna Karenina* the first time.'

'So you at least concede that this is not *Anna Karenina*.'

'When somebody ventures to do something, you don't encourage him, you try to strangle him.'

The discussion stopped there because the bell rang for dinner.

The next day when she arrived he was waiting at the door to the class.

As soon as he set eyes on her, he said, 'Have you read them?'

She realised she should have had learnt some sentences by heart to lie to him.

'Yes.'

'So?'

'They are good.'

'Which one did you like best?'

'All are good.'

'Still ...'

'I think I liked the first one best,' she answered, after thinking for a while.

'Ah, that's the one you liked? Sangbo says that only texts with the warmth of one's experience become good literature.'

Oh, had Sangbo said that? As if that had to be stated by Sangbo. And did he also say that one could write eight different stories from the same experience, only changing the name each time?

The teacher arrived before she could make a reply.

In the evening, Balachandran came with a bundle of books.

He wanted her to sell them for him.

She was astonished.

'If you put your mind to it, Remani, you can. The hostel inmates would surely buy.'

She did not reply.

'Selling this is absolutely necessary to me.'

Even then she said nothing.

'You people have parents. You don't have to worry, do you? You receive regular payments from home. You have all been brought up in the lap of luxury. If you fail to understand this, that's not surprising. I have no one in the world. If I want to study, I have to find the money myself. '

She had heard that he was continuing his studies with great difficulty. But looking at his stiffly-starched shirts and trousers, she had found that difficult to believe.

'Do you know how I managed till last year? A judge wanted a tutor for his son. I managed to get the position. There was an empty room in their padippura. A room full of cobwebs and spiders. I was given that. The judge's wife would give me food twice a day. I taught other children too. That was enough to pay the fees. The next two years, I have to manage with the money from the sale of this book.'

'I will try.'

'I know you are merciful, Remani. To thank you ...'

'You don't have to thank me,' she interrupted him to say.

She took the books from him and left.

When Indira saw her walking in with a bundle of books, she said, 'What now?'

'These are Balachandran's books, Indira. I agreed to sell them for him.'

'This is weird. Are you his sales agent or something, Mani?'

'He needs the money to feed himself.'

'Pity! He is going to starve. With the money he spent on bringing it out, he could have fed himself for two months. He's already thin. Now if he also doesn't get to eat ...'

'For you, Indira, this is fun. For him it's a matter of life. A person's problems ...'

'These are of course not my problems, thank god! The first one: I got only two radicals right when I did the mixture. The second: when I showed the teacher my titre value he said nonsense.'

'Will you please stop? You are acting up. Will you go with me or not, just tell me that.'

'Go where?'

'Do you think I know everyone here? I have to go to their rooms. That's where.'

'Oh, yes, definitely. I have no problem. But to rush to the help of someone who's trying to study by selling stories ...'

'I want none of your talk. Come with me.'

She visited each and every room. She went first to her old friends. They all laughed when told about the author's travails.

She stopped telling his life story after the first couple of attempts. Then she tried a different tack.

'It's only one rupee. Why can't you take one? You spend more on a movie.'

Old acquaintances agreed to buy purely on the strength of their friendship. Among the junior students, her fans bought a couple of books each even before being asked.

About eighty copies were sold in all. She did not get the money in full but some of it she did manage to get.

Eighty rupees for eighty books. Even if she managed to collect the whole, how much would that be?

Indira started again when she was counting the money, 'Mani, don't waste your time selling tickets and collecting money. The kids bought the book because it was the first time. Even then, there's no guessing how many of them would finally pay up.'

'They will all pay. I will make them pay.'

'Thus she saved the great writer from starving to death. Every morsel of bread, nay, every grain of rice that he partook, was soaked in her life blood.'

'Oh, shut up!'

'Let me have my say. After all, I don't get to say it every day. Now Mani, what happened to his milch cow, the judge?'

'He doesn't seem to be staying with them.'

'Why, the milk of human kindness ran dry?'

'I have no idea.'

'The judge might have a couple of nubile young girls. The fellow might have bestowed his love on one. He's the type. He's been bitten badly by the love bug.'

The next day, she gave the money she had collected to him. She felt that he was not paying attention when she explained the details of the sale.

She went to the waiting room during the lunch recess. She persuaded the day scholars also to buy the book. Most of them bought it. Though grumbling under her breath, Indira accompanied her everywhere.

She did not immediately get the money in full. One of her main occupations became collecting the money. Every day, a couple of persons would bring money. Thus, every day there would be some money to be given to Balachandran. He was reluctant to end their meetings quickly. He would never tire of talking to her.

The book sale had become an excuse for talking to her. He would drone on and on and finally end with the story of his life. He would sing a veritable litany of woes for her benefit.

It included the early death of his father and the hardship endured by his mother to bring him up.

When he finally reached the part where his mother died, resting her head in his lap, calling his name, his voice would break and tears would fill his eyes.

He knew that it was through tragedy that he would forge an intimacy with her.

He would never omit to inform her if there happened to be a day's delay in paying his fees. Should she not be made to realise the lack of money?

He was trying to wriggle his way into her life.

He would read all the texts prescribed for examination. Somehow or other, by begging or borrowing, he would get the books. He would read the huge tomes and make notes and give them to her.

She made copies of some, while she only read through the others. To begin with, she was highly sceptical of his notes. But soon she realised something: he knew very well what was required to be done to get through the examination.

She could very well do without plodding through boring critical readings and philological studies. He would go through them all, make notes and share them with her. She need read only the notes. She would not have to sit turning the pages of boring texts. She could devote that time to reading poetry.

Thus the end of the year drew near.

Appettan wrote regularly from Bombay. She replied to his letters.

Chettan never came to the hostel to meet her again. When there was a letter from Ammu they would meet somewhere, either in the library or on the verandah. He was extremely busy with his studies.

The college closed after the examinations. This time she was going home by herself. Gopu had to stay. Gopu and Chettan came to the railway station to see her off.

Achan was home the whole time during the vacation. Amma was in a very bad condition. She sometimes refused to take food. She was forever singing and making a racket. The cradle was still in the room, even though the child for whom it was meant was running around the yard playing. She would not allow it to be removed. Even now, when she was in a good mood, she would pull it with a string and sing.

As for the child, he would not enter the room if you asked him a hundred times. He wanted only Cheriyamma for everything.

The elder sister was forever fighting the younger over the child. Cheriyamma kept out of Amma's way. If by any chance they came face to face, another bitter quarrel would begin.

Mani had been home a full month when Gopu arrived. Having him home was a relief.

There was a letter from Chettan. Achan got it first. He gave it to her but only after opening it and reading it. There was also a warning. 'Don't reply to him. Don't make friends with men.'

There was no news from Appettan. He never wrote to her at home. She could not go and meet Ammu Cheriyamma also. She heard that she too was not keeping well.

Thus she spent that vacation too counting the days.

Chapter 22

Back in college too she was haunted by the feeling that she had no one to call her own. Gopu was not with her that year. He had secured admission to a medical college. His marks were so high that he had no difficulty getting in. So he was gone. The medical college and its hostel were far away. There was no way they could meet as before.

Chettan had also left. As soon as his results were out, he was appointed as lecturer in a college nearby.

There were two new students in the class now. Honours and MA students shared classes. That was how the two were added. One was a girl named Mary. She had passed BA that year. The other was a Gopinatha Menon, who, after having passed BA, spent the next three years of his life involved in politics and literature.

Until a month after the college reopened, she had not even spoken to him. He never spoke to the girls in the class. He rarely, if ever, even came to class. It seemed his studies were not very important to him. He was still involved in politics and journalism. Once in a while he would appear, mark his attendance and leave immediately. Since there was no particular insistence on attendance, the Masters too said nothing.

It was Chettan who introduced her to him. They had been friends for some time, hailing as they did, from the same place. They had been classmates also for a while.

Sometime just before the month of *Chingam*, Chettan had visited the college. His own place of work was not far. He could also meet his old friends.

While she stood talking to Chettan, Menon – it had been one of those days on which he had put in an appearance – came out of the library. Seeing Chettan he drew near.

'Oh, what are you doing here? Have you started attending classes and all?' Chettan asked, laughing.

'Just my luck! What else can I say?' He joined in the laughter.

'Mani, you wouldn't know this guy, would you?'

It was he who answered, 'We have been studying in the same class for roughly a month and a half. And ...'

'And on thirty of those days, you never once came to class,' she filled in.

'Hey, I wasn't absent for thirty days. Don't make me sound that bad.'

'No, if you count every day and take the average, it would come to around thirty.'

'Still, thirty days—'

'Leave it. Mani, have you really grasped the greatness of this man?' Chettan started again.

She stood smiling but did not say anything.

'This man here is the most important personage in my village. He's been part of *satyagraha*s and strikes, has gone underground, has served a prison term and has experienced every kind of hardship. And everything in this young age.'

'Now, what's bitten you?' Menon interrupted him and said.

'There is no end to the thrilling tales of his underground life. For a glass of tea, he ...'

'I am going to finish you off today.'

Since a couple of Chettan's friends came that way, the story was never finished.

Menon stood around talking for some more time and left.

He did not turn up on Monday at all.

The next day Vijaya was absent. There was no class after the first period during the morning session.

A friend came and called Mary away. If she stayed in the class on her own, Balachandran would turn up to buttonhole her. It was better to leave.

Just as she was about to leave, Menon came in, asking whether Chettan had left. She told him that he had. He spent some more time talking about Chettan. He also knew Ammu. The man who married her was his neighbour.

After talking to him for a long time, when she made to leave, he suddenly said, 'Are you the same Mani who wrote in Bhaskaran's autograph?'

'I did write in Chettan's autograph.'

'I happened to see it once. I made up my mind that day to meet Mani.'

Suddenly she recalled what she had scribbled in the autograph. Writing in autograph books was something she did not like. But Chettan insisted and she had written in his autograph. He had told her to write something of her own. It was a time when she was worried about something, maybe about not getting any letters from home. She wrote the first thing that came to mind:

Losing your memories surely is a boon.

'You must tell me some day what made you write that, will you?' Menon continued.

'There's nothing to tell. I thought of something and just wrote.'

'I would like to know just what that something was.'

She only smiled.

After that, they used to meet every day and talk.

One day she was borrowing books from the library when he came in. Her page in the register was open. He approached the table and read through the page.

'Only poetry, nothing else?' he asked when he had finished reading the entries.

'I have no time to read anything else.'

'So you have time to read all this poetry, haven't you?' he said laughing, 'but you don't have time to read anything worthwhile.'

'Only poetry is worthwhile, isn't it?'

'Nothing else would appeal to poetry people, would it? Yet don't you think that you must learn something about the people who inhabit this world?'

'What am I supposed to read, to learn that?'

'Read a little bit of history.'

'Should I go back to turning the pages of my high school history book for that?'

'What's the use of that? Don't you learn only dates there? You must read the history of mankind. Wait. I will get you the books.'

He disappeared among the shelves. He browsed among books for a while and finally returned with one.

'This isn't very hard. Begin with this,' he said, and held it out to her with a smile.

She took it and looked at the name.

'Isn't this the story of the French Revolution? It wouldn't be difficult to read this.'

'No, that's why I chose it.'

She took it with her and finished it quickly.

Their friendship began from that point.

He was a peculiar creature.

He was five or six years older than she. But he had seen much more of life than his years warranted. He had spent almost a year in prison. There was hardly any place where he had not been. He combined politics, meetings and public speaking with his studies.

After college, he usually went straight to some party meeting, which lasted till eight or even ten in the night. He found nothing difficult about sitting up reading till two.

Then after all this, if he felt like it, he would get up in the morning and attend classes. He was a person who believed implicitly in a revolution that would turn the existing social structure upside down. He would even wade through rivers of blood to reach a rosy tomorrow.

She often wondered why he chose to opt for literature instead of economics or politics.

He combined in himself the focused, incisive intelligence of a scientist and the inexorable point of view of a revolutionary.

She felt that talking politics with him was like doing a fitness regimen early in the morning. After half-an-hour of it, you left with renewed energy.

Long, heated arguments between them became common. She found herself unable to concede his point of view that refused to see the individual as being separate from society.

When you divide a hundred thousand with the same number, do you get the individual?

The old question would make him angry.

It was not necessary to consider the individual as being separate from the hundred thousand. There was no harm in sacrificing one for the sake of a noble enterprise.

What is a noble enterprise? Who gets to decide that? Does one among the hundred thousand decide what is good for the rest of them?

Finally, all the talking would make him lose his temper.

She deliberately did not want to understand. She just wanted to confound what was clear as daylight.

She began to love those heated arguments. He also seemed to like them. Every day before he left, he would come and talk to her for some time.

Chapter 23

One day the class was let off at three. Vijaya and Mary left. Mani stood talking to Menon.

She was not aware of time passing. Did the four o'clock bell go? The verandah was beginning to empty.

Balachandran came out from the direction of the library.

'Didn't you hear the bell, Remani?'

He came straight toward her without paying attention to Menon.

She was about to say, 'No, did it really?' But before she could ask, he began again.

'Why are you here after everybody has left?'

She did not like the tone of his voice.

'I am not alone. Can't you see?'

'Oh, yes, you two whispering sweet nothings—'

'Hey, go mind your own business.' It was Menon who said that.

'Let Remani speak. Who are you to say that?' Balachandran was not giving in.

'What right do you have to tell us off?'

'I do have the right.'

'Oh, you have the right? Where did you get it from?'

She waited only thus far into the quarrel. Without waiting around to listen to the whole, she left. Let those two fight it out.

The next day when she reached college, Balachandran was waiting for her on the verandah. He was different from his persona of last evening. The old Balachandran: the same melancholy and the same airs.

Ignoring him, she started to walk away. Was he the type to leave her alone?

'Remani, are you angry with me?' he began.

She walked on without speaking.

'Remani,' he was following her.

Nuisance!

She stopped.

'The things that slipped out yesterday ...'

'Do you have anything other than that to talk about?'

'Remani, when I saw him trying to chat you up ...'

'You are mad.'

'Yes, this is a kind of madness. Everybody says I have become mad.'

'You should go and get help and not do this.'

'Only you can cure me, Remani.'

'Then you are going to remain mad.'

'How can you be so cruel?'

'What nonsense! What are you saying?'

'He asked what right I had to tell you off. You conceded that question with your silence. Maybe I have no right to tell you off. But do I not have the right to love you?'

'Balachandran, you are not giving any thought to what you are saying.'

'No, I know what I am saying. Remani. Before that fellow came, you—'

'Please stop this talk. You shouldn't say such things.'

'Remani, you don't like listening to my talk now. I have come to notice that for some time now. He came between us and spoilt everything.'

'Don't talk nonsense. What did he spoil? You have blown everything unnecessarily out of proportion.'

'He's the reason. Or Remani wouldn't have talked like this. Everybody knows.'

'Stop this nonsense, Balachandran. Never come to me with this kind of talk again.'

'Remani.'

'This is neither the place nor the time for this. Go to class, please.'

She walked to class without waiting to see whether he was following her. Was Menon present? How would she face him? What would he think? What impression did he form about the relationship between her and Balachandran?

As luck would have it, he did not come that day.

After that he did not turn up for a whole week.

That was a relief. By the time he turned up next, he would have forgotten all this.

He came into the class on Monday after noon.

It was evident that he had just got off a train.

As soon as the class was over, he made straight for her.

'Where have you been?' she asked, because it was the polite thing to say.

'I had been to Bombay. I had meant to be back yesterday but was delayed by a day.'

Bombay. Appettan was there.

'Was it fun?'

'Fun? I had been there on some business. I have done the sightseeing before.'

'So you've been there before?'

'Yes,' he paused.

'What happened to the Balachandran affair in the end?' he asked suddenly.

'Affair? What affair?'

'The way the guy tried to tell us off – he's funny.'

She said nothing.

'That day I told my mother about you, Mani.'

'Oh, what did you tell her?'

'That you are a guileless, naïve girl.'

'Do you regard that as a compliment?'

'What do you think?'

'I can't make out.'

She just wanted to put an end to the conversation and leave.

'Alright, when you met me for the first time, what was the impression that you formed?' he was beginning again.

'I don't recall anything specific.'

'No, the first impression is the most important. Even if you change your views later, the first one will lie in your unconscious mind.'

'So you have studied psychology too?'

'Ah, a smattering of that too, yes.'

'So this is a psychological experiment.'

'No, this is an invitation into my life.'

'Oh, Balachandran said—'

'What did he say?'

'The same thing.'

'There is nothing new about this to merit specific mention. Everybody has been talking about it.'

'Who's everybody?'

'Everybody in the college. Who else?'

'You have heard and known about this and was this what you had in mind all these days?'

'Why are you so troubled, Mani?'

'Troubled?'

'I had just this in my mind. Yes, I am ready to marry you. That's what I told my mother.'

'Oh, you have talked—'

'Don't you think that we'd make a very good couple?'

'No.'

'Do you mean to say that you don't enjoy arguing with me?'

'What's the connection between arguing and getting married?'

'Don't you think that we argue because our ideas meet somewhere? Nobody argues with whoever they set their eyes on, do they?'

'Anyway, in my view an inclination to argue isn't basis enough for marriage.'

'Do you mean to say that we share nothing else?'

'Yes, I do.'

'If I were not willing to believe that—'

'Now, to make you believe it—'

'Wait. You may answer me after giving it some thought. When your initial confusion is over, you can mull this over and tell me.'

'There's nothing to mull over.'

'Is this your final answer?'

'Yes.'

'Supposing I am not ready to accept this answer? I don't usually give up something I've set my heart on.'

'This is breaking all bounds of propriety.'

'Propriety ...'

At the far end of the verandah, someone was coming up the stairs.

She was saved.

He stopped what he was about to say.

She left.

Yes, what he said was true.

Naïve girl.

It was because she was foolish that she had to listen to all that.

Oh, if he were to start this kind of talk again – she began to take great care not to be alone. She never remained alone in the class or on the verandah. She would persuade Vijaya to accompany her up to the hostel gate on some pretext or other. When she asked her, Vijaya obliged her willingly. Did Vijaya understand why she was seeking a chaperone instead of going to the hostel on her own? That she went in fear of Gopinatha Menon?

Most probably everybody in the college knew.

How shameful!

Chapter 24

It was soon after she returned from the half-yearly vacation.

It was Panicker Master who had corrected the answer scripts of the poetry paper. She had done well in that paper.

Master brought the answer scripts to class. Without uttering a word, he opened hers and started to read it out aloud. There was a question about Shelley's poetry. It was her answer to it that he had been reading aloud.

At the time Shelley's poetry had gone to her head. The poet revolutionary filled her head and heart.

Her answer was a paean in prose, a poem with no metre.

It was an essay that went beyond the poems prescribed for study and touched all else; seven to eight pages in her minuscule hand.

Master read out the whole. She listened to it, holding her breath.

When what she had written came out in his deep voice, she felt immense pleasure.

Once he finished reading, he folded it and placing it on the table, sat silently for a while. 'The rest are also good. You all should take a look at her answers.' At last he held it out toward her.

In the small classroom, she only had to stretch her hand out to take it from him. His table and the students' benches were that close. But she rose and took the answer script from him without raising her head.

After classes were over, Balachandran came and got it from her. She got it back in five or six days after everyone had read it. From that day on, Panicker Master's classes were like a celebration to her. She had been in the habit of listening spellbound to his eloquence before as well. Now it was as if everything he said was meant only for her ears. After lecturing for a while, it would be toward her that he would turn and ask whether they had understood him. His eyes would seek her out, it seemed unconsciously, while he was lecturing on something with great enjoyment. While dictating notes, he'd always ask for her notebook to see where he had stopped.

It seemed as though he was teaching solely for her benefit.

She began to count the hours to his classes.

One of those days, Ammu called at the hostel. She was on her way from Singapore. From there she had to take a boat to her village. From the railway station, she came straight, early in the morning, to the hostel. After leaving her there, her husband left on some business or other. He came back to get her only in the evening. They spent the whole time talking.

Ammu was her old self. Nothing about her, neither her chatter nor her laughter, had changed. Marriage had wrought no change in her.

Mani was wearing a large locket on a chain round her neck. It took Ammu's fancy.

'Let's exchange our lockets,' she began with her old zest. Even before she finished saying that, she had removed the pendent with the picture of Lord Krishna from round her neck. She put it in Mani's chain and took Mani's locket.

That became something of an event.

By the time Ammu left it was dark. Neither of them noticed the exchanged lockets.

A couple of days passed. Stories about her new locket began to make the rounds.

It was Saramma of the senior class who started them.

Panicker Master's given name was Krishnan.

It was out of her love for him that she got the locket from somewhere and was wearing it.

It went a step further then. Master returned her love.

That was why he gave her maximum marks in the poetry paper. There was a reason.

He gazed at Mani's face while lecturing.

She had never imagined that the exchange of lockets would lead to such weird interpretations.

As usual, the stories made their rounds and finally reached her ears.

It was through Vijaya's goodness that she came know about them. And that too, after the examinations were over that year, when she returned to college for the reopening.

Unusually, Panicker Master brought the answer scripts of the final examinations to class. She had come first in the finals too. As soon as they received the answer scripts, she noticed the others exchanging meaningful glances among themselves. She could make nothing of them.

That afternoon when Vijaya got her alone, she started.

'If I asked you something, will you tell me the truth, Mani?'

'Oh, Devi! You are beginning with a preamble. This appears to be something serious.'

'It is serious. Will you tell me the truth?'

'I will try hard.'

'Let's joke later. I am going to ask you something in all seriousness.'

'Why don't you come out with it whatever it is?'

'Mani, is there something between you and Panicker Mash?'

'There's not just something but a whole lot. Mash is the best teacher around here. There's no other class that I love so much. I like him much better than I do any other master. I have a feeling he also likes the kind of English I write a little.'

'I don't mean your relationship as teacher and student.'

'Then what? Like are we in love?' She burst out laughing.

Vijaya stood looking at her face. Her laughter stopped on its own.

'Mani, I am telling you out of my regard for you. He can't be trusted. He's aptly named. He's truly Sree Krishna. He flirts with every good-looking girl in the place. None of this is real. Everything's a joke to him.'

'What are you driving at, Vijaya?'

'Where did you get this locket from, Mani?'

'What does that have to do with this?'

'This image of Lord Krishna. You didn't have this round your neck before.'

'Where do you think I got it?'

'They are even saying Mash gave you this.'

'Oh. Mash gave me a locket?'

'I am only asking you about what everyone else has been saying. That's all.'

She then told her everything. The way he looked at her in class and the way he gave her marks in the examinations, everything.

Mani listened to the whole silently.

'So how does this go?' She said at last, 'Do I get a new lover at the rate of one per month or do I change them every week?'

'So I am to understand from this that there's nothing in what people say.' Vijaya paid no attention to her sarcasm. 'I am relieved. I just wanted to give you a warning. I know Mash very well. He's staying in our neighbourhood. He's not the person to play around with.'

Back in her room, she kept thinking about this.

Ammu's Chettan – Balachndran – Gopinatha Menon – Panicker Master – who else's name have they linked to mine, she wondered.

And none of them could awaken what lay dormant in her.

She took a pen and a sheet of paper and sat down.

Whatever passed through her mind took shape as words on a page.

My lamp was never lit.
I waited
Painting my earthenware lamp in beautiful colours,
Filling it with perfumed oil,
Placing a wick, ever so soft, in it—
I waited
But
The lamp was never lit. Fireflies came.
Their cold fire did not light the lamp.
Lightning streaked through the sanctum
It singed the edge of the wick
It did not light the lamp.
My lamp was never lit
Till the very end.
Should I wait with this unlit lamp?
Will my waiting never, ever end?
Will my lamp never be lit?

She had been given to reading a lot of Tagore's poetry those days.

Chapter 25

When she looked at what she had written in the morning, she had the feeling that it was not bad. A few days ago, Panicker Mash had told her to write something for the college magazine. He had done so in class.

Why not give this to him?

She went to college with her poem copied on a fair sheet of paper. Since there was time before the bell went, she made straight for Panicker Master's room. He had arrived.

'I'd appreciate it if you'd publish this in the college magazine,' she said, placing the sheet of paper on his table.

'Oh God, couldn't you have brought it sooner than this? The magazine's gone to press. Let me see. If they haven't finished printing it, I will include this.'

'It's in Malayalam, isn't it?' he continued, turning the paper over and looking.

'Should I take it to the Department of Malayalam, sir?'

'No need. I'll give it to them.'

He read the whole poem and looked closely at her.

'Leave it here. I'll deal with this.'

He said, never taking his eyes off her face.

At the door, she paused to look back and found him sitting there, still holding the sheet of paper.

The next day, as he left after his class, Master said, 'Remani, I'd like to meet you. Please come to my room at noon.'

She finished lunch early and went to his room. There was another person also in the room. She did not pay him much attention.

The smell of cigarettes filled the room.

'There's a problem.'

Master said when she went and stood near the table.

'Another person has written a poem exactly like Remani's. If we carried both anybody would think one of you must have copied from the other. A coincidence. It's very surprising.'

'Don't carry mine, sir. You carry the other,' she said when she heard his words.

'There's something else too. The other poem was submitted early. It's already gone to press. The printing is over. Now the page will have to be removed from every copy and a printed copy of this will have to be inserted.'

'No sir, no one can possibly take that much trouble.'

'Well, I think there's nothing else to be done.'

Master did not say anything after that.

She hesitated because she was not sure whether she could leave without being told. No one spoke.

For no reason at all, she felt strange. She turned her head to look.

A pair of piercing eyes were riveted on her.

How strangely bright!

Thin lips, as if drawn carefully by hand, a high bridged nose: she just took these in at a glance. Without waiting for permission, she went out.

Were those eyes following her ...

Two days later, quite by accident, she met their owner on the verandah. This time also she just stole a single glance.

Vijaya had been with her. After they had passed him, she said to Vijaya, 'Do you know who that is?'

'That's the new Malayalam lecturer. His name is Madhava Menon or something. He's supposed to be good.'

'He's never taken classes for us. Wasn't he here then?'

'No, he joined only recently. I think he was working somewhere else.'

For some reason, those eyes refused to fade from her mind.

There was a notice asking everyone to get a copy of the college magazine. After signing her name and receiving a copy from the store, the first thing she did was to turn the pages to locate the poem.

It was the first in the Malayalam section.

The lamp was not lit. This complaint was the refrain. The beginning was the same. The lines differed here and there. The central idea was the same. Most of the lines were similar too.

Who took the unlit lamp and placed it outside?

Who else was complaining about an unlit lamp at the same time as she was weeping over her own unlit lamp?

The poem was signed P.M.M. only.

Who was this P.M.M.? Whom to ask to find out?

She was standing there holding the magazine in her hand when Vijaya came that way.

'Who is this P.M.M., Vijaya?'

'Which P.M.M.?'

'The person who wrote this.' She showed her the page.

'P.M.M. could be Madhava Menon. P. Madhava Menon. I heard someone say that he writes poetry.'

'Who is Madhava Menon?'

'The new lecturer in the Malayalam department. Mani, you asked me about him when we met him on the verandah.'

'Is that him?'

'Must be. I heard the intermediate students say that the magazine carried their teacher's poem.'

Those bright eyes.

A couple of days later, she had to go to the college office on some business. She was alone. She could get no one to go with her.

She came back through the western verandah.

One could walk along it, looking at the backwater. The verandah was deserted.

Students hadn't returned from their lunch recess.

She walked on, looking at the water, and was soon lost in a daydream. She was woken out of it by someone humming a song somewhere.

There was someone standing at the window of Panicker Mash's room.

It was him.

Those fine well-shaped lips, as if drawn by hand, were humming the song.

He was standing sideways. Only his profile could be seen.

Hair combed back with no parting. Wide forehead, whose outline had already begun to encroach on the hairline on one side, making it recede.

His long fingers, placed on the window sill, held a smouldering cigarette.

Looking fixedly at the picture that he made, framed within the window, she walked on, step by step.

Someone was coming up from behind at a distance, talking loudly.

Suddenly he turned. She had almost reached the window. She had to pass under that gaze. With great difficulty, she made her way past, almost dragging her feet. It seemed to her that she had taken an aeon to take those four steps.

As luck would have it, the room was in a corner. She turned away from his line of vision and stopped, holding on to wooden hand rails for support. Her heart was still pounding.

What is this mesmerising power—

She stood still for quite some time, looking into the distance. When she was breathing normally again, she slowly climbed down the stairs and left.

She heard nothing that was said in the class. That face in profile and those magnetic eyes – they filled her mind.

She tried to pay attention to the class. However hard she tried, she could see before her eyes, only the figure at the window, a cigarette dangling from his fingers.

Was there no way of getting rid of it?

For two days, she deliberately did not go anywhere near the western verandah. On the third day, her feet moved there of their own will.

There were other people in Panicker Master's room. She heard someone talking loudly. There was nobody outside. And she did not have the courage to look in.

She had to return with nothing specific achieved.

A heavy weight lay on her mind the whole day.

What was happening to her? She had no peace of mind till she saw him somehow, somewhere. Where was she headed?

To reach the first floor, there was a narrow flight of stairs near the library. The steps were so narrow that two people could hardly climb up at the same time. Usually only girls used it. The teachers also used it when it was not crowded.

One afternoon she met him on the stairs. She had almost reached the top of the stairs and he was beginning to go down. Seeing her, he made way for her. She knew who it was even without lifting her face.

In a day or two she discovered on her own, without being told by any one, that he came for lunch to Panicker Mash's room. He went back down the narrow stairs.

At the top of the stairs was a pair of twin pillars. A person could very easily hide behind it. One day when she saw him coming, she moved behind the pillars. From there she could watch him till he went down most of the stairs.

He could not see her. That also was a discovery. Slowly that became a routine: standing watch behind the pillar. She knew roughly what time he would take the stairs. If she reached the place by that time, she would be able to see him, if only for two minutes, without herself being discovered. That would suffice till the next afternoon.

Had he known that she was secretly watching him?

Chapter 26

Onam vacation time. As the last day of the term approached, she grew tense. Fourteen days, two weeks! She would not be able to see him even once.

Never had she left for home with such reluctance.

The two weeks were spent wandering restlessly about the house.

It was Onam and she had to do more than her share of chores. As usual, Cheriyamma came down with a fever which lasted five or six days. Though she hardly got time to mope about, a kind of unease lay on her mind constantly.

Somehow she plodded through the interminable days.

On the day the college reopened after the vacation, she left for college early. She did not meet him anywhere on the verandah.

It must have been an hour into the first class. She had been sitting with her eyes planted firmly on the page of the book but her mind was wandering somewhere else.

She heard someone wearing a pair of shoes walk along the verandah outside the class room. For a moment, the footfall stopped in front of the room. Without really being aware of it, she raised her head.

It was him.

Their eyes met. She lowered her head.

The footfall resumed immediately.

He was gone.

A tempest was raging in her mind.

Did he come to see me, she wondered. If not, why did he stop at least for a moment near the door?

Was it, she wondered, for her sake that he came by early in the morning, unusually, that way? She could not believe it.

To see her, he – even thinking on those lines was sweet.

She took her place behind the pillar as usual that afternoon also. He had been walking quickly but he slowed down when he neared the pillar. And he took his time going down the stairs. She stood watching, never taking her eyes off him.

The meetings in the morning became routine. Before the first class of the day was over, he would pass by her class once. He would also glance at the class.

She'd be sitting on pins till the familiar footfall came near. The nearer the sound the stronger grew her heart beat.

Till she heard it, she would be waiting. Once she had, she gave herself over to chewing the cud of that memory.

To wait behind a pillar at noon to steal just a glance—

The whole world had shrunk to just one person. The whole universe revolved around that person.

A glance, a footfall, was enough to set her ardour brimming over.

The tense string of a *veena*: one touch and it resonates unendingly.

Is life so multitudinous?

Does it have space for such varied emotional experiences?

Can it be that what has till yesterday been flowing, stumbling over a wide, flat expanse of land, today become a laughing waterfall?

Has the lamp finally been lit?

What was this power which has lifted her off the ground? Was this the love that poets celebrate? Can you describe this glorious feeling with that ordinary word – a word bandied about here and there?

An ethereal feeling which warms the blood, which spreads light all around.

Every moment a song was taking shape in her mind.

The futile mourning over a piece of clod stopped.

New and ever newer thoughts.

All the creative power within her was rearing its head. Feelings, by themselves, were assuming the shape of words.

> I am placing at the feet of my idol a garland of unforgettable moments.
> With every breath I am making a bouquet to be presented to him.
> Do you remember the moment you entered this barren life, a song on your lips?
> Oh, was that day like any other?
> Was there no difference?
> Did the sun come up, slowly and hesitantly, over the hills that day too?
> Was there nothing special about that moment when you came and stood, like a rainbow on my path?
> At the precise moment did not the drums of the Gods sound? Was not there a shower of petals?
> And were celestial beings not astonished at a mere clod being transformed utterly thus?

Admiration—

The incomparable moment—

Her notebook filled with poems.

Quite recently, Chettan had joined the college as a teacher. The very same day in the afternoon, he came to meet her.

While talking of this and that, he told her that he and Madhava Menon had been colleagues. Before joining this college, he had been working in the college in which Chettan had been working till recently.

They were very close.

When he met her sometime later, he asked, 'No poems? Don't you write anything these days?'

She had some reservations about publishing those poems, which revealed her soul. Then she thought, whatever was there in them would be understood only by a single person. Why worry over them?

She chose one or two and gave them to Chettan, with the proviso that they be published under the assumed name 'A Female Acolyte'. He agreed. He only remarked, after going through them, that they were love poems.

Both came out at the same time in two different magazines published from the place. None of her friends discovered that it was she who had written them. They never thought that she, who had no reservations about publishing under her own name, would opt for a pen name now. They never even suspected they were written by her. That was exactly what she wanted.

She never felt anything when they had spread tales about her. They never even bothered her a bit. But when she was in complete inner turmoil, she could not bear the thought of people finding out about it. No one must know about it.

Chapter 27

Christmas vacation arrived. She wrote home an excuse for not coming over during the vacation. She claimed she had a lot to study, as she had her final examinations that year. If she stayed there, she had at least some chance of seeing him. If she went home, as she did during the Onam vacation ...

Every day she went to college at the regular hour. The library would be open. Someone would always be there. She would take her place at a table in a deserted corner. She had a chosen location. If she sat there, she had a clear view of the verandah and anyone who walked past. She always sat there and never went anywhere else.

With no specific plan in mind, she had gone to the college the day after it closed for the vacation. She only had the intense desire to see him. It was when she was tired of wandering round the campus that she had planted herself in the library. She sat there before an open book for a long time. It was almost noon. Suddenly she heard the familiar footfall from outside. She lifted her head. It was him.

He looked in and saw her. Then he just walked away.

Waiting in the library became a routine: the next day, the day after that and so on.

She heard someone ask the librarian, 'Does this master have any special class? He was here yesterday too.'

'Special class for Malayalam? Nobody there has any special class. Wonder why he turns up every day? One meets him almost daily.'

Did this mean that he too, like her, was taking the trouble of coming to college just for the momentary pleasure of a meeting?

It would be scandalous for a teacher and his girl student to stay talking in nooks and corners.

He never spoke to her. That was never felt to be a necessity. Was it not among ordinary friends that talking was a necessity? Where was the need for the lips to be involved when kindred souls communed with each other? Words would vitiate the harmony of their inner music.

The first week of the vacation was spent thus. Early on a Monday morning Gopu came. Achan had sent him to fetch her home.

'Is Amma in bad shape, Gopu?' That was the first question she instinctively asked.

'No, there's nothing wrong.'

'Then is Kochaniyan—?'

'No, nobody is ill.'

'Then why do I have to come? When I wrote that I wasn't planning to come this time, nobody said anything and now one week into the vacation, I have to come. If only they had told me then, I could have come with you. They think of this only now. Hardly six days of the vacation are left. What am I supposed to pull off by rushing over there?'

'I don't know. Achan told me to fetch you.'

'For no reason at all—'

Why not categorically refuse to go? In that case Achan—

But if she were to go how would she manage without seeing him tomorrow and the day after? What would he think if he did not find her in the library?

If she did not go – if Achan lost his temper—

And to send Gopu, who was home on vacation, here—

There could be something.

'He told me to be back this day. If we start by the twelve o'clock train, we will be home by evening,' Gopu said, putting an end to her introspection.

She changed her sari, took five or six books just for the sake of it and, after getting permission from Miss Sarada, started out.

It was really dark by the time they reached home, because there was a long delay before they caught the bus home.

Achan was pacing about in the front yard. He asked Gopu why they were late. He gave no sign of having seen her at all.

The only person who was enthused by her coming was Kochaniyan, who clung to her. He even slept in her bed.

The next day too nobody told her why she was summoned home. Nobody gave any sign that anything untoward had taken place. She was angry and unhappy. She tried shutting herself in her room with a book. Her mind was not there. She did not even open the book.

He must have gone to the library and left. And she was sitting here, behind a closed door.

In the afternoon, there were three or four visitors. She paid no attention to them. Cheriyamma was busy making coffee and preparing a snack with *aval*. There was a flurry of activity in the kitchen. She did not go to her help.

When everything was ready, Cheriyamma herself took them to the front porch.

Some time passed. Cheriyamma came in slowly and said, 'Mani, your father wants you.'

'Aren't those people there?'

She asked.

'He asked to you to come over.'

Without pausing to think further, she went.

Apart from Achan, there were three other people on the front porch. A grey-haired old man was spreading lime on betel leaf. There was a young man, his eyes fixed on the door to the interior of the house. There was also another bald man wearing a blue shirt. He was also preparing to chew paan.

She went and stood looking at her father with a question in her eyes. Nobody spoke.

'This is my daughter,' Achan said after a brief pause.

'Are you studying in college?' the old man asked, by way of small talk.

'Yes,' she replied.

There was silence again. The young man sat, looking at her.

'So this is your Christmas vacation. When does college reopen?'

That was from the blue shirt.

'Next Monday,' she replied, prompted by common courtesy alone.

The young man had still not taken his eyes off her face. Suddenly, she understood. The significance of everything dawned on her.

Everything was clear.

What a fool she had been, not to think of this possibility! She was being exhibited like a domestic animal. Oh, God!

'You may go now, Mani,' Achan said.

She came away.

She stood, grasping the bars of the window in the inner hall.

They have summoned her home, not breathing a word to her. And from a long way away, for this, this shameful thing.

At last she heard movement on the porch. They were leaving.

After accompanying them to the gate, Achan returned to the porch and called Cheriyamma.

Cheriyamma hovered near the door of the porch. She moved into the corridor.

'Everything is okay. They are willing,' stretching himself on the easy chair, Achan said, 'They will be here next week to fix a date. Tell Mani.'

How easily done!

'She's here,' Cheriyamma said quietly.

'Ah, good. You have no objection, do you, Mani?'

'Isn't it a little late to ask me that? You said you were fixing the date, didn't you?' She was trembling with anger.

'There is no need to ask you for your consent. You only have to obey.'

'A person whom I have never seen or heard about ...'

'You have seen him today. He is the person who was sitting in the middle. Now you will hear: his name is Gangadharan Nair. He's working in Madras. He gets a salary of a hundred rupees. He's his father's only son.'

'I have seen and heard about him now!'

'Only an engagement ceremony is planned for now. The wedding will be only after your examinations. I would like to see you pass your course after having put you through college.'

'Let me also have my say. You will only hold the engagement ceremony. Nothing else is going to happen.' Just where did she gain so much courage?

'Hm. Why?'

'This is not going to happen.'

'Is that for you to decide?'

'This is my life. I also have the right to decide.'

'Oh, is that so? And since when did you get this right?'

She said nothing.

A few minutes passed.

'So you won't listen to me.'

'I can't.'

'You can't? Why?'

He rose. A faint smile appeared on his face.

The only thing she wanted at that moment was to get away. The same feeling she had experienced in her childhood.

'Why don't you speak? You have nothing to say?'

There was the same coldness in his voice as before.

She said nothing.

'There is that handsome fool, Ettan. The loser who keeps moaning that he has no father. Are you waiting for him?'

She felt as if someone had slapped her.

The poor man—

'Yes, that's it. I am waiting for Appettan to come.'

'Okay. Have it your way. I will have nothing more to do with you. You do whatever you like.'

If she stayed there, she might be provoked into saying something. She bit down on her lips and walked in.

Achan left the next day. She left on Friday. Achan did not return till she left.

Since it was vacation, the library was not open on Saturdays. So there was no point in rushing back. She had to be patient till Monday.

On Monday, he did not appear even past his usual time.

She grew tense. What would he have thought?

What would he have thought, when he did not find her in the library where he had taken the trouble to go looking for her?

Would he not come again?

Then—

She heard the footfall when it was almost time for the bell.

Ah! She was relieved.

It was a load off her mind.

Life returned to its old rhythm.

The days were filled with poetry.

After that day, Gopinatha Menon never spoke to her. On the rare days he put in an appearance in class, he pretended not to notice her.

Seeing him moping about the place she even toyed with the idea of barging in and talking to him.

It was a time when she felt friendly toward everybody and everything.

Why should he alone be sad? Why cannot everybody be happy?

Since she stopped talking to Menon, Balachandran had taken to treating her as he used to before. He would regularly bring notes he had made and essays he had written. She would not even touch them. It was Vijaya who benefited. She would copy everything and, when she was done, Mani would return them. Balachandran might even have been aware of what was actually happening. Still, he did not change his routine. Thus questions which were frequently asked in the examination passed through her hands.

Appettan used to write now and then. Ettan was not keeping well. He was thinking of returning home. Her replies were sunny. The light in her mind streamed out on to her letters.

Chapter 28

It was Panicker Master's class. He was teaching Rossetti's poem.

'Blessed Damozel' – he was reading and explicating it.

She leaned out from the gold bar of Heaven and looked down. Her eyes were deep as waters stilled at dusk. She had lilies in her hand and stars in her hair.

Deep eyes.

Eyes flowing over with radiance.

The lines in his deep voice echoed in her ears.

Bright eyes.

Mani was lost in a dream.

Her hands moved on the page lying in front of her.

Large, well-opened eyes.

Eyes that shed moonlight.

She sat lost in her dream for some time.

When she woke from her trance, there were two eyes on the notebook. She was surprised. How did that happen? They were so life-like. Under the straight thin eyebrows, eyes that shone like diamonds. Eyes which were always in her mind – she sat looking at them.

She looked up when the sound in the room suddenly stopped.

Master had finished reading and put away his book.

'Take down notes for some time. Where did we stop yesterday? Give me your book, please,' he held out his hand.

How could she give him the book?

It had the sketch.

The only other occupant of the front bench was Vijaya.

The other girl was absent.

Vijaya never gave her book to the teacher. Her hand was so bad as to be almost illegible.

Master was sitting with his hand held out toward her. What would he think?

She turned the page and showed him where they had stopped the previous day. He read the last line.

Please don't let him turn the page, don't let him think of looking at the next page – while she was praying, he turned the page.

The sketch she had made.

The lips curved in a smile.

She thought she was going to be chided, for doodling while he was taking class.

Suddenly, his face changed and his forehead creased.

Did the likeness occur to him too?

They were friends.

For a minute, he kept looking at the sketch. Then he gave her a questioning look and returned her book. He started dictating notes. He was distracted. He stopped every now and again.

She took the notes down mechanically and was hardly aware of what she was taking down. The same evening she met Chettan after classes. He was coming out after engaging a class. She spent some time asking after Ammu, who had just had a baby.

'Oh, Mani, Panicker Mash said he wanted to meet you,' Chettan said just as she stared to walk away. 'I almost forgot. He told me specifically to tell you. Please meet him in his room whenever it is convenient to you.'

She just said 'Hm' and left.

What did he want to talk to her? Why did he want her to meet him? What was it that he so urgently wanted to talk about?

What would she say if Master asked her something?

She kept turning the questions over and over in her mind and finally she did not go.

The next day they had a class with him. So he knew that she was present in the college.

He must have thought that she deliberately did not go and meet him.

A couple of days passed. Panicker Master's classes were becoming difficult to deal with. She had the feeling that he was constantly watching her.

There were not many days left to the examination. Classes were almost over.

One day, when she came down the narrow staircase, Panicker Master was just coming out of the library. There was no means of escape. She had to pass right in front of him.

Seeing her, he stopped. She could not but stop.

'Remani, don't you have any plans for appearing for the examinations this year?'

That was how he started. 'The way you act, one would think that you have made up your mind to appear for it only next year. That's why I am asking.'

She did not speak, but stood, hanging her head. 'Have you forgotten that you have to appear for the final examination this year?' he continued, 'Have you given any thought where you are headed? When one sees gifted students wilfully starting on such a course – have you forgotten that your objective in coming here was to study?'

Still she said nothing. What was there to say?

On the floor above the bell rang.

'It still isn't too late. You can still do well if you put your mind to it.' Master left only after adding that too.

She had listened to this just when she was sailing down, after her regular caper behind the pillar, with her head full of moonlight. His words did not seem very important. Two weeks and the classes would be over. There was a month to go before the examination. She would sit and mug up. After all, Master himself agreed that she was smart.

She could do it. A month was more than enough. It was only recently that she had let things slip. She only had to put her mind to it.

Chapter 29

She had just emerged from her bath that Sunday when somebody came to fetch her. There was a visitor for her.

Indira went down to see who it was and came back.

'It's Mash, Ammu's brother.'

Chettan? He had never visited the hostel in the past two years, ever since that day he took leave of her and left.

What happened? Was Ammu ill?

She wiped off the powder which she was beginning to dust on her face, tied her long hair to a knot at the end and went down quickly.

'Ammu is okay, isn't she, Chetta?' That was what she asked as soon as she set eyes on him.

'No. I came to talk to you about something else.' He ran his eyes round the room.

There were three or four persons there. There was only one room for visitors.

She stood talking of Ammu.

All those present in the room were Chettan's students. One by one, all of them left.

They were alone in the room. 'Mani,' he said after some time. 'I heard that you were not paying enough attention to your studies. What's wrong?'

Chettan was also starting to sermonise.

For God's sake hold your tongue, and let me love.

She recalled Donne's verse she had seen quoted somewhere.

Leave me alone, let me love.

Why do these people not understand?

All I wish is to be left alone.

Chettan was looking steadily at her: a look that scoured out everything in her heart.

'Mani,' he called her, his eyes still fixed on her face.

'Hm.'

'Really? Between you and Madhava Menon ...'

'Chetta!'

'Were all those songs of love really meant for him? Mani, was it because of him that you changed from being a devotee of love to an actual lover?'

'I am still a devotee, Chetta. I still worship beauty but it's not external beauty.'

'How did you come to know of his inner beauty?'

'Not through intellect but through the heart.'

'Mani, he's not as sublime a person as you think.'

'Let me venerate him. Why do you have to break my idol?'

'What madness is this? Don't you see that this is ruining everything else?'

'Nothing is going to be ruined. Even if everything else were ...' she stopped.

For a while both of them did not speak.

'Do you actually know anything about him to admire him so blindly?' Chettan began again.

'No, I don't. I never felt the need to know.'

'Don't you have any thought for tomorrow, Mani? And no plans either?'

'Today is so sweet, Chetta, why should I think about tomorrow?'

'Mani, please talk like human beings. Come down from among the clouds.'

'Why do all of you have this urge to bring me down? Let me live in the present without waiting for tomorrow.'

'This is like a disease.'

'Oh, what shall I say to that?'

'Don't say anything.'

'Mani, he's dirt poor. His family of six is entirely dependent on his salary.'

She laughed out aloud.

'Hm. Now what?'

'No, nothing.'

'He has four sisters, one elder to him and three younger, all unmarried. There's also his mother. He has a responsibility toward all of them.'

'So?'

'Can he think of marriage until he finds husbands for them all?'

'Who brought up the question of marriage here, Chetta? Even so, what if I am prepared to wait?'

'You stand dazzled by the radiance of the flame tree in full bloom. He doesn't deserve a sacrifice on this scale.'

'Sacrifice, Chetta? Is this sacrifice? I cannot act in any other way but this. And don't you think I should also be convinced that it is by the flowers of the flame tree that I am dazzled? You have just told me that he is a good son and a good brother. Does that make his worth go up or down?'

'Forget all that. He cannot share your tender emotions, Mani. Just because someone writes verse, it doesn't mean that he possesses a poet's heart. He writes with his head not his heart. He's purely materialistic and also an opportunist. His principles are utterly utilitarian. He never does anything unless there's something in it for him. Income and expenditure are strictly tallied there; he wouldn't make allowance even for a grain of rice.

'I have shared a room with him for a year. I know him, I know him very well. It is with that knowledge that I speak to you. He's not the person you take him to be. If he's determined to get ahead, he'd trample a heart lying in his way, however precious that heart may be.'

'Are you finished, Chetta?'

'I know you don't take it in the spirit in which I tell you this. You might also recall that old incident. But to cast me in the role of a jilted lover blinded by envy would be ...'

'Chetta!'

'Leave it. I think of you as another Ammu. I have the responsibility to protect a younger sister who has no one near to do that, whether she appreciates that or not.'

'Chetta!'

'See, I like him. He has many qualities that deserve respect. But he has no mercy. I cannot stand by and watch Mani's love knocked to pieces against that rock.'

When she remained silent, Chettan continued, 'He doesn't know how to love. He doesn't believe in something like love.

He views it as the frailty of the powerless, something that the powerful can exploit.'

The hostel bell went. It was time for visitors to leave.

'Chetta, the bell has gone,' she said quietly. Chettan pretended not to hear it.

'We were talking about this,' he was beginning again.

'Who are "we"?' she asked.

'I, Panicker Master and Madhavan.'

'Panicker Mash?'

'Actually it was Mash who opened my eyes. I never guessed this, even though I was witness to many things.'

'What has Panicker Master got to do with this?'

'Don't talk in that vein, Mani. He has your best interests at heart. His love is untouched by selfishness. Instead of Madhava Menon, had you loved that man, Mani ...'

'Bravo, excellent choice. Everybody says he's a veritable Lord Krishna.'

'He is a man, a mere man. He's sure to have his failings. Only he doesn't bother to hide what others do. A good woman never came into his life. When someone did ...'

'Forget it, just forget it please. There nothing between us but the bond between a guru and his disciple.'

'It was his interest in his model student's future that prompted him to intervene in this.'

'There was no need for that.'

'Madhavan had no reservations about discussing this with us. He had told Panicker Master everything. Master thought he was just bragging. That was why he had not intervened in anything before this. Now that he has come to know that Mani has taken this seriously ...'

'Just what did he say to Panicker Master? What actually did happen for him to talk about it?'

'Nothing much. But he was reading the workings of your mind as if through a pane of glass. He's intelligent.'

She said nothing.

'And he – it was because I was close to both that Mash called me too – never told me anything. Till now, he has never spoken a word about this to me. He hasn't, because he knew I wouldn't let him play his little games here. Now that both of us cornered him and asked him what his intentions were ...'

'Oh, you cornered him and asked him—'

'Yes, we asked him to his face, whether he was serious about what he was doing.'

'Just what is he doing? Two persons have set out to question his integrity! Who asked you to take up my case?'

'I know you are getting angry, Mani. Just wait till you hear what he—'

'No, I don't have to listen to this.'

'You have to listen. No matter how angry you get, Mani, I will save you from him.'

'I don't want to listen to this.'

'You have to. He said if Gopu was willing to marry one of his sisters, he would marry you, Mani. If that is not possible, this is also not possible.'

'So you took this that far.'

'He will agree if somebody came to him and suggested that he marry their sister in exchange for a marriage between one of his sisters and that person. He is willing to marry Gopu's sister if Gopu is willing to marry his sister. He is not marrying Mani the individual.'

She felt her head spinning. She stood still, holding to the backrest of a bench.

'None of his sisters is good-looking. I have met all four. The youngest is twenty-two. Do you think Gopu will be willing to do that?'

'Please stop the bargaining, Chetta.' How did she manage to raise her voice?

'You two have gone to talk things over. Who asked you to be the go-between? Goodbye. Thank you for your good deed.'

'Wait, let me finish.'

Without waiting around to listen to the rest, she went out.

'Mani ... Mani,' his voice hailed her from behind.

She did not turn to look.

Come to help her!

When she reached her room, Indira and her friend were engaged in serious study. Seeing her, Indira raised an eyebrow questioningly.

She said nothing but went out.

The verandah was full of students. She went up the stairs. There would probably be no one at the corner of the stairs.

She moved slowly along the ledge, holding on to the banisters. She pushed open the window to the west. It was her regular haunt. The lights were opening their eyes on the distant island.

Slowly darkness spread over the waters.

She stood leaning on the window sill, her mind full of bitterness.

Moonlight did not arrive to turn the expanse of water into silver.

A moonless night.

Chapter 30

She awoke next morning wondering whether all this was real or just a dream. Somehow she waited for it to be ten o'clock.

The Professor was supposed to meet them during the first hour. He had not come to college yet. There was no class. The boys left their separate ways. Vijaya went to the library.

She was alone in the room. She stood near the table looking at the door.

Suddenly she started to hear the familiar footfall outside.

She leaned on the table, holding it with both palms. Her throat was beginning to feel dry.

She stood exercising her whole will power, without taking her eyes off the door.

This day those eyes should not have to scour the room.

The sound was approaching.

It was almost near.

A teacher near the table.

Students sitting in a row in front.

A head bent over an open book – a flushed face that was slowly, ever so slowly raised – the eyes turning away in confusion.

He must have been expecting these that day too. She stood leaning on the table like a marble statue.

Two pairs of eyes met.

There were only the two of them in the whole wide world.

A man and a woman.

Two pairs of eyes measured one another.

Was the moment going to last an eternity?

At last the man's eyes fell.

What did he see in that seemingly endless moment?

Broken dreams? Utter contempt? A challenge to his masculinity? What did he read in those large, well-opened, black eyes?

For the first time, he lowered his head before her.

She felt as though a veil was slipping down before her eyes. Was there a fog before her all these days? Was it through its covering that she found the world colourful? He, a mere man made of clay, dressed in white trousers and a brown bush shirt, walked away from her, without raising his head.

Had everything come to an end with that?

She sat on the table. Her hands and legs were feeling limp.

How long did she continue to sit there?

A bell rang in the distance.

Oh, they have a class. Everybody will be back now.

She picked up her pen and book. She had to get out soon.

When she reached the stairs, there was a tide surging up. They were moving from one class to the next: must be intermediate students. There was a veritable army of them.

How long would it take the crowd to thin?

From the northern side another group came to make their way down. It was best to join them.

Those who were going up on one side, those who were coming down on the other, formed lines. She went down mechanically, keeping her eyes straight. The proximity of human bodies at a time when she craved solitude was suffocating.

She reached the hostel without meeting anyone on the verandah. The key was on the window sill. She threw her books on to the table, drew the bolt of the door and lay down.

A shaft of light was coming into the room through the half-open eastern window. Fine particles of dust danced in the rays. They moved in circles, going up and down, meeting and dodging one another.

She lay looking at them.

The sun rose. The shaft of light slowly shifted from inside the room.

There was only emptiness in the room.

She lay straight, looking up, her head resting on her hands. The roof was whitewashed concrete. There was not even a scratch on it. Would it be possible to whitewash the walls of one's mind like this?

Not leaving even a trace of the past.

The past.

Was everything not over?

Everything.

Could everything become meaningless within the span of a few hours like this?

Still, did life go on as before?

In some corner of the earth, the idol of a foolish girl called Mani crumbled to dust. Should the world come to a standstill over that?

Really?

Should the solar system stop its revolution because I, Mani, have become a corpse?

Did something really happen this day? Was this day's scene really necessary to believe in the truth of what Chettan had said?

Oh, between them, Chettan and he had settled everything. Then why did he turn up at the usual time? Was that to test his hold over her?

It grew noisy outside. Everybody must have turned up for lunch.

Someone was knocking on the door.

She pretended to be asleep. There was no getting away with it. Whoever was knocking had no intention of stopping. At last she got up and opened the door. It was Vijaya.

'What happened, Mani? I reached the class only after Mash was in the class. It was then that I knew that you weren't there. We had class during the third hour also. Why did you leave after coming to class in the morning?'

Was talking such a difficult thing?

'I felt faint. I came here to lie down.'

'Are you better now?'

'It's not gone yet.'

'Why did you feel lightheaded?'

Vijaya sat down near her and felt her forehead. 'You must have sat up all night studying. That must be it.'

She only smiled.

'You must have a wall if you want to paint a mural. Mugging up for the exam is fine but you shouldn't neglect your body. After all, you have to write that exam.'

Again she tried to smile.

'Had your lunch, Mani?'

'Yes.' It would be easier to lie.

Vijaya sat turning over the pages of a notebook for some time.

'Panicker Master asked where you were, Mani.'

'Oh, did he?'

'Hm. I said you had come in the morning and that I hadn't seen you after that. I don't know what he made of that.'

Vijaya looked at her watch and rose. 'It's nearly two. Let me go.'

'Hm.'

'Mani, you should really rest today. Don't read anything just for one day.'

'Alright.'

She closed the door and left.

So Master did ask after her. Chettan and Mash – they had set out to help her. Poor men.

What did they accomplish, except perhaps put out the light in another being's life?

That he was willing to exchange his body, trade his flesh if you would—

Was not loyalty to one's sisters a good thing? Had he asked her to wait till they were married off—

This was not that.

Promises had not been broken. That was true. Because there had never been promises.

There was nothing.

Dare he say that?

Was it only one's word that was sacrosanct?

Had he meant to nip the bud of love, could he not have done that in the beginning? Why did he allow it to thrive, watering it and letting it bask in the early morning sun? If he could do this much, where did sincerity come into it now?

He might have thought that making her wait and then deceiving her would be worse. He had shown at least that much mercy.

But there was no need.

Had he said, hold this to my lips, let me drain it to the dregs—

Had he said, leave your floral offerings at my feet, let me trample them—

Deception would have definitely been better than this trade off.

Chapter 31

Vijaya and Mary came looking for her when she did not put in an appearance in class the next day. She spent that day too feigning illness.

With her drawn and pinched face and unkempt and unwashed hair, she really did look ill.

At any rate, she was not in the frame of mind to wonder what anybody else might think. They asked her why she was lying down. She answered them that she was not feeling well. She did not think beyond that.

Vijaya, who knew her only too well, did not probe further.

The week passed in this manner.

She never went to college. She could not bear to go there and risk a chance encounter with him.

Even otherwise she did not feel up to getting out of bed.

All her senses had stopped functioning.

When Indira insisted, she made a pretense of eating, in an effort to buy peace. The rest of the time she spent in bed.

No one bothered to check what the MA and other senior students were doing in the hostel.

Vijaya called on her one more day. Then she stopped, perhaps feeling that Mani did not really welcome her visits.

The classes came to an end that Friday. The next month was to be their study holiday. When the first hour was over, Vijaya and Mary came to the hostel. This was their last class. She simply had to go over with them.

The boys were firmly of the belief that she was availing of leave to study for the examination. They had sent Vijaya with specific instructions to drag her to class.

She did not even stir from where she lay. Vijaya left feeling hurt.

Classes concluded. There was an air of heaviness about the hostel. The junior classes had examinations. The others were preparing for them.

When Indira protested too much, she would take her book in hand.

Indira's refrain was: are you planning to sit for the exams only next March? Have you no intention of appearing for them this year?

Indira would make her sit up till half past ten.

The Sunday after she stopped attending classes, Ammu's Chettan came to meet her. She sent Indira to tell him that she was not keeping well and could not meet him.

Indira had never approved of her talking to Chettan, so with a little persuasion she agreed to meet him and give him her message.

She was missing for some time. She came back, looking grave. She came straight in and sat on Mani's table.

She sat looking at her quietly for some time and began: 'What is the meaning of all this, Mani?'

Oh, Chettan had not wasted time. He had told Indira about her stupidity. She hoped he had not revealed all.

'Now, Mani, I must ask you, what are you about?' She had hoped Indira would give up if she kept quiet. She did not. Why can't people mind their own business?

'Where do you suppose this is going to end? Don't you think you should harden your heart a little more? It's foolish—'

'Indira, can't you stop this sermonising? I am chock-full of well-meant advice. Can't you all find anyone but me to bestow your wise counsel? I am lying here. I am not disturbing any of you. I didn't ask you for advice. Can't you wait till I do?'

She stopped talking.

Indira did not say a word.

Slowly, tears welled up in her eyes and rolled down her cheeks.

Mani just lay there watching tears fill her eyes and flow down.

Indira sat there for some more time and left silently. The day of the examination finally arrived. A couple of the girls were down with fever. Another girl had a hysteric episode on the eve of the examination. Some of the girls who had gone to seek Miss Sarada's blessings burst into tears.

There was utter confusion.

Mani had just skimmed through the portions here and there and had not studied at all well. She had no idea what to do. Sometimes she would think that she would rather not appear for the examination that year. It was only because Vijaya had come to the hostel to take her along that she went and got the hall ticket.

By half past nine Indira had changed her sari and asked her, 'Aren't you coming, Mani?'

This was the first time Indira was talking to her after the previous day's incident.

She went and sat in the hall. She was given the question paper. She skimmed through it and felt her head spinning. She knew nothing. The paper was 'Old English'. The marking system went something like that for mathematics. You got no marks if your answers are not precise.

She barely knew the answers to two of the questions.

She sat, holding the paper. Why not decide to give it a miss this year? She could always withdraw her candidature, claiming she did not want to appear this year.

But then—

She would have to be back here. No, that she could not.

Would Achan allow her to opt out next year?

If she failed now – at least then she could try saying that she did not want to study anymore. The other was not an option. She could not come back.

If she was going to fail it was okay by her. She did not care.

Her neighbour stood up, asking for an extra sheet.

Mani unscrewed the cap of her fountain pen.

The examinations took place one by one, as per schedule.

Ten days.

Three hours per day.

She would leave the hall before time. If she waited for the bell, she would have to meet the others outside on the verandah. She would have to talk to them. If she left early, she could circumvent that eventuality.

At any rate, she never knew enough answers to fill the three hours.

She managed to write the papers with literary content fairly well and did very badly in those that required intensive study.

The examinations somehow got over.

Now there remained the 'viva', which required the candidate to answer questions orally. There was a week to the viva.

She did not want to go home and return for the viva. She spent the week there like an automaton.

Two days following the final examinations are generally held to be celebration time. Indira and the others went out every evening. Only she shut herself in her room.

Nothing happened to bridge the distance between her and Indira. She somehow managed to live through the seven days.

The 'viva' was on a Monday, at two in the afternoon.

Indira had a practical examination which would start in the morning and go on till evening. Organic Chemistry, a subject of which Indira was a little afraid. She started to fill her pen with ink. She managed to spill it on the table and her saree. She was nervous.

Mani silently went up to her and took the pen from her.

She finished filling the pen with ink. Indira was standing near the window looking out.

What if she was late?

'Indira,' Mani called at last.

She turned, wiping her face with the end of her saree. She took the pen from her and left silently.

It was at noon that Mani had to go. She set off at half past one.

There was no getting away this time. Everybody would be there: Balachandran and Menon and all. Would Panicker Master also be there?

Let them be. Let every one of them be.

It was Balachandran who came to meet her first. 'Remani, how did you do in the exam? You must have done well. Will you get the first rank?'

She smiled. The others arrived by then. Only Menon did not ask her anything.

She had to wait for some time. She was called in only after a couple of others had been. Her only thought by then had been to somehow get through the ordeal and leave.

The Professor was there, along with two others from outside. They started with Philology and asked her the meaning of a word which she managed to give. Then they asked her to explain the etymology of the word, which also she knew because it was from the portion that she had studied. But she was not entirely happy with her answer. Nothing came out right.

She did suffer from 'an inability to recall, at the opportune moment, the art and artifice of war.'*

They asked many more questions, none of which she answered satisfactorily. She fumbled through another fifteen minutes.

When she was allowed to leave, she slipped out in relief.

---

* *Author's note*: From 'Karnaparva' of Ezhuthachan's *Mahabharata*.

That was the last straw. If there had been any hope before, with this that too was lost.

Those who were waiting outside for their turn never guessed any of this when they saw her emerge from the room, holding her head high. Or did they, and they just pretended not to?

She was able to leave only after spending a few minutes there also.

Vijaya was almost in tears. Balachandran had brought his autograph book. Everybody was busy saying goodbye. Only Menon did not speak to her. She bid farewell to everyone and left.

Ah. Now she would never have to go down those stairs. This would be the last time she would be walking along this verandah. She would not have to walk again on the sand at the back of the gas plant. She would never again have to set foot in this cursed place.

The night was spent packing. Indira had an examination the next day but still she helped out with it.

It was when she emptied her study drawer that she found them: a bunch of letters, all unopened.

For five or six weeks, she had never been in the habit of opening the mail. She wondered who they were from and what they had written about.

She threw them into the box. Tearing them open also required effort.

The train was at half past eleven in the morning. Indira's examination will start at ten, so she wouldn't be able to see her off at the station.

When she was leaving finally, there was no one even to see her off. Gopu had been gone for a month.

Indira was ready by a quarter past nine. Even though the ink had not run out in her pen Mani filled it for her.

'Mani,' Indira called her, standing near the table, ready to leave.

'Indira.'

'If you share your sorrow with people whom you really like, it won't hang heavily on you. I had wanted to tell you this all this while. I didn't dare. I don't think that you would act on it, Mani, but I'd regret it if I didn't tell you.'

'Don't worry, Indira. Fools deserve to get hurt.'

'No, Mani, don't say that.'

'You shouldn't waste these last minutes thinking about this. Don't you have nice things to talk about? Go and do well in your practicals.'

'Mani.'

'Indira.'

After waiting for a while, she slowly went out.

At ten o'clock she called a rickshaw, loaded her luggage and started out. She had never had to travel on her own like this.

As she was moving to the ticket counter, someone hailed her from behind.

Chettan.

'Come with me. I will get the ticket for you.'

Poor man, he had come to see her off.

Chettan came with the ticket. The two of them stood wordlessly by her luggage on the platform.

The train crawled into the station.

He had the luggage carried into the ladies' compartment. She boarded the train.

It was very crowded. When the crowd in the passage thinned a bit, she moved to the door. Chettan had not left.

The bell rang. The train whistled in return.

Chuk ... chuk ... chuk ...

'Mani, will you write?'

She only smiled.

Chapter 32

There followed days filled with darkness. She never stepped out of the gate. She never even climbed to the top of the hill.

One day, when Mammali brought some provisions from the market, she was on the porch doing something. He unloaded everything and shaking out his towel, put it on his shoulder.

'When did you arrive, Ammukutti? Mammali didn't get to meet you till now.'

'I have been here almost a month.'

'Mammali had been here the other day but didn't see you then.'

'I must have been inside.'

'Do you get letters from the young master, Ammukkutti? Mammali has no news of him.'

'Do you mean Appettan of Kochachan's house? No. Mammali, couldn't you have asked Cheriyamma?'

'When that lady returns, the boy will be with her, won't he? Then there would be no need to ask.'

'So Cheriyamma is not here?'

'Didn't you know about this, Ammukutti? They wouldn't have written to you because they don't want to displease *valiyeman*.'

'Where have they gone?'

'He came home because he was not well. And here there was a lot of commotion with ayurvedic potions and what not. The doctor was brought in when things got really bad. And the doctor said he must be taken to hospital immediately. By that time the young man had become like a bent coconut spine. What a hard time the lady had!'

'Where was he taken?'

'To Coimbatore or some such place.'

'What was wrong with him, Mammali?'

'He had a bad cough, and also fever. It was after stopping the fever with an injection that he was taken.'

'How long has it been since he was taken, Mammali?'

'It must be two or three months. Wasn't he laid up here for about two weeks? By then he was taken.'

Cheriyamma came out after her bath to hang out the washing.

'So you are here, Mammali. Thank God. We have no sugar left for the morning coffee.'

Mani went in.

The unopened letters at the bottom of her box.

He must have written to her about his illness.

When he got worse, he must have written about that too. When he wrote to her again and again, and received no reply, what would he have thought?

Persistent fever and cough—

Now if she wanted to write, she did not know his address. Where was she to reach him?

Anyway, what was she to write after this long silence?

The days crawled by.

She did not get to hear more news of Appettan. Mammali had none either. And even if she wanted to ask, he was hardly ever to be seen these days. He had to carry the provisions to their house only once in a while. Thus the month of *Midhunam* arrived. She read in the newspaper that the results of Honours and other courses would be declared in a couple of days. It was

Gopu who had shown her the news item. She did not bother to read the news papers.

She had no special interest even then. It was the same to her, whether they came out tomorrow or the day after.

Gopu waited at the bus stand to get a copy of the newspaper as soon as possible. No, there was nothing in it.

It took almost a week for the results to be declared. No one waited for the newspaper that day. It was in the evening that she got it. She had passed.

Recommended BA.

It meant that after three years of study she was not qualified to receive an Honours degree but could only be recommended to receive a BA degree.

Study three and receive a degree which requires only two years of study.

It was Gopu who looked for the results in the newspaper. He quietly placed the paper on the table and left. It was some time after that that she looked at it.

The very first failure. Spending all that money and the trouble staying in a hostel had all gone waste. An ordinary BA degree would have been obtained with much less trouble. Three years wasted. Three years in a lifetime.

What was she going to do with all the years that now lay ahead?

Was her life valuable enough to warrant mourning the loss of three years?

There was nothing to think about now.

Everything was over.

She lived like an automaton, evincing interest in nothing.

She neither cried nor threw hysterics.

Everybody knew that she had not done well but nobody let on that they knew. Nobody bothered to console her either.

Anyway, who was there to do that?

She felt that Gopu accorded her a greater measure of attention. Every evening on his return from his evening walk, he would find some pretext to spend at least ten minutes talking to her before he left to take his bath. Sometimes she almost laughed at his efforts to find a topic for conversation.

It was during such a conversation that one day he told her that Appettan was back. It had been a long time since Appettan's name fell from his tongue. It could have been in an effort to mitigate her sorrow in her failure that he mentioned it.

It seems he had met Ammu Cheriyamma in the temple. She just told him that they had come back because Appettan was much better. Then a couple of weeks later, he met Appettan himself and talked to him.

He was not returning to Bombay. The place did not agree with him. He wanted to find some employment in the village.

What job was a person with a pass in the school final exam going to get?

It was time for Gopu to return. She was sitting idle in the eastern room when he came in and spent some time standing about here and there and clearing his throat. She said nothing.

'Aren't you coming back to college?' he finally began.

'What for?'

'What else will you do? You will receive an MA degree if you put in one more year of study.'

'I am not studying anymore.'

'*Oppole*!'

How long has it been since he called her that!

'Oppole, forget the past. Think of what good lies ahead.'

'I have no desire to do that.'

'Nothing has happened here to bring on this kind of despair. Examinations are a matter of luck. Just because you had bad luck once – Come, we will go together. Come with me.'

'No, I won't.'

'I have already spoken to Achan. He agreed to let you go back to study.'

'I am not willing to study.'

'Then what are you planning to do?'

'Nothing. There's nothing to do.'

'How long will you remain like this?'

'Let me try this for some time. Then I will know.'

'Is this your well-considered opinion?'

'Yes.'

He left.

Cheriyamma never spoke to her. Achan never let on that he even saw her. The days were spent in doing nothing, her mind shying away from the effort of having to think even. She was hardly aware of the day or the date. Day followed night in succession.

Gopu's letters would come. With great difficulty, she would arouse herself to read them but never answered them. Cheriyamma never asked her to help with the chores. She never did them on her own either. If Kochaniyan came to her with his doubts, she would wriggle out under some pretext or other but never bothered to explain anything to him.

Chapter 33

On his way back from school in the evening, Kochaniyan brought her a letter. Whenever she had letters, it was he who brought them to her. The postman would meet him somewhere on the way and give them to him.

Gopu never sent anything in a cover, preferring to use a postcard or an inland letter card. Who was this who had sent her something in a cover?

Oh, what did it matter who it was?

She opened it without paying attention to the address. With the very first sentence, she understood. Appettan—

It was long. She had to sit somewhere quiet to read it.

There was space enough to sit on the low-lying cashew tree in the eastern part of their compound. If you stand there, you can see the palliyal and the paddy fields.

She went out into the grounds and sat leaning on the branch of the cashew tree. She took out the letter again from its cover.

Mani,

It has been six months since I received anything written in your hand.

During those six months – how much pain—

Mani, why did it not occur to you to at least throw a word toward me?

A word carrying the warmth of those fingers.

It would have been elixir to my wounds.

I am not complaining, Mani. There is a limit to what a human being can take. When it crossed the limit, you became silent. You did not know what to say. Isn't that what happened, Mani? If there is any reason other than that behind your silence—

It does not bear thinking about.

I have so much to tell you, Mani. I don't have the courage to tell you in person. So I am copying the pain throbbing in my chest on lifeless paper and sending it off to you. Mani, won't you see my thirsty soul among the black letters staring at you from the white paper? Tell me, won't you?

I am rising from your past like a tormented ghost.

Mani, do you remember how you used to stand on the other side of the fence when I came to water the vegetables in the palliyal? How simple life was in those days! Why did we have to grow past that stage?

Mani, you also have tasted failure, haven't you? Gopu told me about the examinations. Is that why you became silent? Couldn't you have shared the troubles in your heart with me?

The two of us like this—

Oh, why did those days have to pass?

How much water has flowed past over our heads after that?

Today, I am just refuse spat out by disease.

Such as I am—

Why should I drag this out, let me ask you straight, whatever I have to.

I have no right to ask you this now. How many dreams had I woven around this moment, when I would ask you this question! How long have I waited for the right opportunity—

Did I ever imagine that I would be obliged to ask you this in this manner?

Dearest, lean on me, here, on this strong chest—

Let's move, shoulder to shoulder, through this path strewn with thorns. When you are exhausted, place your hand on my shoulder. Or hold my hands tight. Will you come?

Don't you find loneliness unbearable on this thoroughfare? Let's become one. Offer shade to each other. Beloved, will you come?

The question every man wants to ask.

Isn't this the same that every woman wants to hear? A dependable support during a difficult journey.

I have no right to ask you this question now. I have nothing to offer you – except for the pain in my life and the need of my heart.

Mani, I am extending my hand in supplication to you. Giving is a greater pleasure than taking. The needy are beggars.

The poverty of the soul—

I cannot bear living on my own any longer, Mani.

Doesn't there come a point when you are drained of all your will power? There is no going beyond that point.

I have no right over you. Mani, your life is not meant to be tied to that of a consumptive.
I have no money to offer you instead of health. Neither do I have position. Nor is there any hope of advancement in life.
A consumptive school master in a primary school in an obscure village—
Demanding this of you, Mani, is in itself sinful of me.
But don't I have a right? Doesn't even a consumptive have a right?
A right to long for some warmth and light in his life—
Mani, the doctors sent me away, saying that I have been completely cured.
Ever since I was old enough to think for myself, you, Mani, have been the queen in all my dreams of the future.
Many, many hopes—
When I was in Bombay, Amma had written to me that you rejected a good proposal of marriage citing my name. When I received that particular letter from Amma, I was jubilant: the day I came to know that you had rejected another for me—
Oh, why did I not come and carry you away?
I waited for a better job. My Mani shouldn't be the wife of a mere office clerk. And what happened next?
A consumptive school master coughing out his life force.
Mani, why did it have to be like this? Why did I have to be a clerk in an airless office? Why did I have to fall ill?
Does God stand to lose anything if the two of us were happy for a while?
When I look, there's only darkness ahead. I am scared.
No, I can't live on my own.
Tell me, will you take this tired life in hand?
Ettan

The sheet of paper slipped and fell on her lap. She threw herself on the hard, rough branch of the cashew tree.

Tell me, will you take this tired life in hand?

Take this life in hand?

Take this life in hand?

A dog barked somewhere near. She raised her head.

The thin sheet of paper slipped from her lap and was lying at a distance. She picked it up and returned to her perch on the tree.

Appettan's wife – Poor Appettan. Kochachan's son.

They will share her health between them.

The consumptive's wife.

So what?

A meaningless life.

Let this benefit at least him. Let this be of use to a needy person.

If she could live for another person, perhaps it would lessen her ego. Actuated by sympathy—

She would thus forget the past.

Devi! That would be a relief.

She rose and walked away.

The white fruit of sacrifice was dangling before her. She had only to extend her hand.

She had meant to answer him the same day. When she sat down with pen and paper, she had nothing to write. She put it off till the next day. When she had made up her mind about what to write, she stopped thinking about it. Her mind became inert as before. She kept putting it off till a whole week passed.

Achan was not home that Monday evening when Appettan came in.

She was standing on the porch. How different he looked. He even seemed to have shrunk in height.

He stood for some time near the door. She also did not move. For a moment her eyes met his. Did they hold all the pain since creation?

When it was no longer possible for her to bear his immovable stance, she called softly, 'Appetta!'

Even then he said nothing.

He walked in. He went straight to the eastern room. That was where she used to sit and study. Her table and chair were still there. They belonged to Kochaniyan now. Ettan went straight and fell into the chair: 'Did you get my letter, Mani?'

'Yes, I did.'

Then there was nothing.

She stood looking out through the window.

When she turned at a sound, he was lying with his head resting on the table.

His face was gaunt.

The movement of the lump in his throat was painfully obvious.

A look on his face that craved sympathy—

'What you need is not a wife but a bottle of Waterbury's Compound.' That was something she once read in a bad story.

What you need is not a wife but a bottle of Waterbury's Compound.

What is needed is not a wife but medicine. Waterbury's Compound.

Oh God! Had it been the other pair of eyes that had been fixed thus on me, she thought, those large, brilliant eyes – had it been them—

No, she could bear it no longer.

Burying her face in her hands, she ran out of the room.

This was more than a human being could endure.

When she returned in a short while, there was on one in the room.

It was growing dark.

She untied the makeshift gate at the back of the house and climbed to the top of the hill.

The line of blue mountains was invisible. There was not even profound emptiness. Some rich man, who had just returned from Singapore, had bought the place and fenced it in. On one side, there was a plantation surrounded by a fence. On the other side, eager preparations were on for building a new house. The foundation had already been laid. Only the space for a narrow footpath had been left.

Blue mountains would no longer reach out to fold her in their embrace. They will not whisper words of consolation in her ears.

The only thing left was the whistling, slightly offended in tone, of the casuarinas trees planted along the fence erected by the rich man.

She leaned on the half-finished foundation of the house. Her eyes, unused to tears, slowly filled with tears. Tears, like drops of pearl, rolled down her cheeks, searing her, hurting her.

Chapter 34

So what she had been thinking all this time was pointless. Did this mean that there were live embers underneath what she had taken to be a heap of ashes? Sympathy, tenderness, duty – was that particular desire stronger than these?

Was she only actuated by the bitterness of loss all this while? Was she only a mere woman who hankered after the unattainable?

When someone needy stood in front of her, she could not even nod in assent. What must the poor man have done? Would he come again?

She waited for five or six days. For a couple of days, she waited for Kochaniyan to come back from school, in the hope that he would bring a letter from him. No, there was nothing.

If his need was real, would he not come, once again looking for her?

If it was difficult for him to come, could he not at least write to her? No, this was not important to him.

It was fine by her. If he could not be bothered to come again—

Slowly, the same emptiness as before began to fill her life.

Long letters would arrive from Gopu, describing his college life. He had never been in the habit of writing regularly to anyone. There was a letter from him soon after he left after the vacation. The manager of a school in the locality was his acquaintance. There was a vacancy in the school. The manager was willing to offer it to her. Would she accept it?

She wrote him the same day:

> *I am not in the mental state to do anything, Aniya. It is not that I haven't tried. I can't. Give me some more time.*

That was the end of the job offer. Chettan wrote to her a couple of times. She never replied to his letters.

Achan never gave any indication of being aware of her presence in the same house—

Now Chettichiyar's daughter was Ammu Cheriyamma's maid. That was how she came to know: Appettan was ill again. Every day, as soon as Chettichiyar arrived, she would ask her about his illness. Was he better?

Too early to say anything. He was still unwell. It was almost Christmas. Appettan was still sick. Every day, a car was being sent to fetch a doctor. To give him an injection.

What if she wrote to him? Or visited him? Would he like it?

Many days were spent hesitating.

It was almost dusk on a Friday. She was standing on the porch when she saw Ammu Cheriyamma going to the kaavu with oil and wick and all.

She followed her in a while. She wanted to meet her when she returned. She had to ask her for news in person. She felt she could not walk as far as the kaavu, so she decided to wait for her on the way.

It was a long time before she returned.

At last she appeared. Her hair had gone completely gray. Did she have this stoop before?

She was walking along looking down. She saw her only when she drew almost level with her. She tried to smile.

'How's Appettan now, Cheriyamme?'

'There's no improvement.'

'Isn't the doctor visiting regularly?

'Yes, he does. But one must take the medicine if one wants to get well. He refuses to take anything. He asks me why he should want to be rid of his disease. What's written in my fate is something terrible.'

'Does he refuse to see the doctor when he comes?'

'No, he meets him.'

She did not actually stop to talk to her but replied, walking forward, 'He would say there was no need to call in the doctor. But when the doctor came he wouldn't say anything to him. Once the doctor left he wouldn't pay attention to anything he said. That's how it is. The doctor keeps talking about going somewhere else to stay. Appa wouldn't listen. It was because we went and stayed in Coimbatore that he got well really quick. The doctor says there are other places where he could go but who is going to listen? I mortgaged the eastern paddy field to Varrier and got the money ready the other day. When I talk to him about going he won't listen. He says peculiar things to me, telling me that I would be rid of my burden and all. I haven't time to stop, Ammu. He must be asking for me. Bye.'

They had reached the bridge.

'Where are you going Ammu, this late in the evening?'

'Coming with you, Cheriyamme.'

'At this untimely hour? No, Ammu. There's no one there to see you back home.'

'You don't have to see me home.'

'Your father will raise hell if you are not home by night. If you came without asking him—'

'If I asked him he wouldn't let me go. There's no need to ask.'

'Won't he be angry when you go back home in the morning, Ammu?'

'I am not going back in the morning.'

'Then how long are you planning to stay?'

'Did you not go with Kochachan, Cheriyamme?'

'Oh, my daughter, what are you saying? That was wishful thinking. It isn't meant to be. Otherwise, why should he go down with this disease?'

'The disease doesn't matter. It will be cured.'

'Of course it will be, but you are young—'

'Cheriyamme, if I offered to go with him, Appettan would go to Coimbatore or wherever. At least I think he would. Then—'

'But you are also my child, Ammu. How can you—'

'Appettan is willing. If you have some objection, Cheriyamme—'

'Objection? Who, me?'

'Okay then, walk on. Let's go.'

'My daughter!'

'Come, Cheriyamme.'

She climbed down to the ledge bordering the paddy field and walked on.

On Translating Rajelakshmy

The peculiar use of tenses in Malayalam has always been designated a problem area for the translator. Surprisingly enough, tenses did not pose much of a problem in translating these stories into English, but changes in perspective did. The peculiar genius of the Malayalam language permits one to achieve the intimacy of a first-person narrative without specifically using the first-person pronoun *njan*. This is possible because Malayalam has *tan* which can be used in a reflexive sense. It is not easy to achieve the same tonal quality in English. At times a choice had to be made and the immediacy of a first-person narrative had to be sacrificed for the sake of clarity. In stories like 'History Did Not Repeat Itself' and 'In the Abode of God', whenever there is a shift in perspective, it is to denote physical movement on the part of the protagonist. In the case of the former, the shift takes place only twice in the course of the story. It could not be retained without jeopardising the entire tone of the story and hence the first-person perspective was maintained throughout. 'In the Abode of God' is a much more complex piece involving a good many shifts in perspective. The third-person narrative was confined to physical movements and interspersed with the first-person to achieve a measure of intimacy. For instance,

> She stood bewildered in front of the door of that famous temple's *gopuram*.
>
> Do the sad eyes of those who hold me dear follow me here?
> It is a sea of strange faces that is behind me.
>
> 'In the Abode of God', this volume

In the Malayalam original, the title of the story 'In the Abode of God' is *Devalayathil* which might have been translated as 'In the Temple'. Since it was felt that the choice of *devalayam*, a word of Sanskrit origin, in preference to other more commonly used words denoting a temple was significant, an attempt to achieve the same tonal quality was made. In all the other stories, shifts in perspective are denoted by pointers within the narrative. For instance, we have:

> Oh damn! She said to herself, may be they were afraid that I might start to bawl—
>
> 'The Apology', this volume

Culture-specific terms relating to items of dress and religious rituals abound in the stories, especially in 'In the Abode of God' and 'A Winding Sheet for Mathai'. In the latter, Rosa asks for a 'nadan', which is a *mundu* of coarse, unbleached cloth. It rhymes with the term (*mooduvan*) that she employs to denote a winding sheet. But in very rare cases alliteration has been achieved exactly where they occur in the original. For instance, in 'Suicide', the protagonist's brother is fond of reading aloud the deaths and disasters column, which is *marana maaranangal* in the original. In the case of terms relating to rituals, approximate equivalents are provided in some instances, whereas in some others the original term has been retained as such. Kinship terms too crop up in the stories, presenting problems to the translator. The term '*oppol*' for one's elder sister is one that is peculiar to the northern dialect of Malayalam. But it had to be retained, because social custom requires it that one does not address or even refer to one's elders in the family by name. As in the case of kinship terms, there are specific terms for people who do menial jobs in a household. For instance, in the story 'The Defeated One', Ravi's mother and grandmother are referred to as servant maids. Actually, the original term means a person employed to dehusk rice and as such, it places them one rung lower down the hierarchy since a servant maid enjoys greater powers and might even be a favourite one. Rajelakshmy, fortunately enough, is not given to using too many culture-specific proverbs. Only four cases cropped up during translation. For one, an English equivalent was available – in 'A Pretty Girl and Her Pals', Lalitha is advised that a bird in the hand is worth two in the bush. The original proverb, translated, reads: 'The crow in your hand is better than the cuckoo/koel in the forest'; this was chosen in the interest of faithfulness to the text. Again the same principle was applied to the following sentence in 'The Daughter': 'And the cat thought no one would know if it lapped up the milk with its eyes shut' could have been translated as 'And you thought you could get away with playing the ostrich.'

A major casualty has been the racy dialect considered one of Rajelakshmy's strong points. There was no way in which it could be brought out in translation. And, unlike in the case of her novels, she has peopled some of her stories with protagonists who have a decidedly urban background. In such stories, the conversation, or even the narrative, often lapses into English in the original. When the whole thing is in English, it is easy enough to denote it in translation. ('She lapsed into English to thank him ...' and 'He wrote in English ...') but when a character lapses into English right in the middle of a conversation, it is well-nigh impossible to bring it out. For instance, in 'A Teacher is Born', when Ravi accuses Indira of being born with a sick conscience, he does so in English, and that too in the middle of a conversation. Indira keeps repeating the sentence to herself at various points in the narrative, again in English. Since the fact that it is in English is not very crucial to the development of the story, it was left out.

Explanatory notes have been provided separately in the glossary for items which are culture-specific.

Glossary

ammavan	one's maternal uncle
ammu	a term of endearment for a girl
Aniyan/Kochaniyan	younger brother but could be given names too
appam	a kind of rice cake or bread, a ritual offering
aval/avil	rice, pounded and flattened
bhoota	male spirit
Changampuzha (and Edappalli)	Changampuzha Krishna Pillai and Edappalli Raghavan Pillai wrote in the 1930s. Together they breathed new life into Malayalam poetry of their times. Changampuza's most important work is *Remanan*, a pastoral play in verse is on the death of Edappalli who committed suicide in 1936
chanthu	black unguent made from burnt rice, ragi, etc. used by women before the advent of bindis
Chechi	elder sister
Cheriyamma	aunt, either one's father's sister or mother's
cheruma	person belonging to the pulaya, paraya or kurava caste
Chettan/Ettan	strictly means elder brother. The term is used to refer to one's cousins and even acquaintances who should be accorded the respect due to an elder brother
Chettathiyamma	elder brother's wife
chettichiyar	a woman of the chetti or vaisya caste of Tamil origin
Chingam	August–September
chinnan	one of the five breaths supposed to be taken by one at the time of death
chuttuvilakku	an offering as part of which all the lamps on the outer walls of temple are lit
deepam	literally, lamp. At dusk, a lamp is lighted and carried to the front porch by a maiden (usually the daughter of the house) who calls out 'deepam'

edakka	a percussion instrument
Edavam	May–June
etham	a pulley and plank arrangement to draw water from a pond or well for irrigation
imbidi/kochambidi	respectful forms of address to women/girls of a higher caste
incha	soap bark tree, the crushed bark is used to scrub the body
gopuram	a temple-tower, especially the front one
kaithapoo	'Kaitha' is the screw-pine. Its inflorescence has a sweet smell.
Kaalan	Yama, the god of death
kaavu	sacred grove
kachamundu	a mundu of coarse material
kindi	a kind of bell-metal ewer with a spout at the bottom
kochamma	lady of the house
kontattam	spiced and salted rice batter dried in the sun
koothu	here a puppet show version of the classical art form
koppu	the measure of rice and victuals given to a tenant by his landlord on the first day of Onam
kuthuvilakku	a lamp with a long handle
kutta/kutti	terms of endearment for a boy and a girl respectively
maddalam	a percussion instrument
Makaram	January-February
mandapam	a pillared platform inside a temple
master/*Mash*/mistress	Master and teacher are English loan words in Malayalam and are commonly used in the Malayalam word order. The corrupted form of Master is *Mash*. Thus Kumaran Master, Devaki Mistress, Leela Teacher, etc.
Mathai	a corrupt form of Mathew
Medam	April–May
Midhunam	June–July
mooppan	person belonging to the vaisya or vaniya caste
mul	bleached cloth; 703 is a brand name
murapennu	roughly means, the betrothed. A female cousin whom one can marry as per kinship rules

mundu	a long piece of cloth worn around the waist
nadan mundu	coarse, unbleached mundu or dhoti
nagaswaram	a double reed wind instrument
nalukettu	a house built in the traditional style of Kerala, around an open courtyard in the middle
nampoothiri	a caste of Malayali brahmins
nellu kuthukari	a woman who lives by de-husking rice
nilavilakku	a bronze lamp with an open flat receptacle for oil, supported by a long stem attached to a base. Wicks are laid in the oil and lit
niramala	an offering at Bhagavati temples, in which the idol is covered in garlands
nirapara	a *para*, or container for measuring rice, filled with grain on auspicious occasions
njattuvela	literally the *vela* or the time of *njayar* or the sun. When the sun moves into the constellation of Thiruvathira, it results in heavy rains for the crops
onnara	'onnara' literally means one-and-a-half. Onnara is a kind of mundu which is one-and-a-half times longer than a usual mundu and is used also as an undergarment. 'Jagannathan' denotes cloth woven in Orissa
Oppol/Oppole	one's elder sister; a kinship term peculiar to the northern dialect
Ousep	a corrupt form of Joseph
padippura	a gate house
palliyal	a terraced hill slope for cultivation
pandal	a temporary shed-like structure erected for festivals and marriages
paattu	a ritual offering of songs
Pakkara	a corrupt form of Bhaskara; here, a term of endearment
Parith	a corrupt form of Paris
payasam	thin milk pudding
poothan	attendant of Bhagavati
PSP	Praja Socialist Party
pulaya	name of a dalit caste
rakshasa	demon of Hindu mythology
rasnadi powder	an ayurvedic preparation, meant to be rubbed on the head immediately after bath
rompa	Tamil word meaning many, a lot, etc.

saare	a corrupt form of 'sir' used to address both male and female officers in government institutions in Kerala
Sarvodaya	a social movement of the 1950s in which reformers promoted a society that Gandhi envisioned
thampuran	Kshatriya chieftain
tharavad	ancestral seat of a family
thira	a ritual performance common in Malabar
thodi	yard around the house. Malayalis make a distinction between *mittam* and thodi. Mittam is the yard immediately surrounding a house, an open but bounded space always swept clean and sometimes beautified with sand. Thodi, on the other hand, is more extensive and full of vegetation and served varied purposes, even acting as open air toilets for men and children of the house
Thommi	a corrupt, shortened form of Thomas, used also as a term of endearment
tulasi *thara*	tulasi is the basil plant. In Hindu houses, it is customary to have a *thara* or a brick structure filled with soil for planting the tulasi plant. It is located on the eastern side of the house
Unniarcha	a beautiful woman celebrated in folk ballads of Northern Kerala for her valour
Uthradam	the first day of Onam
valiyeman	literally, big master
Valiyechi	eldest sister
Valiyettan	eldest of one's brothers
vela	the festival
vellanedyam	rice offering to the God
vilakkathrol	midwife; she belonged to the barber caste
yakshi	supernatural enchantress of popular myth